NICHOLSON

THE ORDNANCE SURVEY GUIDE TO THE WATERWAYS

1 SOUTH

Series editor: David Perrott

Robert Nicholson Publications

Also available in this series:

Nicholson/Ordnance Survey Guide to the Waterways 2. Central
Nicholson/Ordnance Survey Guide to the Waterways 3. North
Nicholson/Ordnance Survey Guide to the River Thames (and Wey)

*The indication of a towpath in this book
does not necessarily imply a public right
of way. If you are in any doubt, check
before you proceed with the latest published Ordnance Survey map.*
Pathfinder Series (1:25 000 scale or 2½ in to
1 mile). These OS walker and rambler maps show the
countryside in great detail, including rights
of way in England and Wales.
Landranger Series (1:50 000 scale or about 1¼ in
to 1 mile). This OS series covers the country
in 204 sheets and is ideal for detailed
exploring by car or on foot.

First published 1983 by **Robert Nicholson**
Publications Limited, 17 Conway Street,
London W1P 6JD and **Ordnance Survey**,
Romsey Road, Maybush, Southampton SO9 4DH.

2nd edition 1985

© Text, Robert Nicholson Publications Limited 1985

Original research: Paul Atterbury, Andrew Darwin
and David Perrott

Thanks are extended to the Electric Boat
Association who supplied information on recharging
points, the Kennet & Avon Canal Trust, Ray Arnold,
and the staff of British Waterways Board.

Cover photograph: Derek Pratt

Great care has been taken throughout this book
to be accurate, but the publishers cannot accept
any responsibility for any errors which appear
or their consequences.

Typeset by Rowland Phototypesetting Ltd,
Bury St Edmunds, Suffolk
Printed in Great Britain by
Blantyre Printing and Binding Co Ltd
Blantyre, Glasgow

ISBN 0 905522 73 7

INTRODUCTION

The canals and navigable rivers of Britain were built as a system of new trade routes at a time when roads were virtually non-existent. After their boom period in the late 18th and early 19th centuries, they gradually declined in the face of fierce competition from the new railway companies, and large-scale commercial carrying ended by the time of the Second World War, when many of the routes had slipped into decay and ruin. It is true that in a few areas goods continue to be carried profitably to this day, but for the majority of canals it was the new traffic of pleasure boats that provided the impetus for rescue and restoration.

The founding of the Inland Waterways Association by L.T.C. Rolt and Robert Aickman in 1946 brought together enthusiasts from all over the country who were to campaign to save and restore these 2000 miles of navigable waterways that are so much a part of our history. More and more people are now realising that what had been abandoned as little more than a muddy ditch and a convenient place to dump rubbish can be transformed into a linear park, full of interest and a place of recreation for all.

There is something for everyone in the canals: engineering feats like aqueducts, tunnels and flights of locks (all of which amazed a world that had seen nothing like it since Roman times); the brightly decorated narrow boats which used to throng the waterways; the wealth of birds, animals and plants on canal banks; the mellow, unpretentious architecture of canalside buildings like pubs, stables, lock cottages and warehouses; and the sheer beauty and quiet isolation that is a feature of so many English canals.

Use this book to discover the waterways for yourself; it is one of four volumes covering the South, Centre and North of England together with the rivers Thames and Wey, published jointly by Nicholson and the Ordnance Survey, in response to public demand.

CONTENTS

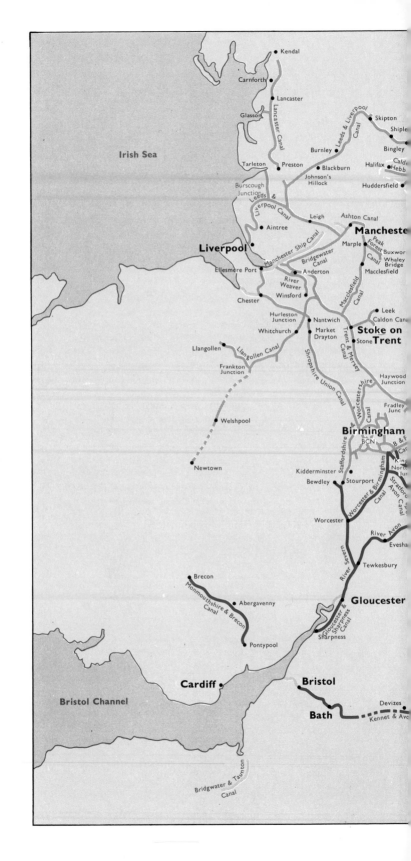

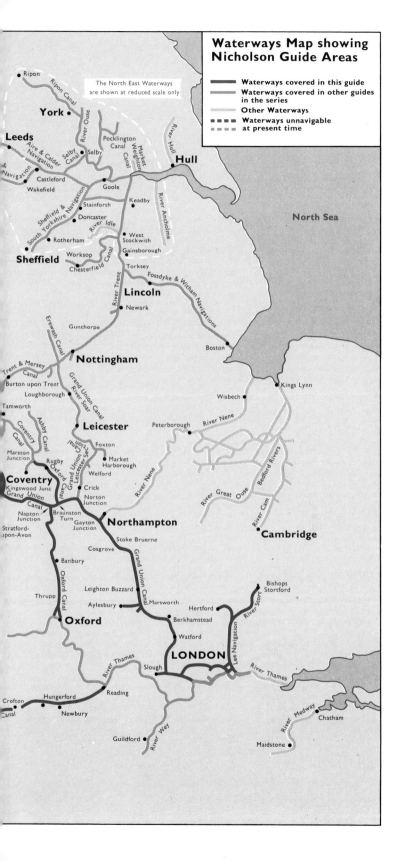

Waterways Map showing Nicholson Guide Areas

——— Waterways covered in this guide
——— Waterways covered in other guides in the series
——— Other Waterways
▬ ▬ ▬ Waterways unnavigable at present time
- - - -

The North East Waterways are shown at reduced scale only

Ripon
Ripon Canal
York
Leeds
Aire & Calder Navigation
River Ouse
Pocklington Canal
Selby Canal
Selby
Market Weighton Canal
River Hull
Hull
Castleford
Goole
Wakefield
Keadby
River Ancholme
North Sea
Stainforth
Sheffield & South Yorkshire Navigation
Doncaster
River Idle
West Stockwith
Rotherham
Gainsborough
Worksop
Chesterfield Canal
Torksey
Sheffield
River Trent
Lincoln
Fossdyke & Witham Navigations
Newark
Erewash Canal
Gunthorpe
Boston
Nottingham
Kings Lynn
Trent & Mersey Canal
Burton upon Trent
Grand Union Canal
River Soar
Loughborough
Wisbech
Tamworth
River Nene
Coventry Canal
Ashby Canal
Leicester
Peterborough
River Nene
Marston Junction
Oxford Canal
Foxton
Rugby
Market Harborough
Grand Union Canal Leicester Section
Welford
Bedford Rivers
Coventry
Crick
River Great Ouse
River Cam
Kingswood Junc
Grand Union Canal
Norton Junction
Napton Junction
Braunston Turn
Gayton Junction
Cambridge
Stratford-upon-Avon
Northampton
Stoke Bruerne
Grand Union Canal
Cosgrove
Banbury
Bishops Stortford
Oxford Canal
Leighton Buzzard
Thrupp
Aylesbury
Marsworth
Hertford
River Stort
Oxford
Grand Union Canal
Berkhamstead
Watford
Lee Navigation
LONDON
River Thames
Slough
River Thames
Crofton Canal
Hungerford
Reading
River Medway
Chatham
Newbury
River Wey
Maidstone
Guildford

HOW TO USE THIS GUIDE

The maps are drawn at a scale of two inches to one mile. Adjacent to each map section is a description of the countryside and places of interest together with a commentary on the course of the canal or river. Details of boatyards correspond to the symbol ⑧ on the map, and pubs 🅿 near the waterway are also named and in some cases described. Those with a restaurant are indicated by the symbol ✕ and wine bars and licensed premises by ▾. Other symbols used on the maps are:

Locks, with number and 'rise'. The symbol points uphill.

Staircase locks.

Bridge and its number. Many are named.

Tunnel—often described in the text.

Aqueduct—often described in the text.

Winding hole—turning point for boats longer than the ordinary width of the canal (it's pronounced as in the wind that blows). Canal junctions are also good places to 'wind'.

Weir.

R is refuse disposal, **S** is sewage or 'Elsan' disposal, **W** is a water point, **P** is petrol, **D** is diesel and **E** is electric boat recharge. Many of these facilities are often available at boatyards; 'pump-out' toilet emptying machines may also be available—see the boatyard entries.

A feature of these guides is the 'milestone' which appears on every map thus:

This performs many useful functions. It reminds you of your direction of travel—in this example up the page is towards Napton, down the page is towards Oxford; it denotes distances and indicates the number of locks between the milestone and strategic points (usually junctions) along the waterway—in this example, Napton is 22¼ miles (M) with 22 locks (L) from the 'milestone', and Oxford is 27 miles and 17 locks from the milestone. By deducting the miles and locks on one milestone from those on the next, distances from page to page can be accurately estimated. Using the 'lock-miles' system (see **Planning a cruise**, page 13) the time your journey will take can be calculated, and with a little experience based on your speed of travel and lock operation, your own time formula can be arrived at.

Where this occurs on a map it simply means that the actual route of the waterway would not fit neatly onto the page, so the cartographer has 'bent' the map, using two north points. The navigator on the water, or the walker on the bank, will notice nothing amiss. Distances in this book should be measured along the thick blue line only, not including these gaps.

LOCKS AND THEIR USE

The different locks and their attendant machinery are a source of endless fascination for all waterway users. Understanding why they are there and the principle upon which they work will help you in their use.

A lock is a device for transporting craft from a higher water level to a lower level, or vice versa, for example when a canal crosses a range of hills. It consists of a box with gates at each end, and a separate means of letting water in at the top (higher level) and out at the bottom (lower level). This is controlled by paddles. These paddles may simply open and shut holes in the gates (gate paddles), or they may open and shut underground culverts (ground paddles). A windlass (carried on the boat) is used to wind the paddles open and shut. Whilst locks differ in detail, the following instructions will apply in the case of the vast majority of *narrow* canal locks. Some extra points regarding wide locks are covered later.

A typical narrow lock

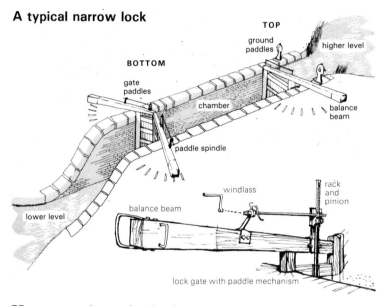

lock gate with paddle mechanism

How to go through a lock

PRELIMINARIES

Stop the boat well outside the lock and secure it. If members of your crew can get off the boat before the lock (at the narrow point under a bridge for example) and run ahead to prepare the lock, this will save time.

GOING UP IN A LOCK (LOCKING UP)

Lock empty—ie water at lower level

Open gate(s)
Drive boat in
Close gate(s)
Check bottom paddles closed
Keep boat near to the bottom of lock
Open top paddles to fill lock
Open top gate(s) when lock is full
Drive boat out
Close top gate(s)
Close top paddles

Lock full—ie water at higher level

Check top gate(s) and paddles closed
Open bottom paddles to drain lock
Open bottom gate(s)
Drive boat in
Close bottom gate(s) and paddles
Keep boat near to the bottom of lock
Open top paddles to fill lock
Open top gate(s) when lock is full
Drive boat out
Close top gate(s)
Close top paddles

GOING DOWN IN A LOCK (LOCKING DOWN)

Lock full—ie water at higher level

Open top gate(s)
Drive boat in
Close top gate(s)
Check top paddles closed
Keep boat near to the bottom of the lock
Open bottom paddles to empty lock
Open bottom gate(s)
Drive boat out
Close bottom gates and paddles

Lock empty—ie water at lower level

Check bottom gate(s) and paddles closed
Open top paddles to fill lock
Open gate(s)
Drive boat in
Close top gate(s) and paddles
Keep boat near to the bottom of the lock
Open bottom paddles to empty lock
Open bottom gate(s)
Drive boat out
Close bottom gate(s) and paddles

If you have to drain or fill a lock in order to enter it, make sure there is no boat approaching that could usefully use the lock before you. Always try to conserve water, which is being continually passed down the canal from its summit and thus requires constant replenishment at a higher level.

SOME GENERAL DO'S AND DONT'S AT LOCKS

Do not leave your windlass slotted onto the paddle spindle—if something slips it could be thrown off and cause injury.

Always leave all gates and paddles closed when you leave, but look out for notices which may give other instructions for the proper operation of a particular lock.

Always wind the paddles down—letting them drop is bad practice, and causes damage.

Beware of protrusions in the side walls of the lock chamber that may damage the boat, and don't use fenders in narrow locks—they may jam.

When opening and closing lock gates, keep to the landward side of the balance beam.

Don't rush around at locks, especially in wet weather, when the sides are slippery. Never jump across partly opened gates.

Always make the safety of the crew and boat your prime concern and remember that if things do start to go wrong, you can stop everything by closing the paddles.

There is no reason why your children, wearing buoyancy aids and properly supervised, should not help at locks—it is all part of the fun, after all—but impress upon them the potential dangers, and establish some common-sense rules. You have no authority over other people's children, and their participation should be discouraged. Great difficulties could ensue should they be injured in any way.

Beware of fierce top gate paddles, especially in wide locks.

Don't leave your windlass behind; hundreds are lost this way each year.

WIDE LOCKS

Taking a narrow boat (7ft beam) through a wide lock (14ft) can present special difficulties, especially when locking up. If all the top paddles were to be opened fully at the same time, the boat would be buffeted considerably. The diagram below illustrates one method of ensuring a smooth passage. The stern line held ashore will provide added security.

Locking up in a wide lock
(a suggested technique)

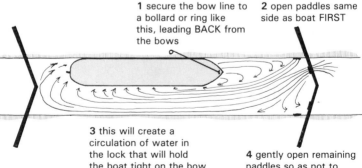

1 secure the bow line to a bollard or ring like this, leading BACK from the bows

2 open paddles same side as boat FIRST

3 this will create a circulation of water in the lock that will hold the boat tight on the bow line and hard against the side of the lock

4 gently open remaining paddles so as not to disrupt the circulation already established

STAIRCASE LOCKS

Where the top gates of one lock are the bottom gates of the next. Usually there is a board nearby giving operating instructions—read it carefully and make sure you understand it before you start. And remember: in a narrow staircase you can't pass a boat coming the other way.

Even young children can help, if properly supervised, but you must make sure life jackets are worn all the time when near the water. *David Perrott*.

GENERAL CRUISING INFORMATION

The vast majority of the waterways covered in this series are controlled by the British Waterways Board. All craft using BWB canals must be licensed and those using BWB rivers must be registered. Charges are based on the length of the boat and a canal craft licence covers all the navigable waterways under the Board's control. Permits for permanent mooring on the canals are also issued by the Board. Apply in each case to:

Craft Licensing Office,
Willow Grange,
Church Road,
Watford WD1 3QA.
(Watford 26422).

The Licensing Office will also supply a list of all BWB rivers and canals. Other river navigation authorities relevant to this book are mentioned where appropriate.

Getting afloat

There is no better way of discovering the joys of canals than by getting afloat. The best thing is to hire a boat for a week or a fortnight from one of the boatyards on the canals. (Each boatyard has an entry in the text, and most of them offer craft for hire; brochures may be easily obtained from such boatyards.)

General cruising

Most canals are saucer-shaped in section and so are deepest in the middle. Very few have more than 3–4ft of water and many have much less. Try to keep to the middle of the channel except on bends, where the deepest water is on the *outside* of the bend. When you meet another boat, the rule is to keep to the right, slow down, and aim to miss the approaching boat by a couple of yards: do not steer right over to the bank or you will most likely run aground. The deeper the draught of the boat, the more important it is to keep in the middle of the deep water, and so this must be considered when passing other boats. If you meet a loaded working boat, keep right out of the way. Working boats should always be given precedence, for their time is money. If you meet a boat being towed from the bank, pass it on the outside rather than intercept the towing line. When overtaking, keep the other boat on your starboard, or right, side.

Speed

There is a general speed limit of 4mph on most British Waterways Board canals. This is not just an arbitrary limit: there is no need to go any faster, and in many cases it is impossible to cruise even at this speed. Canals were not built

for motor boats, and so the banks are easily damaged by excessive wash and turbulence. Erosion of the banks makes the canal more shallow, which in turn makes running aground a more frequent occurrence. So keep to the limits and try not to aggravate the situation. It is easy to see when a boat is creating excessive turbulence by looking at the wash—if it is 'breaking' or causing large waves, you are going too fast and should slow down.

Slow down also when passing moored craft, engineering works and anglers.

Slow down when there is a lot of floating rubbish on the water: old planks and plastic bags may mean underwater obstacles that can damage a boat or its propeller if hit hard. Try to drift over obvious obstructions in neutral.

Slow down when approaching blind corners, narrow bridges and junctions.

Running aground

The effective end of commercial traffic on the narrow canals has resulted in canals being shallower than ever. Running aground is a fairly common event, but is rarely serious, as the canal bed is usually soft. If you run aground, try first of all to pull the boat off by gently reversing the engine. If this fails, use the pole as a lever against the bank or some solid object, in combination with a tow rope being pulled from the bank. Do not keep revving the engine in reverse if it is obviously having no effect. Another way is to get your crew to rock the boat from side to side while using the pole or mooring lines. If all else fails, lighten your load; make all the crew leave the boat except the helmsman, and then it will often float off quite easily.

Remember that if you run aground once, it is likely to happen again as it indicates a particularly shallow stretch—or that you are out of the channel. If you are continually bumping the bottom in a shallow stretch, it may be that you are going too fast, causing the boat to 'dig in' at the back. Going less fast may make things more comfortable.

In a town it is common to run aground on sunken rubbish; this is most likely to occur near bridges and housing estates. Use the same methods, but be very careful as these hard objects can easily damage your boat or propeller.

Remember that winding holes are often silted up—do not go further in than you have to.

Mooring

All boats carry metal stakes and a mallet. These are used for mooring when there are no rings or bollards in sight, which is usually the case. Generally speaking you may moor anywhere to

BWB property but there are certain basic rules. Avoid mooring anywhere that could cause an obstruction to other boats; do not moor on a bend or a narrow stretch, do not moor abreast boats already moored. Never moor in a lock, and do not be tempted to tie up in a tunnel or under a bridge if it is raining. Pick a stretch where there is a reasonable depth of water at the bank, otherwise the boat may bump and scrape the canal bed—an unpleasant sensation if you are trying to sleep. For reasons of peace and quiet and privacy it is best to moor away from main roads and railway lines.

Never stretch your mooring lines across the towpath; you may trip someone up and face a claim for damages.

There is no need to show a riding light at night, except on major rivers and busy commercial canals.

Beware of mooring at unrecognised sites in cities—you may attract the unwelcome attention of vandals.

So long as you are sensible and keep to the rules, mooring can be a pleasant gesture of individuality.

Knots

A simple and easy way of securing a rope to a bollard or mooring stake is to use a couple of round turns and a half hitch made with a loop and pulled tight. This can be released quickly by pulling the loose end, which will have been left tidily coiled.

When leaving a mooring, coil all the ropes up again. They will then be out of the way, but ready if needed in a hurry. Many a sailor has fallen overboard after tripping on an uncoiled rope.

Fixed bridges

At most bridges the canal becomes very narrow, a means of saving building costs developed by the engineers. As a result, careful navigation is called for if you are to avoid hitting either the bridge sides with the hull or the arch with the cabin top. As when entering a lock, the best way to tackle 'bridgeholes' is to slow down well in advance and aim to go straight through, keeping a steady course. Adjustments should be kept to a minimum for it is easy to start the boat zig-zagging, which will inevitably end in a collision. One technique is to gauge the width of the approaching bridgehole relative to the width of the boat, and then watch one side only, aiming to miss that side by a small margin—say 6in; the smaller you can make the margin, the less chance you have of hitting the other side of

the bridge. If you do hit the bridge sides when going slowly it is not likely to do much damage; it will merely strengthen your resolve to do better next time.

Moveable bridges

Swing and lift bridges are an attractive feature of some canals and cannot be ignored as they often rest only 2 or 3ft above the water. They are moved by being swivelled horizontally, or raised vertically. Operation is usually manual, although some have gearing to ease the movement. There are one or two mechanised versions; these have clear instructions at control points. Before operating any bridge make sure that approaching road traffic is aware of your intention to open the bridge. Use protective barriers if there are any and remember to close the bridge again after you.

Some lift bridges are *very unstable*, and could close while your boat is passing underneath, with disastrous consequences. For this reason it is prudent to have your strongest (or heaviest) crew member hold it open until the boat is clear. Many swing bridges are very heavy to operate, and require two strong people to move them.

Tunnels

Many people consider a canal incomplete without one or two tunnels, and certainly they are an exciting feature of any trip. Nearly all are easy to navigate, although there are a few basic rules:

Make sure your boat has a good headlight in working order and *always* use it.

If it is a narrow tunnel (ie 7ft) make sure there is no boat coming the other way *before* you enter. Craft of 7ft beam can pass in some wide tunnels—slow right down when you meet to lessen the almost inevitable bump.

In most tunnels the roof drips constantly, especially under ventilation shafts. Put on a raincoat and some form of hat before going in.

A notice on the tunnel portal will give its length, in yards, and will say whether unpowered craft are permitted to use it.

Where there are restrictions on time of entry, and one-way systems, these must be adhered to. To meet head on half way through a long narrow tunnel would create great difficulties.

Care of the engine

Canal boats are generally powered by either diesel, petrol or two-stoke engines. If you hire a hire craft, the boatyard will give you instructions for your daily maintenance, which will no doubt include some or all of the following:

Every day before starting off, you should:

Check the oil level in the engine.
Check the fuel level in the tank.

If your engine is water-cooled, check that the filter near the intake is clean and weedfree. Otherwise the engine will over-heat, which could cause serious damage.

Check the level of distilled water in the battery, and ensure that it is charging correctly.

Lubricate any parts of the engine, gearbox

or steering that need daily attention.

Check that the propeller is free of weeds, wire, plastic bags and any other rubbish. The propeller and the water filter should be checked whenever there is any suspicion of obstruction or overheating—which may mean several times a day.

Pump the bilges everyday

When navigating in shallow water, keep in mind the exposed position of the propeller. If you hit any underwater obstruction put the engine into neutral immediately. When running over any large floating object put the engine into neutral and wait for the object to appear astern before re-engaging the drive.

Fuel

Petrol engines and petrol/oil outboards are catered for by some boatyards and all road-side fuel stations. Fuel stations on roads near the canal are shown in the guide, and these should be considered when planning your day's cruise. Running out is inconvenient; remember you may have to walk several miles carrying a heavy can.

Diesel-powered craft, and narrowboats in particular, can usually cruise for over two weeks before needing to be refilled. Those using diesel-powered hire craft rarely need to be concerned about fuel. Those with their own boats, however, should bear in mind that boatyards are few and far between on some parts of the network, and should a diesel-powered boat run out of fuel, the system will need to be bled before the engine can run again. Most boatyards sell marine diesel (indicated ⒟ in the text), which is cheaper than the road fuel.

Electrically powered boats

These are becoming very popular on the inland waterways, in view of their quietness and lack of environmental pollution. Indicated ⒠ under the **BOATYARD** heading are those establishments known to offer recharging facilities—polite enquiry by electric boat users will certainly reveal more. If you are lucky enough to be using this form of power, please note the following.

All boats using this information are assumed to have a battery charger on board and 50 metres of cable fitted with standard 13 amp terminals. You are advised to offer a £2 fee (1984) for an overnight re-charge if not equipped to measure what you take.

It is essential for the safety of the boater, the owner of the supply and the general public that a proper residual current circuit breaker (RCD) be carried by the boat and fitted between the boat's cable and the supply unless the supply is already so protected. The RCD must be tested for correct operation before battery charging starts.

Water

Fresh water taps occur irregularly along the canals, usually at boatyards, BWB depots, or by lock cottages. These are marked on the maps in the guide. Ensure that there is a long water hose on the boat (BWB taps have a ½-inch slip-on hose connection). Fill up every day.

Lavatories

Some canal boats are fitted with chemical lavatories which have to be emptied from time to time. Never empty them over the side or tip them into the bushes. Use the sewage disposal points marked on the map ⒮, for which you will need a BWB key, or at boatyards. Many boats now have pump-out toilets, which must be emptied with a special machine—usually at boatyards and indicated in the text. This symbol at the canalside indicates just such a 'pump-out station' (although not all boatyards with the facility display it). Expect to have to pay.

Some BWB depots and boatyards have lavatories for the use of boat crews; again, you may need your BWB key.

Litter

Some canals are in a poor state today because they have long been misused as unofficial dumps for rubbish, especially in towns. Out of sight is only out of mind until some object is tangled round your propeller. So keep all rubbish until you can dispose of it at a refuse disposal point, indicated ⒭ on the map, or at a boatyard equipped to deal with it.

Byelaws

Although no-one needs a 'driving licence' to navigate a boat, boat users should remember that they have certain responsibilities to others on the waterways. Prospective navigators are advised to obtain a copy of the byelaws relevant to the waterways on which they are to travel.

Stoppages

Although the BWB and other navigation authorities plan their maintenance for the winter months, it often becomes necessary to carry out repairs during the cruising season. Many of the structures on the canal system are beginning to show their age (especially the tunnels) and repairs are a lengthy and costly affair, sometimes resulting in stoppages lasting many years. A long dry spell can lower water levels and restrict lock operation, and of course a canal bank can breach at any time.

To avoid disappointment it is wise to check that your planned route is clear before you set off, and that there are no time restrictions on locks that may upset your schedule. Those using hire craft may be able to get this information from their boatyard, although some are surprisingly lax. It is best to check for yourself by ringing the BWB Area Amenity Assistants (listed at the end of this book) or the relevant navigation authority. News of any last minute stoppages is available on 'Canalphone', as a recorded message. Ring (01)-723 8486 for the North and Midlands, or (01)-723 8487 for the South and Midlands. Check before you go.

PLANNING A CRUISE

It is wise when planning a cruise to establish a means of calculating the time it takes to travel any given length of canal. This ensures that you can reliably work out whether you will reach a shop or pub before closing time. And of course for those who have hired their boat for a week, it is vital to return on time to the starting point.

The time taken to navigate any canal depends, of course, on the average cruising speed of your boat and the amount of time it takes to negotiate the locks along the way. Remember that there is in any case an overall legal speed limit of 4 mph on all canals. In practice, 3 mph is a realistic canal cruising speed for most boats and 2 mph is the maximum which can be achieved on shallow canals, such as the Peak Forest.

To the uninitiated, 3 mph may sound an unbearably slow rate of progress through the countryside; but a few hours of gentle cruising on a fine day is usually enough to convert most people to this pace. For only by proceeding at walking pace can you appreciate the peace and beauty of the countryside, watch the bird life, and see the scurry of voles, rats and other creatures as they suddenly notice the slowly approaching boat.

The length of time taken to work through a lock depends on several things: whether the lock is full or empty, wide or narrow, deep or shallow. It depends on the number and size of the paddles that control the sluices, on the presence or otherwise of other boats near the lock, and of course on the number and competence of the boat crew. Most people take around 10 minutes on average to work through a typical lock—or, to put it another way, they take as long to get through a lock as they would have taken to travel another ½ mile at 3 mph. Herein lies the basis for a simple method of estimating time required to travel along a given length of canal: take the number of miles to be travelled and add half the number of locks to be negotiated on the way. This gives the number of 'lock-miles'. Divide this by your average cruising speed, and the result is the approximate length of time it will take, in hours. Thus if you intend to travel 30 miles, and there are 42 locks along the way, the calculation is as follows: 30 + (42 divided by 2) = 30 + 21 = 51 lock-miles. 51 divided by 3 (mph) = 17 hours. So this particular journey will take you around 17 hours, assuming your average cruising speed to be 3

mph and assuming you take about 10 minutes to get through the average lock. (If you're a beginner, it might take a little longer than this to start with.) The length of your journey and the number of locks can easily be calculated using the 'milestones' that appear on every map in this series of guides. To refine the system, simply tailor it more closely to the actual cruising speed of your boat and the efficiency of your lock-operating technique.

An excellent fortnight's trip, for example, would be the circuit formed by the River Soar and Trent and Mersey, Coventry, Oxford and Grand Union (Leicester Section) canals. This is 170 miles and 74 locks long (about 70 hours cruising time), and takes you through some of the very best parts of Leicestershire. You will see the Foxton staircase locks, Braunston Tunnel and the delightful canal village of Shardlow, and if you have time to spare you can explore the lock-free Ashby Canal (22 miles long—2 days there and back) or the meandering course of the unspoilt Market Harborough arm, 5 miles long.

A good round trip in terms of contrasts would be the Grand Union main line, north Oxford, Coventry and Birmingham & Fazeley canals, which at 106 miles and 88 locks (about 50 hours cruising time) would be an energetic week's cruising. On this route you could see Braunston and Hillmorton, the long level of the north Oxford and Coventry Canals broken by the 11 locks at Atherstone, and then the industrial outpost of Fazeley. Once out in Warwickshire, you encounter the 5 wide but modern locks at Knowle and the 21 locks of the Hatton Flight. Then you are in the valley of the Warwickshire Avon, and after passing Warwick and Leamington Spa you start locking up out of the valley again to rejoin the Oxford Canal at Napton.

These are just two examples of the many circular cruising routes available—a glance at the planning map on pages 4 and 5 will reveal many more. Of course, there is also much to be said for a straight out and back cruise—it will all look different when you are coming the other way, and you can arrange to re-visit that favourite pub again. The whole secret is to allow plenty of time, for shopping, for exploring and for gentle cruising. Many a holiday has been spoilt by becoming a race against time.

See also 'Stoppages' in the **General Cruising Information** *section.*

Good, quiet moorings in Middlewich. *David Perrott*

RIVER AVON

Maximum dimensions

Length: 70'
Beam: 13' 6"
Draught: 3' 6"
Headroom: 8' (at normal levels)

Mileage

Avon Lock, TEWKESBURY to:
Pershore Lock: 14½
Evesham Lock: 25¾
Bidford Bridge: 32¾
Tramway Bridge, STRATFORD: 42¼
Alveston Sluice: 45½

Locks: 17

Rising at Welford on the Leicestershire and Northamptonshire boundary and joining the River Severn at Tewkesbury, the River Avon was first made navigable to Stratford by William Sandys of Fladbury during the period 1636–39, with plans to extend eventually to Warwick.

In 1717 the ownership of the river was split into the Upper and Lower Avon, the dividing line being Workman Bridge, Evesham; following several changes in ownership, the Upper river was purchased by the Great Western Railway in 1863. By refusing tolls they avoided the obligation to maintain the river and as a result within 10 years it was in a ruinous state. In 1875 all traffic on the Upper Avon had ceased.

Although deteriorating gradually, the Lower Avon did remain navigable to Pershore until it was bought, for £1500, by C. D. Barwell in 1950. At this time the Lower Avon Navigation Trust was formed and restoration began, with navigation being restored to the Bridge Inn, Offenham (the present administrative boundary between the Lower and Upper river) by June 1964. In July of that year, the southern section of the Stratford-on-Avon Canal from Kingswood Junction to Stratford was also re-opened, making the restoration of the Upper Avon the next logical step. But with no right of access to the river, a non-effective navigation authority, all but 2 of the weirs collapsed and the locks in complete ruin, it seemed an all but impossible task.

Under the leadership of David Hutchings MBE the Upper Avon Navigation Trust was formed in 1965, and in 1969 work began. An appeal was made to raise £300,000 and eventually over a third of this sum was given by one anonymous donor. Despite enormous difficulties, the Upper river was officially opened by HM Queen Elizabeth the Queen Mother on the 1st June 1974. A truly magnificent achievement for private initiative and volunteer labour.

Cruising on the Avon

This is a river navigation, and as such can present problems to those more accustomed to the still waters of the canals. Just 36 hours of summer rain can put sufficient 'fresh' water into the river to make passage hazardous—the 'pull' upstream of the weirs increases, cross-currents below the weirs become fierce and the water 'piles up' as it rushes through narrow bridge holes. *When this happens, all boats must moor up out of the main stream and wait for the level to return to normal.* If you are in any doubt, phone your hire company or seek expert advice.

All the locks on the river are wide locks, and those on the Upper Avon demonstrate considerable ingenuity in the re-cycling of gates and paddle gear from other canals and rivers—as a consequence some of the locks are difficult to operate, and require a good deal of physical strength. Do not believe that a cruise on this part of the river will necessarily be restful.

Finally, those accustomed to the cosy informality and 'go as you please' atmosphere of the narrow canals will not be impressed by the plethora of 'Private' and 'No Mooring' notices. Many landowners and local authorities have yet to come to terms with the river, especially the Upper river, as a navigation, and boaters can begin to feel distinctly unloved. Many villages are sited back from the river, away from the floods, and the scenery is generally that of quiet water-meadows with prolific bird life. However, those who plan their journey carefully and avoid the crowded summer peak period will find much to enjoy.

The Lower and Upper Navigation Trusts are charities operated almost entirely by volunteers. Boat crews can help them to keep down their costs by observing their rules and requests. They should also be acquainted with the relevant bye-laws, and ensure that their craft is equipped with such items as an anchor made off to a chain and warp, a bow fender and so on. Remember also:

Power gives way to sail.

Maximum speed—Lower Avon 6 mph, Upper Avon 4 mph.

Watch out for anglers, and slow down.

Keep off private land.

Keep well away from weirs and slow down when approaching locks or blind corners.

Moor only at recognised sites, moor economically, and be prepared to 'breast up' (moor side by side) where this does not obstruct traffic. Moorings are *very* limited and marked **M** on the maps.

Lower Avon Navigation Trust
(Tewkesbury to Offenham Ferry)
Gable End, The Holloway, Pershore, Worcs.
Tel: Pershore 52517.

Upper Avon Navigation Trust
(Offenham Ferry to Alveston Sluice)
Avon House, Harvington, Evesham, Worcs.
Tel: Evesham 870526.

Tewkesbury

The River Avon joins the Severn some 600
yards below Mythe Bridge. A short distance
upstream is the attractive Avon Lock,
mechanised and with a resident lock keeper
(Tewkesbury 292129). The moorings on the
Mill Avon (the branch leading to the 12thC
Abbey Mill) are a convenient base from which
to explore the town. Continuing upstream
through the narrow navigation arch of King
John's Bridge (built circa 1200 and widened in
1964) the river widens, passing a marina on its
way into open farmland and water-meadows, a
reach extensively used by the local sailing
clubs. There is no longer a ferry at Twyning,
and moorings are limited to those of the
attractive Fleet Inn, where a lane beside the
pub leads to the small village.

Navigational note
Craft entering the Avon from the Severn should
be wary of a shallow spit projecting south west
from the north bank at the junction of the 2
rivers. When approaching from upstream on
the Severn, do not cut the corner but steer close
to the south side of the junction. Craft leaving
the Avon and wishing to proceed upstream on
the Severn should not turn north until Mythe
Bridge can be seen in its entirety.
Craft navigating between the Severn and the
Avon Lock should steer a course close to the
Town Quay and Healing's Mill, thus avoiding
the mudbank opposite. Note that Avon Lock is
operated by a resident lock-keeper—do not
disturb him outside of his usual operating
times, which are posted by the lock. Keep your
craft clear of the lock wall nearest the lock
house, as there are 3 metal bosses that stand
proud of the wall, and may catch your boat
when ascending or descending.
When entering the Avon from the lock, and
when passing through the centre arch of King
John's Bridge, visibility is restricted, and great
care should be taken.

Tewkesbury
Glos. EC Thur. MD Wed. Sat. All services. An
historic town at the junction of the rivers Avon
and Severn, with many attractive and ancient
buildings to see, chief among these being of
course the Abbey. One of the more unusual
aspects of Tewkesbury is the great number of
tiny alleys leading off the main street that it is
the backbone of the town. These alleys yield
tempting views of discreet cottages, gardens,
back walls and private yards. One of
these—Baptist Chapel Court—leads to the old
chapel, built around 1655. This tiny, simple
building and its little burial ground reflect well
the modest aspirations of the minority Baptist
movement. There are very many other
buildings of great interest throughout
Tewkesbury, chiefly of the timbered variety,
with overhanging gables. Some have curious
names like 'House of the Nodding Gables' and
'Ancient Drudge'. There is also a liberal
scattering of historic pubs, notably the Hop
Pole Inn (associated with Dickens' 'Pickwick
Papers') and the Bell hotel, an Elizabethan
building which was Abel Fletcher's home in the
book 'John Halifax, Gentlemen'.
Tewkesbury Abbey This superb building is
cathedral-like in proportions and is generally
reckoned to be one of the finest Norman
churches in the country. It is contemporary
with Gloucester Cathedral, and has the same
type of vast cylindrical arches the length of the
nave. This massive scale is repeated throughout
the building: the beautifully decorated central
tower, 46ft square and over 130ft high, is the
largest Norman tower in existence. The
recessed arch that frames the mighty west
window is over 60ft high. The Abbey's interior
is no less splendid than the exterior, and
contains interesting monuments, notably the
Despencer and Beauchamp tombs. The Abbey,
which was completed in about 1120, was part of
a Benedictine monastery until this was
threatened with dissolution by King Henry
VIII in 1539. The townspeople bought the
Abbey—for £453—to save it from demolition,
and it became the town's parish church.
The Abbey Cottages Church St. The most
unusual buildings in Tewkesbury must surely
be the row of medieval shops near the Abbey.

These 25 cottages were rescued from dereliction and threatened demolition when it was realised that they are unique in this country. As built, in about 1450, they were made of wattle and daub in a heavy timber framework. The ground floor consisted of trodden earth, the windows had no glass, and there was no chimney in the roof—the smoke from the fireplace escaped through a hole under the eaves. The shutters covering the big window facing the street folded down to form a shop counter. One of the houses has been restored to this original state and may be visited: the others have been modified to provide pleasantly discreet modern houses. The restoration of this terrace won a Civic Trust award.

Tewkesbury Museum Barton St. A small museum in a delightfully irregular timber-framed house. Displays of local history, costumes and furniture. Also a large model of the Battle of Tewkesbury. *Open weekdays during the summer.*

Barton Fair takes place in Tewkesbury every 10th October except when that date falls on a Sunday. One of the oldest fairs in the country, it used to be held at the monastery gate.

Tewkesbury Steam Fair and Organ Festival every July, in the meadows by the Avon. This is becoming an important event on steam enthusiasts' calendars, attracting increasing numbers of cherished traction engines, steam rollers and miscellaneous fairground machinery every year.

Battle of Tewkesbury 4th May 1471 The last decisive battle in the Wars of the Roses, fought to the south of the town, where the Lancastrians, under Queen Margaret's commanders Somerset, Wenlock and Devonshire were defeated by Edward IV's Yorkists under Edward, Gloucester and Hastings.
Tourist Information Tewkesbury 295027.

BOATYARDS

Ⓑ **The Tewkesbury Yacht Marina** Bredon Rd (Tewkesbury 293737). Ⓡ Ⓢ Ⓦ Ⓟ Ⓓ Pump-out, gas, boat-building and repairs, chandlery, toilets, showers, winter storage, mooring (ring in advance). *Closed Sat afternoons and Sun.*
Ⓑ **Telestar Pleasure Cruisers** 185 Queen's Rd (Tewkesbury 294088). On the Mill Avon by Abbey Mill. Cruiser hire, day boat hire, 47-seater trip boat 'Avon Belle'. Maps, books, overnight and long-term moorings. BWB & Avon licences.

MOORING

See also Boatyards and Pubs. Overnight moorings on Mill Avon by Healing's Mill, below King John's Bridge on west bank, and below Avon Lock at the Town Quay.

PUBS

Many pubs and hotels in Tewkesbury, including
🍺 **Bell** Church St. 12thC inn opposite the Abbey.
🍺 **Berkeley Arms** Church St. 17thC.
🍺 **Olde Black Bear** High St. Said to be the oldest inn in Gloucestershire.
🍺 **Riverside** On the Mill Avon. Mooring by arrangement.
🍺✗ **Royal Hop Pole Hotel** On the Mill Avon near Abbey Mill. Lunch and dinner, mooring by arrangement.
🍺**Fleet Inn** Twyning. Riverside with gardens, overnight mooring by arrangement.
🍺**Village Inn** Twyning.

Bredon Hill seen from Twyning. The Avon is quite wide here. *David Perrott*

Bredon

A half a mile above Twyning the M5 motorway
crosses the flood plain on a high embankment,
beyond which is the village of Bredon, where
the fine 14thC Tithe Barn can be seen from the
river. There are many moored cruisers and tidy
gardens making the river-front attractive and
interesting.

The river is wide to Strensham Lock, and is
used extensively by the unusually named
Severn Sailing Club. Below the lock a pipe
bridge carries the Coventry Water Main over
the navigation, and beyond this the weir spills
into the river, creating a very strong cross
current when there is 'fresh' water in the river.
The lock is operated by a resident lock keeper
(Evesham 750355) who lives in the old Mill
House. A limited number of moorings are
available by arrangement with him, but
unfortunately the small shop no longer
operates.

The river now starts to meander around
Eckington village, passing under a railway
bridge carrying the main Exeter to Newcastle
upon Tyne line before reaching Eckington
Bridge, a many-arched and irregular 16thC
structure, still in good condition.

Bredon
Hereford & Worcs. P.O. Stores, A substantial
and attractive village with many fine timbered
buildings. Close to the river is a 14thC Tithe
Barn (National Trust), 124ft long and once one
of the best preserved in the country, where
grain—paid as taxes to the church—was once
stored. Severely damaged by fire, it has now
been rebuilt. The Church of St Giles has a
vaulted Norman porch, and dates from
c1180—it was mentioned by John Masefield in
'All the land from Ludlow Town to Bredon
Church's spire'. Bredon Hill, which dominates
the river for several miles, rises to 961ft some 3
miles to the north east—it is said that 8 or more
counties can be seen from its summit on a fine
day. On the southern slope is an 18thC
castellated folly, Bell's Castle, and on the top is
a 2ndC BC hill fort containing Parson's Folly, a
prominent tower built late 18thC. The hill was
celebrated in A. E. Houseman's 'A Shropshire
Lad.'

Strensham
Hereford & Worcs. Birthplace of Samuel Butler
(1612–1680), verse satirist and secretary to
Judge Thomas Jeffrey, who lived in the 16thC
house by the well-sited Church of St Phillip and
St James, which has a painted gallery and 2 fine
brasses of the Russells, once the Lords of the
Manor. The key is kept at the farm.

Eckington
Hereford & Worcs. P.O. Stores. A dormitory
village of little interest except for Holy Trinity
Church, which dates from the 12thC, and 3
pubs. Walk from Strensham Lock or
Eckington Bridge.

BOATYARDS

Ⓑ **Bredon Boatyard** Dock Lane, Bredon.
(Bredon 72795). Hire boats. Limited mooring
(all that is available in Bredon) by prior
arrangement.

MOORING

See also Boatyards. Overnight mooring by prior
arrangement with the lock keeper at Strensham
(Evesham 750352).

PUBS

Royal Oak Bredon.
Fox & Hounds Bredon. Thatched 15thC
inn with garden.
Crown Inn Eckington.
Bell Inn Eckington.
Anchor Inn Cotheridge Lane, Eckington.
Wadworth's real ale.

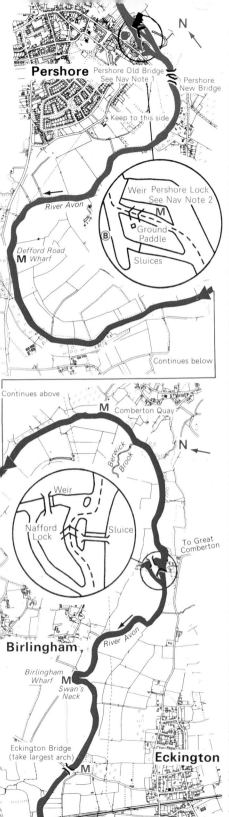

Pershore

Above Eckington Bridge the river meanders beside the ever-present Bredon Hill, turning a full 180 degrees at the Swan's Neck. Nafford Lock adjoins the wilderness of Nafford Island, a nature reserve, and a path leads from here to Birlingham, 1 mile to the north west. The swing bridge across the lock must be left closed on leaving. The path over the sluice leads to Eckington, Woollas Hall and Great Comberton but alas, there are no moorings by the lock, the next being those at Comberton Quay. There is little to see from the river until Pershore is reached.

Navigational note

1 The 2 bridges at Pershore are extremely difficult to navigate when there is 'fresh' water in the river. The navigable arches align awkwardly and the current rushes around the piers of the old bridge, causing considerable turbulence.
2 Pershore Lock. When *filling* the chamber to lock up, open the ground paddle first, then open the gate paddle when it is submerged. When *emptying* the chamber to lock down, ensure the ground paddle is closed.

Woollas Hall

A mile south of Nafford Lock. A fine Elizabethan manor house with a three-storey porch, now divided into flats. Beyond the hall, a track climbs to the summit of Bredon Hill.

Great Comberton

Hereford & Worcs. Stores. One of the timeless small villages which surround Bredon Hill—Little Comberton, Bricklehampton and especially Elmley Castle, with its half-timbered cottages and Church of St Mary containing fine 17thC monuments are worth visiting.

Pershore

Hereford & Worcs. All services, and swimming baths by the river. A busy market town with many well kept Georgian buildings, set among fruit farms and market gardens. The fine 6-arched 14thC bridge over the Avon no longer carries traffic—a 3-arched structure built in 1928 now takes the load. The Abbey, now the Parish Church of Holy Cross, was built on the site of a wooden building erected in AD689 by King Oswald. This was replaced in 983 by a new building commissioned by Ethelwold, and again by a later Norman building, finally consecrated in 1239. In 1288 a fire destroyed part of the abbey (and much of the town) resulting in much rebuilding before the dissolution in 1539. Restoration was by Scott 1862–65. Of the original Norman building, the nave, crossing and transepts survive. The church of St Andrew, very close by, is now a community centre. Perrott House in Bridge Street was built in 1760 by George Perrott, when he purchased the Lower Avon Navigation.

BOATYARDS

Ⓑ **Millside Boatyard** 37a Bridge St, Pershore. (Pershore 2849). W P D Slipway, gas, boat and engine repairs, mooring, chandlery, toilets, winter storage.

MOORING

See also Boatyards and Pubs. There are good overnight moorings above Eckington Bridge, and less attractive ones at Birlingham Wharf (Swan's Neck), Comberton Quay and Defford Road Wharf. The Recreation Ground moorings above Pershore Lock are convenient for the town, and thus very popular. There is also limited mooring below the lock.

PUBS

Old Mill Elmley Castle. Food, garden.
Plough Inn Elmley Castle. Own brew cider.
Queen Elizabeth Elmley Castle. Food, garden.
Cider House Woodmancote, Defford. Draught cider, no beer.
Defford Arms Garden.
Angel Inn Pershore. Riverside garden. Mooring by arrangement.
Brandy Cask Pershore. Mooring by arrangement.
Star Inn Bridge St, Pershore. Riverside garden. Mooring by arrangement.

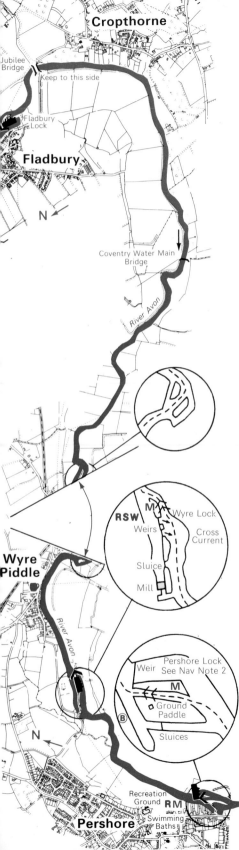

Wyre Piddle

The reach between the locks at Pershore and
Wyre Piddle is the shortest on the navigation,
being just one mile. Wyre Mill, called by the
traveller Charles Showell 'the ugliest, of which
the Avon is ashamed' is now used by the Lower
Avon Navigation Trust as a sailing and social
club. The lock is diamond-shaped, the last of
its kind on the river. Approaching from
downstream the weir creates a strong cross
current, especially after prolonged rain. Wyre
Piddle (the Piddle Brook runs behind the
village) spreads around the outside of a wide
bend, with gardens down to the river, and the
Anchor Inn providing a useful mooring for
patrons.

The villages then skirt the flood plain of the
Avon, and there is little to see except for the
wild life—those interested in herons will be
particularly pleased. Beyond the Coventry
Water Main Bridge the village of Cropthorne
sits on higher ground to the south east. Below
Jubilee Bridge are the remains of the last flash
lock on the river, dismantled in 1961.

Wyre Piddle
Hereford & Worcs. P.O. Stores. A main road
village with no public mooring. The church has
a Norman chancel arch and font, and an early
English bellcote.

Cropthorne
Hereford & Worcs. Store. An attractive village of
thatch and timbers on the 'Spring blossom
route'. Much local fruit and vegetable produce
is sold from small roadside stalls in this area.

MOORING

See also Pubs and Restaurants. There are
overnight moorings in the weir stream at Wyre
Lock.

PUBS & RESTAURANTS

Anchor Inn Wyre Piddle. Bar meals and
restaurant, large riverside garden and the only
mooring for the village, by arrangement only.
Riverdale Restaurant by Jubilee Bridge.
Overnight mooring by arrangement. W
New Inn Cropthorne.

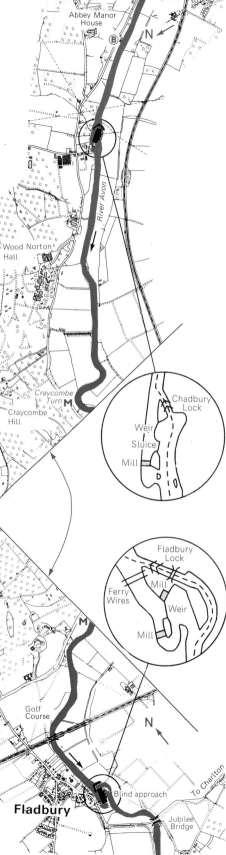

Fladbury

The approach channel below Fladbury Lock is
extremely narrow and steep sided, with
restricted vision. The lock walls narrow
towards the base and this should be borne in
mind when 2 craft lock down together. The
beautiful Fladbury Mill overlooks the weir—it
was in use as recently as 1930, and ferry wires,
difficult to see from upstream, stretch across
the weir stream. On the north side, beyond the
railway bridge carrying the main London to
Worcester line, is Evesham golf course. Above
Craycombe Turn are extensive woodlands,
while to the south lie the inevitable
water-meadows, with few buildings or roads
near the river. There is another handsome mill
at Chadbury Lock, which was restored in
1952–53, the first major project carried out by
the Lower Avon Navigation Trust, who were
helped by the Royal Engineers. Beyond the
lock, the river passes the Abbey Manor House,
and a boatyard, before passing through
Evesham in a wide loop.

Fladbury
Hereford & Worcs. P.O. Stores. A picturesque
village of half-timbered houses and cottages
around a square, once the home of William
Sandys, who began making the Avon navigable
in 1636. The Church of St John Baptist has a
fine 14thC rib-vaulted porch and contains some
fine brasses to John Throckmorton and his
wife. About 1 mile to the north east is
Craycombe House, built c1791 by George
Byfield for George Perrott (see Pershore) and
later restored by the author Francis Brett
Young, who lived here from 1932 until he went
to South Africa after the Second World War.
Wood Norton Above the north bank below
Chadbury Lock. Once the seat of the Duc
d'Aumale and later the Duc d'Orleans,
pretender to the throne of France, it now
houses an engineering school run by the BBC,
who have built some incongruous modern
buildings to accompany the mansion.
Abbey Manor House 1 mile above Chadbury
Lock, on the north bank, c1840. An obelisk in
the grounds overlooks the site of the Battle of
Evesham, 4 August 1265, when Simon de
Montfort and his rebel barons were defeated by
the Royalists under Prince Edward, resulting in
some 4000 deaths. Another memorial, the
Leicester Tower, built c1840, is visible in the
woodland.

BOATYARDS

Ⓑ **Sankey Marine** Worcester Road, below the
Abbey Manor House (Evesham 2338). Ⓟ Ⓓ
Slipway, gas, boat and outboard sales,
overnight moorings by arrangement. Passing
hire craft are charged for water, which is
available free above the railway bridge.

MOORING

See also Boatyards. Overnight mooring available
at Craycombe Turn.

PUBS

🍺 **Anchor** Fladbury.
🍺 **Chequers** Fladbury.
🍺 **Gardener's Arms** The Green, Charlton.

Evesham

Care should be taken approaching Hampton Ferry, where a wire stretches across the river—this will be lowered when the ferry man hears 3 long blasts of your hooter. Above the ferry to the west is Clarke's Hill, where the monks of Evesham once grew vines. Beyond the A435 road bridge the Abbey Public Park opens out to the north, with riverside gardens giving way to the borough moorings and Workman Gardens to the east, below the handsome Workman Bridge, built in 1856. After passing through the centre arch of the bridge, you will see the lock to the left past the old mill stream. There is a resident lock keeper here (Evesham 6511), who lives in an unusual triangular house built in 1972 to span the chamber of an earlier lock. He has a small shop and sells Lower Avon Navigation Trust licences. Craft should keep well away from the weir above the lock, passing close to the boatyard on the opposite bank. The river is then once again in open country, entering the Vale of Evesham, a major fruit and vegetable growing area.
The Bridge Inn at Offenham marks the official boundary between the Lower and Upper Navigations; the wooden bridge is no longer there, but a cable ferry operates, and a lookout should be kept for this obstruction.

Evesham
Hereford & Worcs. EC Wed. All Services. A town which owes the major part of its prosperity to the fruit and vegetable growing in the Vale of Evesham—in the spring a mass of blossom, and in the autumn rich in local produce. All that remains of the once-important Benedictine abbey, founded in 714 by Bishop Egwin and dissolved by Henry VIII in 1539, is the fine timbered gatehouse, a detached bell tower (1533) and a few ruins. Close by there are elegant Georgian buildings and half-timbered houses, Booth Hall (late 15thC) being a fine example. Close to the bell tower are 2 notable churches—St Lawrence (16thC) and All Saints (12thC). There is an annual regatta on Spring Bank Holiday, rowing boats can be hired and an ex-Thames steamer, the Gaiety, does trips.
Information Centre Evesham 6944
Offenham
Hereford & Worcs. EC Sat. P.O.Tel, Stores. 12 centuries ago this was the headquarters of Offa, King of Mercia; today it is one of the few English villages to possess a maypole. The village has grown considerably, and of the original Church of St Mary and St Milburga only the tower remains.

BOATYARDS

Ⓑ **Evesham Marina** Kings Rd. (Evesham 47813). Ⓡ Ⓢ Ⓦ Ⓓ Ⓔ Pump-out, gas, repairs, slipway, boat building, repairs, craneage, breakdown service. Narrow boat hire. Overnight mooring.
Ⓑ **Abbots Salford Marine** (Evesham 870244). Ⓦ Moorings, supplies, gas. *Closed Nov–Feb.*

MOORING

See also Boatyards and Pubs. There is a single overnight mooring, for a fee, below the A435 bridge on the south side, and extensive borough moorings by Workman Gardens, for a fee. Weir Meadow Caravan Park, between Workman Bridge and the lock, has overnight moorings with full facilities for craft up to 24ft long. By arrangement, ring Evesham 2417.

PUBS

🍺 **Cider Mill** Hampton.
Plenty of pubs in Evesham.
🍺✕ **Northwich Arms Hotel** Waterside, Evesham. Grill and Buttery. Moorings opposite, by arrangement.
🍺✕ **Evesham Hotel** Coopers Lane, Evesham. Garden, moorings opposite.
🍺 **Swan** Port St, Evesham. Snacks, garden.
🍺✕ **Bridge Inn** by the ferry, Offenham. Ⓡ Ⓦ Ⓔ Mooring by arrangement.

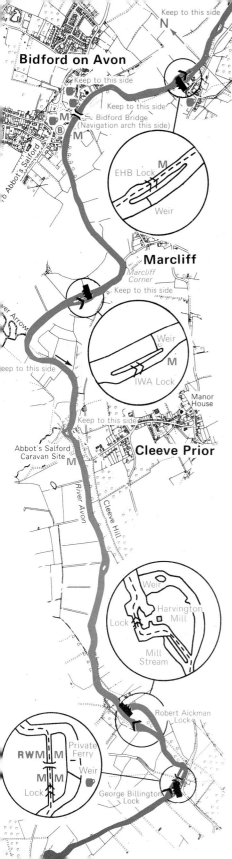

Bidford-on-Avon

George Billington Lock is the first of the new Upper Avon locks, built in the winter of 1969. The unusual flood-proof lock keeper's hut, the 'Offenham light' is a more recent addition. The new lock cut joins the river at right angles, and care should be exercised when rejoining the main course. Robert Aickman Memorial Lock soon follows, overlooked by Harvington Mill, disused since the turn of the century. The original Robert Aickman Lock was the first to be built on the restored Upper Avon, being completed in the summer of 1969, but was re-sited in 1982 due to erosion and silting of the original course. The steep ridge of Cleeve Hill closes from the south to a virtual cliff at the water's edge below Cleeve Prior. The river now heads north away from Marcliff Hill, entering Warwickshire and approaching Bidford on Avon. The village backs onto the north bank, faced by park and meadowland. E. & H. Billington Lock is sited by the pretty hamlet of Barton.

Navigational note
The navigation arch of Bidford Bridge is to the far right when heading upstream.
Middle Littleton
Hereford & Worcs. Walk east from the Fish and Anchor Inn to see the tithe barn (National Trust), 136ft × 32ft, thought to have been built by John de Ombersley, Abbot of Evesham from 1367 to 1377. Nearby is the 17thC stone Manor House and St Nicholas's Church.
Harvington
Hereford & Worcs. P.O. Stores. A typical timbered Worcestershire village. The offices of the Upper Avon Navigation Trust are in the old railway station.
Cleeve Prior
Hereford & Worcs. P.O. Stores. The manor house (private) is a handsome 16thC building, standing in well kept grounds with a fine display of yews. The Church of St Andrew still retains some Norman and Early English work.
Bidford-on-Avon
Warwicks. P.O. Stores, bank. The irregularly arched bridge was built in 1482 by the monks of Alcester, near the site of a Roman ford which was finally removed in 1970. A new bypass has brought peace to this pleasant village of old timbered buildings, amongst which is the solidly built former Falcon Inn—Shakespeare is said to have taken part in a drinking contest here. The Church of St Lawrence, by the river, dates from 1276, but was restored in 1835.

BOATYARDS
ⓑ **Bidford Boats** Riverside House, 4 The Pleck, Bidford-on-Avon (Bidford-on-Avon 773205) Ⓢ Ⓦ Ⓔ Hire cruisers, overnight moorings, slipway.

MOORING
See also Pubs. There are free overnight moorings at George Billington Lock. Overnight moorings are available, for a fee, at Abbots Salford Caravan Site (unfortunately on the opposite bank to Cleeve Prior), and at IWA Lock (free). The public moorings at Bidford are very limited, and access is hampered by a steep slippery bank. There is a single mooring available at Bell Court on the town side, and more at Bidford Boats, both for a fee. Upstream, at Barton, there are free overnight moorings in the lock cut.

PUBS
🍺 **Fish and Anchor Inn** George Billington Lock. Food, gardens. A private ferry crosses the weir stream, allowing access from the moorings.
🍺 **Coach & Horses** Harvington.
🍺✕ **Dog (or Talbot)** Harvington. Garden.
🍺✕ **King's Arms** Cleeve Prior.
🍺 **Bull's Head** Bidford on Avon.
🍺 **Plough Inn** Bidford on Avon.
🍺✕ **White Lion Hotel** Riverside, Bidford on Avon.
In Bidford there is a useful off-licence, with a short-term mooring for customers, below the bridge.
🍺 **Cottage of Content** Barton. 15thC pub with garden by the river. Food.

Welford-on-Avon

Proceeding upstream, craft should follow the narrower right-hand channel below Bidford Grange—there were once 2 mills and a lock here, but now nothing remains. Beyond is the new Pilgrim Lock, built in the winter of 1970. The river flows through attractive meadowland, and pleasant orchards announce the village of Welford-on-Avon and W. A. Cadbury Lock, completed in July 1971. The river meanders round the village, passing a once-fine Victorian house adorned with a grotesque modern chimney, before the multi-arched Binton Bridges, the former mill and the Four Alls pub are reached. Weston-on-Avon lies to the south on a very attractive stretch of deep water with many trees lining the banks.
Luddington Lock was built in spring 1971—there are overnight moorings here, but a sign informs 'sorry, no shop, no pub'.

Hillborough Manor Private. It is thought that Charles II fled here in September 1651 after being defeated by Cromwell at Worcester.
Welford-on-Avon
Warwicks. P.O. Tel. Stores. The Church of St Peter is of Norman and early English origin, situated in the older and more attractive part of what is now a desirable commuter village. There is a maypole, and several pubs. Weston-on-Avon lies a short distance to the east and can be reached by what is, in part, a -riverside walk; visit the Church of All Saints, itself by the river.
Luddington
Warwicks. It is thought that Shakespeare may have been married here, in a church now replaced by a more recent building.

MOORING

See also Pubs. There are free overnight moorings at Pilgrim Lock, W. A. Cadbury Lock, Welford (no access to village), and below Binton Bridges (access to Welford), for a fee. There are also free overnight moorings above Luddington Lock.

PUBS

Four Alls Binton Bridges. A smart riverside pub and restaurant with a garden—its name, in the stained glass of the public bar, is explained thus:

> A King I rule over all
> A parson I pray for all
> A soldier I fight for all
> A farmer I pay for all

Overnight mooring by arrangement. (A similarly named pub, the 'Five-Alls', is situated in Chepstow.)W
Blue Boar 1 mile NW of Binton. Food, garden.
Bell Welford. Food. Children's room.
Shakespeare Inn Welford. 16thC village local that was once a school. Children's play area and barbecue facilities.

Stratford-upon-Avon

The River Stour joins the Avon from the south as Stratford-upon-Avon Racecourse is approached. The disused railway bridge here once carried the line from Stratford to Gloucester.

Weir Brake Lock, which takes its name from the wooded bank to the south east of the river, was completed early in 1973; the weir was completed a few months later. Immediately beyond the disused Stratford to London railway bridge is the very deep Stratford New Lock, reinforced by a series of rectangular steel girder frames to overcome the high ground pressures and overlooked by a monument to celebrate the re-opening of the navigation. On sunny summer weekends the lockside and bridge is thick with gongoozlers enjoying the river, the boats and the extensive parkland. A block of flats now stands on the site of the old Lucy's Mill.

Above the lock the river throngs with cruisers, trip boats and rowing boats, overlooked by the red-brick hulk of the Royal Shakespeare Theatre.

The Stratford-on-Avon canal basin can be seen beyond the entrance lock below Tramway Bridge, which was built in 1823 to carry the Stratford and Moreton Horse Tramway from the Bancroft basin to Moreton-in-Marsh. It is now a footbridge. The 14-arched road bridge was built circa 1480 by Sir Hugh Clopton, once Lord Mayor of London, and was widened in 1814.

The surroundings become quieter as the river gently winds to its effective head of navigation by The Red House, although shallow-draught craft may proceed to just below Alveston Weir.

Stratford-upon-Avon
Warwicks. EC Thur. MD Wed. Fri. All services.
Tourism has been established a very long time in Stratford, ever since 1789 when the first big celebrations in William Shakespeare's honour were organised by the actor David Garrick. They are now held annually on St George's Day, 23rd April, which is believed to be Shakespeare's birthday. An annual Mop Fair on the 12th October reminds the visitor that Stratford was already well established as a market town long before Shakespeare's time. (The first grant for a weekly market was given by King John in 1196.) Today, Stratford is well used to the constant flow of charabancs and tourists, ancient charm vying with the expected commercialism that usually mars popular places like this. There are wide streets of endless low, timbered buildings that house dignified hotels and antique shops: plenty of these are also private houses. On the river, hired punts and rowing boats jostle each other while people picnic on the open parkland on the banks. The Royal Shakespeare Theatre, opened in 1932, is a splendid institution on an enviable site beside the Avon, but the aesthetic appeal of its massive 'industrial' style is limited. It was designed by Elizabeth Scott to replace an earlier theatre, destroyed by fire in 1926.
Shakespeare Birthplace Trust This Trust was founded in 1847 to look after the 5 buildings most closely associated with Shakespeare; 4 of these are in Stratford (listed below) and the other is Mary Arden's cottage at Wilmcote (see page 178). *There is a standard opening time for these properties, any variation on this standard is shown in the individual entries. Open weekdays and Sun afternoons Apr-Oct. Weekdays only Nov-Mar.*
Shakespeare's Birthplace Henley St. An early 16thC half-timbered building containing books, manuscripts and exhibits associated with Shakespeare and rooms furnished in period style. Next door is the Shakespeare Centre. *Open Sun afternoons Nov-Mar.*
Hall's Croft Old Town. A Tudor house complete with period furniture—the home of Shakespeare's daughter Susanna and her husband Dr John Hall.
New Place Chapel St. The foundations of Shakespeare's last home set in a replica of an Elizabethan garden.
Anne Hathaway's Cottage Shottery, 1 mile west of Stratford. Dating from the 15thC this fine thatched farmhouse was once the home of Anne Hathaway before she married William

Shakespeare. It has a mature, typically English garden, and long queues of visitors in the summer. The cottage was badly damaged by fire in 1969, but has since been completely restored. *Open Sun afternoons Nov-Mar.*

Holy Trinity Church attractively situated among trees overlooking the recently restored lock on the river Avon. It is mainly of the 15thC but the spire was rebuilt in 1763. Interesting misericords depict some amusing scenes, and fine monuments include one of William Shakespeare who is buried in the chancel. His tomb bears a curse against anyone who disturbs it.

Shakespeare Memorial Theatre (box office 292271). The home of the Royal Shakespeare Company, who produce Shakespeare plays to a very high standard *from Apr to Dec every year.*

Clopton Bridge A very fine stone bridge over the Avon, originally built by Sir Hugh Clopton c1480–90—he later became Lord Mayor of London. The bridge is close to the canal basin. The brick bridge nearby was built in 1823 to carry a horse-drawn tramway connecting Stratford with Shipston-on-Stour. It is now a footbridge.

Information Centre Judith Shakespeare House, 1 High St, Stratford-on-Avon (293127) Judith Shakespeare was William's younger daughter. In 1616 she married and moved into this former tavern, once called The Cage. It is a characteristic Elizabethan building of 3 storeys. Judith Shakespeare is buried in the graveyard of Holy Trinity church in Stratford.

BOATYARDS

There are trip boats and many rowing and motor boats for hire in Stratford-upon-Avon.
Ⓑ **Stratford Marine**, by Clopton Bridge, Stratford-upon-Avon (Stratford 69669).
Ⓡ Ⓢ Ⓦ Ⓓ Ⓔ Pump-out, gas, chandlery, narrow boat hire, repairs, toilets, showers, overnight mooring.

MOORING

See also Boatyards. There are free overnight moorings at Weir Brake Lock, below Stratford New Lock, by the Recreation Ground opposite the theatre, in the Stratford Canal Basin, and at the Old Bathing Place ¾ mile above Clopton Bridge.

PUBS

Plenty in Stratford-upon-Avon, many named for the benefit of visitors, such as 'The Pen and Parchment'. Also:
🍺 **Black Swan** Waterside. Known also as the 'Dirty Duck'.
🍺 **Cross Keys** Ely St, near the High St.
🍺 **Old Tramway Inn** Shipston Rd.
🍺 **Queens Head** Ely St. Known as Doug & Edna's bar.
🍺 **Red Lion** Warwick Rd. Snacks.
🍺✕ **Shakespeare Hotel** Chapel St. Visit the 'Froth and Elbow' bar!
🍺 **White Swan Hotel** Rother St. Has fine early wall painting.
🍺 **Ferry Inn** Alveston. Food, garden.
🍺 **Alveston Manor** Hotel. Banbury Rd. Food.

Peace and quiet on the Upper Avon. *David Perrott*

GRAND UNION

Maximum dimensions

Regents canal
Length: 72'
Beam: 14' 6"
Headroom: 9'
Brentford and Paddington to Birmingham
(Camp Hill top lock)
Length: 72'
Beam: 12' 6"
Headroom: 7' 11"
Norton Junction to Foxton Junction
Length: 72'
Beam: 7'
Headroom: 7' 6"
Market Harborough to Leicester
Length: 72'
Beam: 10'
Headroom: 7'
Aylesbury and Northampton Arms
Length: 72'
Beam: 7'
Headroom: 7'

Mileage

Thames, BRENTFORD to:
Bull's Bridge: 6
Black Jack's Lock: 15
Watford: 21
Berkhamsted: 31½
Bulbourne: 38
Leighton Buzzard: 47½
Fenny Stratford: 55
Cosgrove: 66
Stoke Bruerne: 72
Gayton Junction: 76
Buckby Locks: 88
Braunston: 93½
Napton Junction: 98½
Leamington Spa: 109
Shrewley: 115½
Salford Junction: 135½

Locks: 165
Paddington Arm: 13¾
No locks

The Grand Union Canal is unique among English canals in being composed of at least 8 separate canals. This system links London with Birmingham, Leicester and Nottingham. Up to the 1920s all these canals were owned and operated by quite separate companies: there were 5 between London and Birmingham alone.

The original—and still the most important—part of the system was the Grand Junction Canal. This was constructed at the turn of the 18thC to provide a short cut between Braunston on the Oxford canal and Brentford, west of London on the Thames. Previously, all London-bound traffic from the Midlands had to follow the winding, narrow Fazeley, Coventry and Oxford canals down to Oxford, there to tranship into lighters to make the 100-mile trip downriver to Brentford and London. The new Grand Junction Canal cut this distance by fully 60 miles, and with its 14ft wide locks and numerous branches to important towns rapidly became busy and profitable. The building of wide locks to take 70-ton barges was a brave attempt to persuade neighbouring canal companies—the Oxford, Coventry and the distant Trent and Mersey—to widen their navigations and establish a 70-ton barge standard throughout the waterways of the Midlands. Unfortunately the other companies were deterred by the cost of widening, and to this day those same canals—and many others—can only pass boats 7ft wide. The history of the English canals might have turned out very differently had the Grand Junction's attempt succeeded.

The mere proposal of the building of the Grand Junction Canal was enough to generate and justify plans for other canals linked to it. Before the Grand Junction itself was completed, independent canals were built linking it in a direct line to Warwick and Birmingham, and a little later a connection was established from the Grand Junction to Market Harborough and Leicester, and thence via the canalised River Soar to the Trent. Unfortunately, part of this line was eventually built with narrow locks, thereby sealing the fate of the Grand Junction's wide canals scheme.

Meanwhile in London in 1812 the Regent's Canal Company was formed to cut a new canal from the Grand Junction's very busy Paddington Arm, round London to Limehouse, where a big dock was planned at the junction with the Thames. This was duly opened in 1820, narrowly escaping conversion at an early stage into a railway, and proved extremely successful. Ten years later a 1½-mile-long canal—the Hertford Union—was built: this remains a useful short cut from Regent's Canal to the River Lee.

These were the canals that made up the spine of southern England's transport system until the advent of the railways. When in this century the Regents Canal Company acquired the Grand Junction and others, the whole system was integrated as the Grand Union Canal company in 1929. The new company, aided by the Government, in 1932 launched a massive programme of modernisation: widening the 52 locks from Braunston to Birmingham, piling and dredging, etc. But when the grant was all spent, the task was unfinished and broad beam boats never became common on the Grand Union canal.

The great attempt to break loose from narrow boat carrying had failed, and after this the Grand Union could only begin to decline. Now narrow boat carrying on the canal is virtually finished, although there is still some barge trade at the London end.

Limehouse

In the Greater London area little specific information is given that does not relate directly to the canal; but canalside pubs and restaurants are included together with some nearby places to eat and drink. Places and features of interest can be found in Nicholson's 'London Guide'. The Regent's Canal begins at Limehouse Basin (previously known as Regent's Canal Dock) in London's dockland and climbs up round central London towards Paddington. It is mostly flanked by the backs of houses and factories which usually contain the canal in a remarkably private and peaceful world of its own. The towpath can now be followed from Salmon Lane Lock along the whole length of the Regent's Canal to West London, and there are frequent access points. The booklet 'London Is—Canal Walks' gives full details (available from the BWB or London Tourist Board). East of Kensal Green access gates may be locked during hours of darkness. In Islington a BWB Sanitary Station padlock key will open access gates—other boroughs may follow this example in due course. There is still a small trade on the canal, mostly in timber. The entrance to the Regent's canal and to the River Lee Navigation from the Thames is through a big ship lock and across Limehouse Basin. The ship lock is only opened during the 3 hours preceding every high water; any queries should be put to the Section Office on 01-790 3444.
The Hertford Union Canal (often known as Duckett's), is a useful short cut between the Regent's Canal and the Lee Navigation, running along the attractive Victoria Park.

Victoria Park Hackney. Beside the canal. Almost 300 acres of parkland which comes as a relief after so much townscape. Designed by James Pennthorne, a protégé of Nash, and laid out between 1842 and 1845.
Limehouse Basin Limehouse. The terminus of the Regent's Canal and of the Lee Navigation where they meet the Thames, the basin used to be crowded with ships, barges and narrow-boats. Once known as the Regent's Canal Dock, this basin is now the subject of a plan to develop a marina incorporating housing, offices, pubs and shops, at a cost of £70 million over a period of 6 years. There is still a good deal of barge traffic here, and visiting pleasure craft should take care.

PUBS

- **Freemason** Salmon Lane E14.
- **Vulcan** Salmon Lane E14.
- **Royal Cricketers** 211 Old Ford Road E3. Bar food, garden. [E]

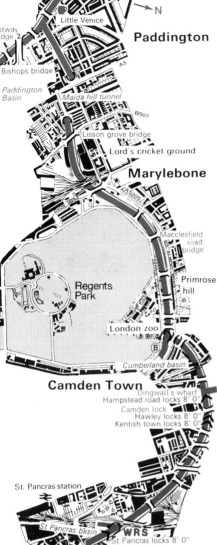

Within the map the following labels appear:

Ha'penny bridge
N
Little Venice
Westway bridge 2
Bishops bridge
Paddington Basin
Paddington
A5
Maida hill tunnel
B507
Lisson grove bridge
Lord's cricket ground
Marylebone
A5205
Macclesfield road bridge
Regents Park
Primrose hill
London zoo
Cumberland basin
B
Camden Town
Dingwall's wharf
Hampstead road locks 8' 0"
Camden lock
Hawley locks 8' 0"
Kentish town locks 8' 0"
St. Pancras station
St Pancras basin
W R S
St Pancras locks 8' 0"
St Pancras
Battlebridge basin
W S
18M 4L
Bull's Bridge
Limehouse Bsn
4½M 8L
Islington tunnel
Islington
City road locks 8' 0" R S W
City Road basin
Wenlock basin
Sturts locks 8' 0"

Regent's Park

The canal continues to climb, passing 2 large basins before plunging under Islington through a ½-mile tunnel (forbidden to unpowered craft), then round the back of St Pancras and Camden Town. Here, at Camden High Road, the top locks are reached and the long level begins (27 miles of canal without a lock). Near the top lock is a castellated youth club; boatmen should beware of the many young persons rowing and canoeing nearby, and at Hampstead Road Locks the BWB have a canal information centre in the lock cottage. Soon the industrial surroundings melt away and, rounding a right-angled bend, the canal suddenly enters London Zoo and Regent's Park—which look splendid from the water. (Do *not* attempt to tie up and walk into the Zoo without paying.) The canal continues through a long wooded cutting, then leaves Regent's Park and skirts the former Marylebone goods yard—now a housing estate—beyond which is the short Maida Hill tunnel. One emerges into one of the finest stretches of urban canal in the country. Tree-lined and flanked by fine Regency houses, the Regent's Canal ends gloriously at Little Venice. To the left, under the new Westway bridge, is the vast Paddington Basin. To the right is the Paddington Arm of the former Grand Junction Canal. The 2 stop places seen at Little Venice were used for 'gauging' boats for tolls. There may be moorings available in Battlebridge Basin by arrangement with the London Narrow Boat Assoc, 16a New Wharf Rd, N1 (01-837 9256).

Islington Tunnel 960yds long, the tunnel was opened in 1816. In 1826 a towing boat was introduced, which pulled itself to and fro along a chain laid on the canal bed. This system remained until the 1930s.

Regent's Park Originally part of Henry VIII's great hunting forest in the 16thC. In 1811 the Prince Regent planned to connect the park and a new palace via the newly built Regent Street to Carlton House. Although never completed, the design by John Nash is very impressive: the park is surrounded by handsome Regency terraces and gateways. The sanctuary and the north east corner of the park are excellent points for watching migrant birds, including willow warblers, chiffchaff, white throats, redstarts and redpolls.

London Zoo Regent's Park. The canal passes along the edge of the Zoo, one of the largest in the world. Lord Snowdon's aviary can be seen from the canal. The Zoo was originally laid out by Decimus Burton in 1827, but since then many famous architects have designed special animal houses *Closed Christmas.*

Cumberland Basin A small canal basin by the Zoo which used to form the junction of the Regent's Canal main line with an arm that led off round the park to Cumberland Market near Euston Station. Much of the arm was filled in after the last war and the Zoo car park now sits on top of it. Cumberland Basin is now full of moored boats; there is also a floating restaurant.

Lord's Cricket Ground St John's Wood Rd NW8 (01-289 1615). The ground of the MCC, which is also the governing body for British cricket. Test match in *Jun or Jul.*

Canalside walk From Lisson Grove (at the east end of Maida Hill tunnel) to Regent's Park Zoo, 2 miles of the canal towpath make one of London's most attractive waterside walks. The bridges are nicely painted and wooden seats installed at intervals. With the ducks, the overhanging trees, the passing boats and London Zoo on either side, this is a remarkable stretch of urban canal.

Little Venice A very canal-conscious area centred on the junction of the Regent's and Grand Junction canals, famous for its elegant houses, colourful boats and excellent canalside views. The island and pool were named after Robert Browning. The area is sometimes referred to as Paddington Stop.

BOATYARDS

BWB St Pancras Basin Camley St NW1. R S
Permanent moorings and slipway. Apply to St
Pancras Yacht Club (01-278 2805).
London Narrow Boat Assoc 16a New Wharf
Rd N1 (01-837 9256)). W S E
B **Turner Marinas** 57 Fitzroy Rd NW1.
(01-722 9806). R W E Slipway, chandlery,
toilets, engine repairs. Moorings at Little
Venice, Cumberland Basin and Lisson Grove.

BOAT TRIPS

BWB Zoo Waterbuses Delamere Terrace W2.
(01-286 6101). A boat leaves from Little Venice
for a 40-minute trip through Regent's park into
the Zoo.
Jason's Trip 60 Blomfield Rd W9. (01-286
3428). A traditional canal narrow boat leaves
the Canaletto Gallery, a converted barge, for a
1½-hour trip through Regent's Park and Zoo to
Hampstead Road locks. Commentary during
return trip. Telephone for departure times.
Advisable to book. E
Jenny Wren Cruises 250 Camden High St
NW1. (01-485 6210). 1½-hour trip on narrow
boat through Regent's Park and the Zoo, under
the Maida Hill tunnel, round the island in
Little Venice and back. Telephone for times
and availability.
Glideways Cockaigne Cruises 152
Sewardstone Rd, E2. (01-981 4678). A *Sunday*
waterbus service from Camden Lock to
Victoria Park. 2 hrs.

PUBS & RESTAURANTS

Paddington Stop 54 Formosa St W9. Food,
overnight mooring. E
Warwick Castle Warwick Place W9. At
Little Venice and decorated with prints of the
old canal system. Bar lunches.
Gallery Boat Prince Albert Rd NW1
(01-485-8137). Converted floating barge at
Cumberland Basin. Chinese (Peking-style)
restaurant. *Open Mon–Sun LD*.
Narrow Boat 119 St Peter St, Islington.
Canalside. Food. Pub with strong canal flavour.
Island Queen 87 Noel Rd, Islington
(01-226 0307). Near City Road Basin. Busy 'in'
pub. Snacks only for lunch.
Le Routier Camden Lock, Chalk Farm Rd
NW1 (01-485 0360). Well-situated overlooking
the canal, various craft workshops and brightly
painted barges. Nouvelle cuisine; lots of fresh
fish. Advisable to reserve. *Open Mon–Sun LD*.
Constitution 42 St Pancras Way. Canalside.

Early morning at Hanwell Locks. *David Perrott*

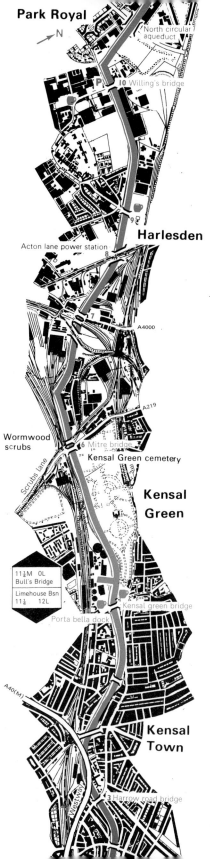

Kensal Green

The Paddington Arm continues west. Starting at a big housing estate, one passes the backs of houses in Harrow Road and then goes along the side of the well-known Kensal Green cemetery. The huge concrete structure sweeping out over the canal is the elevated Westway road. The main Western region tracks run just below the canal to the south, and beyond them can be seen the towers of Wormwood Scrubs. Acton Lane Power Station straddles the canal; not far away are the twin townships of Harlesden and Willesden. The canal crosses the North Circular road on a large aqueduct: a strange contrast between the tranquillity of the canal and the roaring traffic below.

Kensal Green Cemetery North bank of canal. Opened in 1833, the huge cemetery flanks the canal. The monuments are now all romantically overgrown, and scattered among trees. Water gates set in the wall indicate that at one time coffins for burial could be brought up by barge. Leigh Hunt, Thackeray, Macready, Trollope, Wilkie Collins and Blondin are among the famous buried here.
St Mary Magdalene Alongside the canal west of Little Venice. Built by Street, 1868–78, the church with its tall Gothic spire is now curiously isolated among modern flats. The richly decorated crypt is very striking.
Wormwood Scrubs South of canal. Expanse of open space with the famous prison on the southern boundary.

PUBS

🍺 **Plumes** Abbey Rd, Park Royal, by the Guinness Brewery. Bar lunches.
✕ **Porta Bella Dock** Kensal Rd W10 (formerly St Anne's Dock) (01-960 5456). Ⓦ A marina/market/restaurant complex. Regular boat trips from here.
🍺 **Grand Junction Arms** Acton Lane. Harlesden. Canalside. Newly converted pub with strong canal flavour. Food.
🍺 **Plough** Kensal Green bridge.
🍺 **Narrow Boat** 119 St Peter's St, Kensal Green bridge. A fully refurbished Fuller's pub with canalside seating.

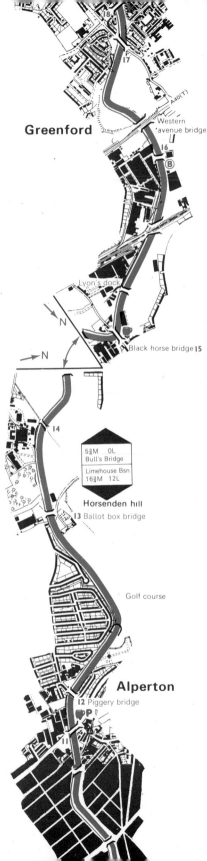

Greenford

The Paddington Arm continues west through
Alperton and Greenford. The surroundings are
mostly flat, but Horsendon Hill and Perivale
Wood provide a long stretch of beautiful hilly
parkland; an old timber yard completes the
rural scene and Sudbury Park Golf Course
adjoins the canal. Soon afterwards the canal
turns south into suburban Middlesex. A feature
of the Arm is the 'horse-dips' or steps leading
down into the water from the towpath. These
were built so that any towing horse that
accidentally fell into the 'cut' could be led along
to one of these steps and hauled up and out.
Otherwise, getting a horse out of the water
could be a long and difficult operation.

BOATYARDS

Ⓑ **Highline Yachting** Rowdell Rd, Northolt
(Iver 651496). Ⓡ Ⓢ Ⓦ Ⓓ Gas, toilet, moorings.

PUBS

🍺 **Civil Engineer** by bridge 18.
🍺✕ **Black Horse** Black Horse Bridge,
Greenford. Canalside. Food, garden.
🍺 **Pleasure Boat** Ealing Rd, Alperton.
Canalside. Food.
🍺 **Ballot Box Inn** Horsenden Lane North.
North of bridge 13.

Greenford

Western
avenue bridge

16

Ⓑ

Lyon's dock

N

N

Black horse bridge **15**

14

5¾M   0L
Bull's Bridge

Limehouse Bsn
16¾M   12L

Horsenden hill

13 Ballot box bridge

Golf course

Alperton

12 Piggery bridge

Bull's Bridge

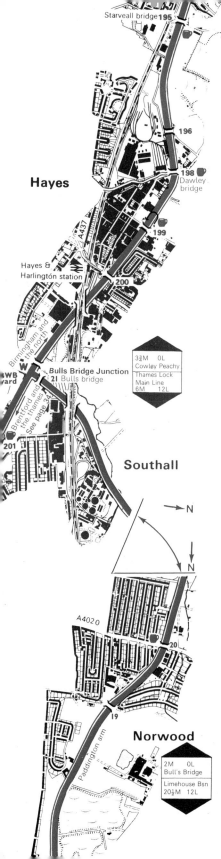

Continuing south through the industrial estate, the Paddington Arm soon reaches the junction with the main line of the Grand Union at Bull's Bridge. Here is a large BWB yard—formerly the Grand Union Canal Carrying Fleet depot—where maintenance boats are built and repaired. Turning left leads east towards Brentford and the Thames: turning right goes to Birmingham and the north. Along here the canal now enters the indivisible conurbation of Hayes, Harlington, West Drayton and Yiewsley: a good area for shops and pubs.

Hayes & Harlington
Middx. EC Wed. Much-industrialised area, home of such famous brand names as Nestlés, Heinz and EMI.
Hayes & Harlington Museum Golden Crescent. A small museum devoted to local history. *Closed Wed afternoon & Sun.*
Southall
Middx. EC Wed. Extensive modern shopping centre.
Martinware Pottery Collection Southall Public Library, Osterley Park Rd. Representative collection of Martinware, including birds, face mugs and grotesqueries. Of exceptional interest to admirers of 'art nouveau'. *Closed Sun.*

BOATYARDS

BWB Bull's Bridge Depot Bull's Bridge, Hayes Rd. Southall. (01-573 2368). D emergency only.
T & D Murrell Bull's Bridge Junction. (01-848 4485). E

BOAT TRIPS

Colne Valley Passenger Boat Services The Toll House, Bull's Bridge Wharf, Southall (01-848 4485). Trips from The Swan & Bottle (bridge 185). Ring for availability.

PUBS

🍺 **The Woolpack** Canalside at bridge 198.
🍺 **Foresters Arms** West Drayton. (80yds from bridge 195). Food.
🍺✕ **Blue Anchor** Hayes. Canalside, at bridge 199. Food.
🍺 **Grand Junction Arms** Southall. (By bridge 201). Canalside. Food. E
🍺 **Hambrough Tavern** Southall. Canalside, at A4020 bridge.

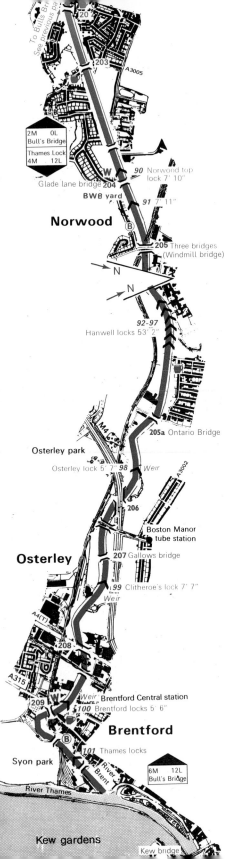

20

203 A 3005

2M 0L
Bull's Bridge

Thames Lock
4M 12L

Glade lane bridge **204** *90* Norwood top
   lock 7' 10"

BWB yard

  91 7' 11"

Norwood

205 Three bridges
(Windmill bridge)

92-97
Hanwell locks 53' 2"

205a Ontario Bridge

Osterley park

Osterley lock 5' 7' *98* Weir

206

  Boston Manor
  tube station

Osterley

207 Gallows bridge

99 Clitheroe's lock 7' 7"
  Weir

208

Weir Brentford Central station
209
100 Brentford locks 5' 6"

Brentford

101 Thames locks

Syon park

6M 12L
Bull's Bridge

River Brent

River Thames

Kew gardens

Kew bridge

Brentford

This section follows the main line of the Grand
Union east from Norwood down to the junction
with the Thames at Brentford. At Norwood is a
BWB maintenance yard; here begins the
11-lock drop to the river, including the
Hanwell flight of 6 locks. Navigators should
note that Norwood top lock is padlocked every
night for safety reasons. (17.00 in winter, 19.00
in summer). It is in parts an interesting and
attractive stretch: Osterley and Syon parks are
nearby. Brentford is still a busy canal depot and
there are several canalside pubs in Norwood.
The river Brent joins the canal at the bottom of
Hanwell locks; there is a rare intersection of
canal, road and railway at the top of these locks
and several of the bridges are of the brick
arched type more commonly seen on the rural
canals. Near the big M4 embankment is a very
attractive cast iron 'roving' bridge, dated 1820.
Towards Brentford, the towing path disappears
under the roof of a large new BWB
warehouse—an odd experience for a walker.
Kew Gardens is just across the Thames. Access
for walkers to the towpath is easily gained at the
top and bottom (from Green Lane) of Hanwell
Locks and at Brentford Locks (from Brentford
High Street), but there is no towpath from
Brentford locks to the Thames. Brentford and
Thames locks are controlled by lock keepers
and are of course subject to the tide. They
operate within 2–2½ hours of high water and
the lock keeper can be informed of your
imminent arrival on 01-560 8941 or 01-568
2779.

Navigational note
The Thames at Brentford is tidal; Teddington
Locks are 5 miles upstream. Application to
navigate the non-tidal Thames should be made
in advance to Thames Water, Nugent House,
Vastern Road, Reading, Berks. Craft entering
the canal from the Thames without the
necessary BWB licence may complete the
formalities at Brentford Depot office at
Brentford Locks. No licence is required on the
tidal river.

Osterley House
Isleworth (01-560 3918). Set in a large park—a
superb remodelled mansion with elegant
interior decorations by Robert Adam, 1760–80.
Gobelins and Beauvais tapestries and fine
carpets. Elizabethan stables in large park. *Open
afternoons. Closed Mon.* Access is unfortunately
on the south side of the M4, 1½ miles from the
canal. But Osterley Park tube station is close to
the entrance, which is just north of the A4.
Boston Manor House Boston Manor Rd,
Brentford, ½ mile north of bridge 208. (01-560
3485). Tudor and Jacobean house with
excellent examples of period ceilings. *Open
summer afternoons.* Nearest tube station: Boston
Manor (¼ mile north of the house).
British Piano Museum High St, Brentford.
(01-560 8108). In the church at the foot of the
tall gas holder east of the locks. Exceptional
collection of automatic, old and odd musical
instruments. Many of them are demonstrated
during the 90-minute guided tour. *Open Sat &
Sun afternoons. Closed Dec–Feb.*
Syon House Brentford. (01-560 0881).
Entrance 300yds west of Brentford Locks on
A315. Seat of the Duke of Northumberland.
Noted for its fine Adam interior and period
furniture, also its paintings. Its historical
associations go back to the 15thC. *Open summer
afternoons. Closed Fri & Sat.*
Syon Park Gardening Centre Park Rd,
Brentford. (01-580 0134). Very wide selection
of plants and gardening equipment for sale.
Syon Park Gardens Brentford. (01-560 0881).
55 acres of Capability Brown gardens. In the
grounds are the Gardening Centre, Live
Butterfly House and Motor Museum. Gardens
closed Xmas day & Box day.
Kew Gardens Kew (01-940 1171). On the
south bank of the Thames, opposite Brentford.
(Access from south side of the Gardens or from
the Thames towpath.) One of the world's great
botanic gardens, with thousands of rare
outdoor and hothouse plants. Kew Palace, also
worth a visit, was built in 1631 in the Dutch
style. *Open daily 10.00–sunset.* The famous
glasshouses *open 13.00, closing times vary.*

BOATYARDS

BWB Norwood Yard at Norwood top lock (01-574 1220) R S W.
Ealing Pleasure Boat Co. Three Bridges, Tentelow Lane, Southall. (01-574 1539) R S W Moorings, chandlery, hire cruisers.
T & D Murrell (01-848 4485). In dock near Norwood top lock. E
BWB Brentford Depot Brentford. A busy warehousing depot near the junction of the canal and the Thames, there are normally lighters and narrow boats still to be seen. The depot is at Brentford Locks, just off Brentford High Street (bridge 209).

PUBS

🍺 **Old Oak Tree** Southall (at bridge 202). Canalside. Food; grocery and tel nearby.
🍺 **Lamb** Norwood (at bridge 203). Canalside. P.O. shops nearby.
🍺 **Fox** Green Lane, Hanwell (at bottom of Hanwell Locks 50yds from canal). Food.
🍺 **Brewery Tavern** off Brentford High St.
🍺 **Northumberland Arms** near Brentford Locks.

Ice and snow at Denham. *Derek Pratt.*

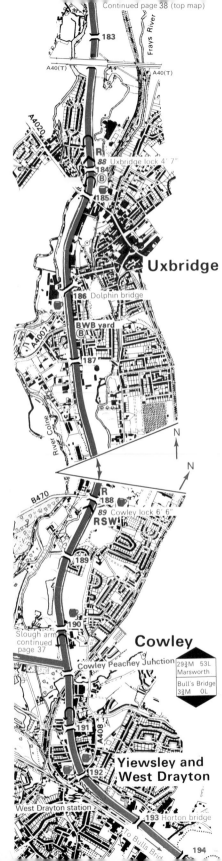

Continued page 38 (top map)

183

A40(T)   A40(T)

R

88 Uxbridge lock 4' 7"

184

B

185

Uxbridge

186 Dolphin bridge

BWB yard

B

187

N

N

R

188

89 Cowley lock 6' 6"

RSW

189

190

Slough arm
continued
page 37

Cowley

Cowley Peachey Junction

29¾M 53L
Marsworth

Bull's Bridge
3¾M   0L

191

192

Yiewsley and
West Drayton

West Drayton station

193 Horton bridge

194

Cowley Peachey
Junction

The canal begins to bend towards the north. At
Cowley Peachey junction, the Slough Arm
branches off to the west. Cowley Lock marks
the end of the 27-mile pound and the start of
the climb up the Colne valley and the Chiltern
hills. Uxbridge, just to the north, signals the
limit of the outer-suburban belt that surrounds
London. Uxbridge Lock has an attractive
setting with its lock cottage, a turnover bridge
and a tall modern flour mill standing nearby in
grounds that are splendidly landscaped down to
the water's edge; ½ mile north is an interesting
contrast between a large and utilitarian concrete
bridge carrying the A40 and a typically modest
brick arched accommodation bridge painted
white.
The Paddington Packet Boat used to run daily
from Paddington to Cowley—one of the few
passenger boats plying regularly along the
Grand Junction Canal. It was pulled by 4 horses
and had precedence over all other boats, so it
covered the 15-mile lock-free run in a time that
was remarkable at the beginning of the 19th
century. A reminder of this boat service
survives in the Paddington Packet Boat Inn at
Cowley.

Yiewsley & West Drayton
*Middx. EC Wed. P.O. Tel. Stores, garage,
station.*
Uxbridge
*Middx. EC Wed. P.O. Tel. Stores, garage,
station, cinema.* The Battle of Britain was
directed by the late Air Marshal Lord Dowding
from the R.A.F. Headquarters in Uxbridge.
The town is not otherwise particularly
noteworthy.
Hanson Museum Uxbridge Library, High St.
Local interest museum. Items relating to the
history of the town and district. *Closed Wed
afternoon.*
Narrowboat 'Pisces' An ex-working canal boat
now owned and operated from Cowley Lock by
the London Borough of Hillingdon. The boat is
used in connection with social education
activities and such activities as are covered by
the Duke of Edinburgh's Award Scheme.
Youth groups and organisations such as
'Gingerbread' may hire it from the Council's
Education Department, 265 High St,
Uxbridge, Middlesex. (Uxbridge 50111).

BOATYARDS

Ⓑ **Denham Yacht Station** by bridge 184.
(Uxbridge 39811). Ⓡ Ⓦ Ⓟ Ⓓ Gas, slipway,
chandlery, boat sales & repairs, toilets, winter
storage. Club house, temporary moorings and
restaurant.
Ⓑ **Uxbridge Boat Centre** Uxbridge Wharf,
Waterloo Rd. (Uxbridge 52019) Ⓡ Ⓢ Ⓦ Ⓓ Ⓔ
Repairs, servicing, chandlery, installations,
DIY facilities, undercover storage, slipway, dry
dock toilets. *Closed Mon.*

PUBS

🍺 **Treaty House** Uxbridge, by bridge 185.
🍺 **Dolphin** Canalside, bridge 186.
🍺 **General Elliott** St John's Rd, Uxbridge.
🍺 **Shovel** Cowley Lock, Iver Lane, Cowley.
Canalside. Food.
🍺 **The Paddington Packet Boat** by bridge 190.
🍺 **Anchor** West Drayton. Canalside, north of
bridge 192.
🍺 **de Burgh Arms** near bridge 192.

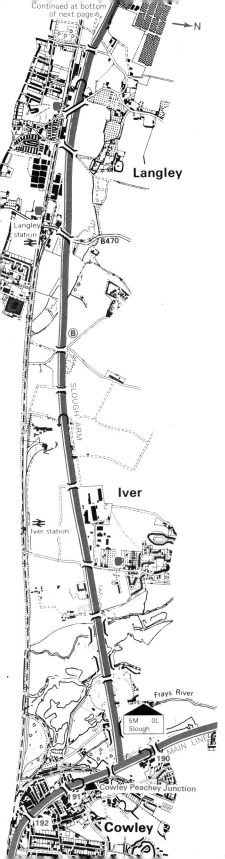

Iver

Striking off to the west from Cowley Peachey Junction, this 5-mile lock-free arm leads in an almost straight line to Slough. Built as late as 1883 (the last canal to be built in Britain except for the Manchester Ship Canal), it sweeps easily over several aqueducts and through a long cutting. There is no trade now on the canal, but there is a very useful boatyard near Iver. West of here the water is amazingly clear, and there are often attractive weeds and reeds to be seen growing in the canal in summer.

Iver
Bucks. EC Wed. P.O. Tel. Stores, garage, station. The church has a Saxon nave with Roman bricks visible in the walls. Norman arches, medieval art and Tudor monuments. The 700-year-old tower owes its great height to the 15thC bell chamber.
Old Slade Nature Reserve 1 mile south of Iver station. Gravel pit taken over by the Berkshire, Buckinghamshire and Oxfordshire Naturalists' Trust and now a wealth of bird and animal life.
Iver Grove Shredding Green, Iver (north of the Boatyard). A fine mansion built by Sir John Vanbrugh in 1724. Not open to the public.

BOATYARDS

ⓑ **Highline Yachting** Mansion Lane, Iver (Iver 651496). ⓇⓈⓌⒹ Mooring, repairs, slipway, hire craft, boat building, gas, chandlery, toilets, showers, winter storage. Also issues a brass plaque to those who navigate to the terminus of the arm—telephone before you start, and be prepared to pay a modest fee.

PUBS

🍺 **Chestnuts** Langley.
🍺 **North Star** by Langley Station.
🍺 **Fox & Pheasant** Thorney Lane, Iver.
🍺✕ **Swan** High St, Iver. Food (*except weekends*).
🍺 **Red Lion** Shredding Green, Iver. Food.
🍺 **Paddington Packet Boat** Cowley Peachey. Food.

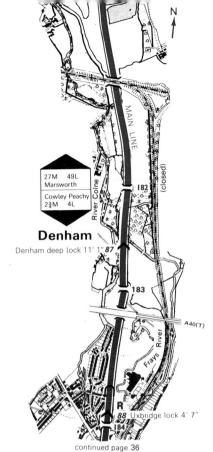

Denham

The main line of the canal continues northwards up to the Colne Valley past the village of Denham and across Harefield Moor, a stretch of common land of considerable interest to naturalists. Denham Lock, with a rise of 11ft 1in, is the deepest on the Grand Union. The large mooring site of the Harefield Cruising Club is in one of the flooded gravel pits that are linked to the canal here.

Langley
Bucks. EC Wed. P.O. Tel. Stores, station. A new town development; but there are unspoiled woodlands at Langley Park.
Denham
Bucks. EC Wed. P.O. Tel. Stores, station. West of the canal and of the River Colne, Denham is split into two parts: the new part is north of the railway. In the old village is the church set among the cottages. It contains a Doom painting of 1460 and some Renaissance effigies and monuments. Denham Court, which stands in the Colne meadows, and Denham Place, the 17thC home of the Vansittart family are both fine examples of English architecture.

PUBS

All these are 1 mile north west of the lock:
- **Falcon** Denham. Snacks.
- **Green Man** Denham.
- **Swan** Denham.

continued page 36

Slough

The Slough Arm continues westwards under the A412 to its terminus, passing dull housing and industrial estates on its way to the terminal basin.

Slough
Berks. EC Wed. MD Tue. P.O. Tel. Stores, garage, station, cinema. This is the largest town in Berkshire; it is a new town, undistinguished architecturally and remembered more for its very wide range of light industries and its great concern for road safety. St Mary's Church is, however, interesting for its stained glass by Kempe and Alfred J. Wolmark: the church was completed in 1876. Herschel Park, in the town centre, is also worth a visit.

PUBS

- **Nags Head** near Slough Basin.
- **Grapes** south of the basin.
- **Rising Sun** further south of the basin.

continued page 37

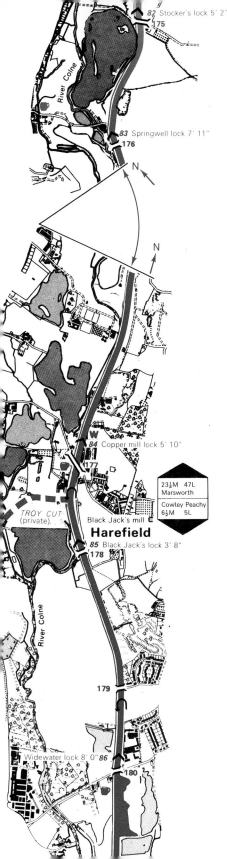

Harefield

Leaving Widewater lock, the canal continues
north up the Colne Valley through a landscape
of interesting contrasts which contains woods,
mills, lakes and a large sewage works. Black
Jack's Lock is beautifully framed by a small
mill and a tiny timbered cottage while Copper
Mill Lock is just upstream of an attractive
group of canalside buildings. Old chalk
quarries adjoin the canal as it turns north east
towards Rickmansworth. Meanwhile flooded,
worked-out gravel pits cover the floor of this
wooded valley. Stockers is yet another lock
with an interesting group of old farm buildings
close by: they date from the 16thC.

Springwell and Stocker's Locks This stretch is
of interest to naturalists: there is a great variety
of plants along here, and disused watercress
beds are nearby. Orchids have been found
growing in the adjacent chalk pits.
Copper Mill An interesting canal settlement.
The big mill was once a paper mill, but after the
canal was built it turned to making copper
sheets for the bottoms of boats. The old cast
iron bridge by the pub has now been replaced
by a concrete one. South of here is the
unnavigable Troy Cut, which leads to the very
ancient Troy Mill.
Harefield
Middx. P.O. Tel. Stores. Harefield represents
the first escape from the stranglehold of outer
London suburbia. The church set at the foot of
the hill is almost a small museum: Norman
masonry, box pews, 16thC screen. 19thC
Gothic gallery, Georgian pulpit, and a huge
collection of monuments including brasses, and
work by Grinling Gibbons, Rysbrack and
Bacon.

PUBS

Whip and Collar north west of bridge 176.
Fisheries Copper Mill Lock, Harefield.
Canalside. Food. $\boxed{\text{E}}$
Horse and Barge Canalside, bridge 180.

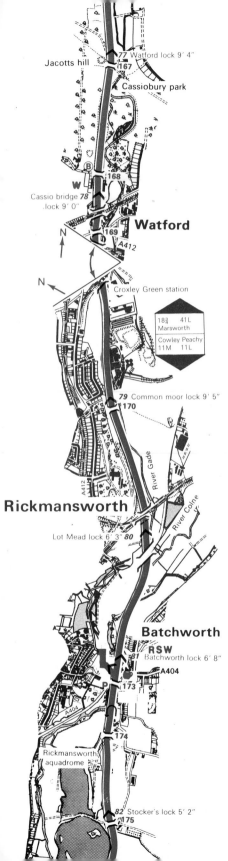

Rickmansworth

Continuing north east, the canal reaches
Batchworth Lock on the outskirts of
Rickmansworth. (There are in fact 2 locks here,
one of them leading up into the River Chess which
is navigable for a short distance.
Northbound navigators should take the right
hand lock to stay on the Grand Union Canal.)
Here the River Colne comes in from the east
and the Chess from the north west, while the
Gade continues to accompany the canal to the
north east. Past Rickmansworth is Common
Moor, north of this is Croxley and the outskirts
of Watford. The canal keeps well away from
this town and climbs instead into the superb
Cassiobury Park, a long and lovely stretch of
wooded parkland. The A404 crosses at
Rickmansworth and the A412 at Croxley.

Cassiobury Park The canal flows through the
park, once part of the 17thC gardens of the
Earls of Essex. The avenue of limes was planted
by Moses Cook in 1672 and many of the trees
are as old as 300 years. The park stretches for
190 acres and is adjoined by Whippendell
Woods. Watford's carnival takes place here
every Whitsun.
Croxley Green
Herts. P.O. Tel. Stores, garage, station. Despite
being swamped by new housing, part of the old
village survives around the green, where there
are several attractive houses. There is a large
medieval barn south of the village.
Rickmansworth
*Herts. EC Wed. P.O. Tel. Stores, station,
cinema.* Very little of the medieval town
remains today: the Vicarage in Church Street
has late medieval timberwork, but 18thC and
19thC alterations are intermingled. Despite
this, there are several other buildings well
worth a look: the 17thC Bury and the
timber-framed but much restored Priory, both
lying near the 19thC Church of St Mary, which
lends a wonderful feeling of unity because it is
almost entirely the work of one man—Sir
Arthur Blomfield. The town centre is north of
bridge 173.
Moor Park Mansion House 1 mile south east
of canal. Fine Palladian house reconstructed in
1727 by Sir James Thornhill and Giacomo
Leoni. Incorporates the house originally built
by James, Duke of Monmouth. Superb interior
decorations by Verrio and Thornhill. *Open Mon
afternoons.*
Rickmansworth Aquadrome Bury &
Batchworth lakes. The canal flows along the
south east edge of the lakes. Facilities for all
types of water sport, especially sailing. Picnic
areas for onlookers, and swimming in Bury
lake. *Open daily.* An aqua show is held *every
Whit Mon.*

BOATYARDS

Ⓑ **Cassio Bridge Marina** Cassio Bridge,
Watford. (Watford 34113). Ⓡ Ⓢ Ⓦ Ⓔ Slipway,
gas, mooring, chandlery, toilets, provisions,
storage. *Closed Sun in winter.*

BOAT TRIPS

Arcturus Cruises Cassio Wharf, Watford. Part
or whole day cruises by narrow boat, for parties
of up to 54 passengers. Public trips *Sun
afternoon* from lock 77. (Enquiries to Welwyn
4528).

PUBS

🍺 **New Halfway House** near Cassio Bridge
(169).
🍺 **Batchworth Arms** near Batchworth Lock.
Food.
🍺 **White Bear** near Batchworth Lock.
Lunches *Mon–Fri.* Bar billiards.

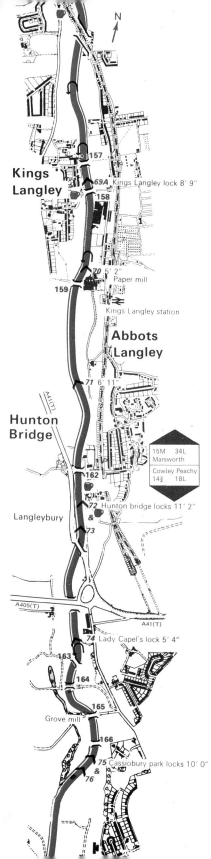

Kings Langley

The canal climbs in a northerly direction through Cassiobury Park past a restored lock cottage to the delightful Grove Mill, an isolated water mill where the mill stream doubles as a private canal arm. Just north of the mill is the deservedly famous ornamental stone bridge ordered by the Earl of Essex before he would allow the Grand Junction Canal Company to cut a navigation through his park. The canal winds considerably along this valley as it follows the course of the River Gade. This results in several wide stretches; do not attempt to turn in these without ascertaining the depth. The M25 north orbital road and the A41 cross the canal as it approaches the lovely village of Hunton Bridge. A little further north is Kings Langley.

Kings Langley
Herts. EC Wed. P.O. Tel. Stores, station. Once a country village but now ravaged by the heavy motor traffic that thunders through the town. Its name derives from its royal associations; there are still the remains of a palace in the town. The tomb of Edmund de Langley, brother of the Black Prince, lies in the Norman Church of All Saints. Sir John Evans, the famous archaeologist, is also buried here.

Abbots Langley
Herts. EC Wed. P.O. Tel. Stores, station (shared with Kings Langley). The Church of St Lawrence has 12thC arcades to the nave and a 14thC south chapel, an octagonal Perpendicular font and a 14thC wall painting of Saints Thomas and Lawrence.

Hunton Bridge
Herts. P.O. Tel. Stores. Peaceful canalside village, with a spired church and the pleasing Langleybury Park.

Aldenham Reservoir This canal feeder reservoir is near Elstree (about 6 miles east of Cassiobury Park). It covers 107 acres and was designated a Country Park in 1971.

PUBS

Red Lion Small unspoilt pub close to bridge 155.
Lots of pubs west of Kings Langley Lock, including:
Swan High St, Kings Langley.
Saracens Head High St, Kings Langley.
Lamb near Kings Langley Lock. Food, garden.
King's Head Hunton Bridge. Food, *except Sun.*
Unicorn Gallows Hill, Hunton Bridge. Food. Quaint 450-year-old pub.
Dog and Partridge Old Mill Lane, Hunton Bridge.

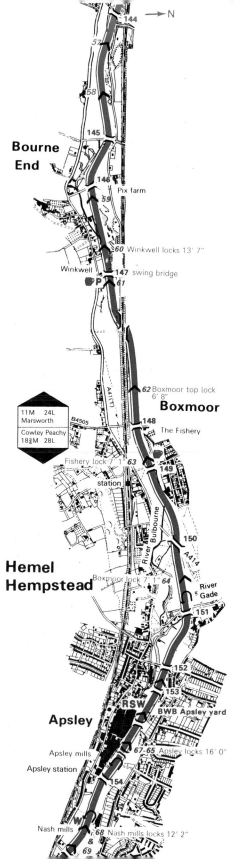

Hemel Hempstead

The canal begins to climb more steeply to the north west, passing several large paper mills in Apsley. The River Gade leaves the canal for Hemel Hempstead, a handsome modern town standing back from the canal beyond spacious urban parkland known as Boxmoor. The canal turns further west, accompanied now by the little River Bulbourne. The busy railway line is never far away, interrupting the peace of this very attractive valley. Watercress beds are to be found along here; they owe their existence to the mineral waters from the many chalk springs of the Chilterns which are the source of the River Bulbourne. The nearby A41 is fortunately shielded by trees; its many petrol stations, pubs and shops may be useful to the canal traveller.

Hemel Hempstead
Herts. EC Wed. MD Thu/Fri/Sat. P.O. Tel. Stores, garage, station, cinema. A developing, well-planned new town with excellent shops.
Piccotts End Medieval Murals 138 Piccotts End. Remarkable 14thC wall paintings in a hall believed to have been a pilgrims' hospice. Also an Elizabethan painted room.

BOATYARDS

BWB Apsley Yard Ebbems Rd. Apsley. (Hemel Hempstead 56910). R W

PUBS

Three Horseshoes Winkwell Boxmoor. By the wheel-operated swing bridge. Canalside. Food.
Fishery Inn Fishery Rd, Boxmoor. Canalside. Food. E
Old Kings Arms High St. Hemel Hempstead. Restaurant (English & Chinese), reductions for children. No meals on *Sun.*
White Hart High St, Hemel Hempstead. Food.
Albion Apsley.

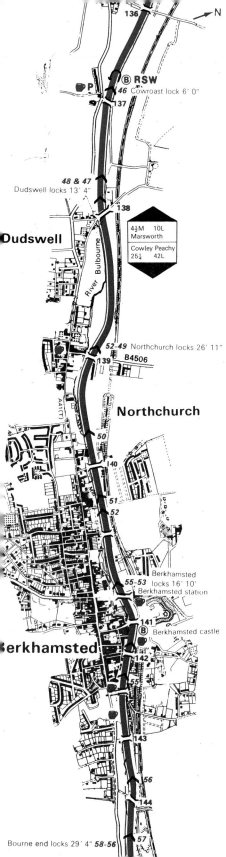

Berkhamsted

The canal now enters Berkhamsted by its back
door and steals inconspicuously through the
middle of the town. Many boats are moored
here, and there are four canalside pubs within a
couple of hundred yards of each other.
Berkhamsted is incidentally the northern limit
of the Grand Union as a barge canal. Leaving
Berkhamsted and still climbing up the
Chilterns, one passes Northchurch, where a
pump draws canal water supplies from a deep
borehole in the chalk beds. The summit level is
reached at Cowroast Lock which, in the days
before the pump was installed at Northchurch,
used to be the scene of long lines of boats tied
up in the dry summers as the canal engineers
struggled to maintain the water supply in the
3-mile summit level—which was constantly
being drained by the use of locks at either end.
(It is perhaps worth noting that every time a
boat crosses this summit level it draws off
nearly 200,000 gallons of water). At Cowroast
Lock the old toll office still stands.

Ashridge House
Herts. 3½ miles north of Berkhamsted. (Little
Gaddesden 3491). Built 1808 as a large
romantic mansion in the Gothic taste by James
Wyatt, the house gives an impression of what
his famous Fonthill must have been like; the
chapel is particularly splendid. The grounds
were laid out by Capability Brown, and altered
later by Repton. (*Telephone for opening times*).
Northchurch
Herts. EC Wed. P.O. Tel. Stores. Built round
the flint church which contains some Saxon
work, and fine 19thC stained glass. In the High
Street are several timber-framed houses.
Berkhamsted
*Herts. EC Wed. MD Sat. P.O. Tel. Stores,
garage, station, cinema.* Good-looking large
town with buildings of all periods, the A41
running through the middle. The High Street is
dominated by the Church of St Peter, which
contains work from practically every period,
including a restoration by Butterfield of 1871.
There are several brasses. Only the ruins of the
Norman castle remain, where William I
received the offer of the English crown in 1066.
The 17thC Sayer almshouses are completely
intact. The Common is known as a haven for
wild birds including nightjars, woodcocks,
grasshopper warblers, redpolls and bramblings.

BOATYARDS

ⓑ **Cowroast Marina** by Cowroast Lock,
Tring. (Tring 3222). ⓌⒹ Pump-out, narrow
boat hire, gas, moorings, wet dock, chandlery,
electric day hire.
ⓑ **Bridgewater Boats** Castle Wharf,
Berkhamsted. (Berkhamsted 3615). ⓌⒹ
Pump-out, gas, narrow boat hire, slipway,
toilets, emergency repairs. *Open Mar–Oct.*

PUBS

ⓟ✕ **Cow Roast** opposite Cowroast Lock.
Restaurant meals.
ⓟ **George & Dragon** Northchurch. Food
(*except Sun*).
ⓟ **Crystal Palace** near Berkhamsted station,
Canalside.
ⓟ **Boat** Gravel path, Berkhamsted. Canalside.
Food at lunchtime.
ⓟ **Rising Sun** George St. Berkhamsted.
Canalside at lock 55. Food.
ⓟ **Swan** High St, Berkhamsted. ¼ mile south
of bridge 141.
ⓟ **Bull Inn** High St, Berkhamsted, below lock
55. Calor gas available. Food.

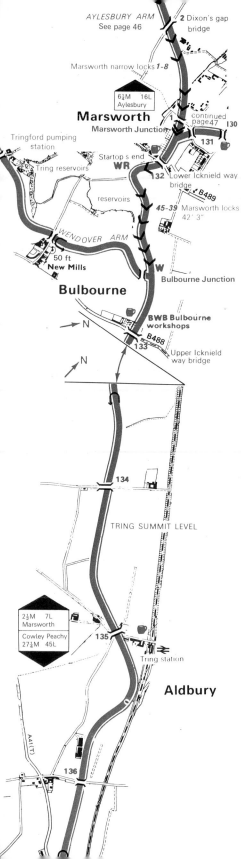

AYLESBURY ARM
See page 46

2 Dixon's gap bridge

Marsworth narrow locks *1-8*

6¼M 16L
Aylesbury

Marsworth

continued page 47

Marsworth Junction

130

131

Tringford pumping station

Startop s end
WR

132 Lower Icknield way bridge

Tring reservoirs

B489

reservoirs

45-39 Marsworth locks 42′ 3″

WENDOVER ARM

50 ft
New Mills

W

Bulbourne Junction

Bulbourne

N

BWB Bulbourne workshops

B488

133 Upper Icknield way bridge

N

134

TRING SUMMIT LEVEL

2¼M 7L
Marsworth

Cowley Peachy
27¼M 45L

135

Tring station

Aldbury

A41(T)

136

Bulbourne

The canal continues north west through the long wooded cutting that contains the Tring summit level. At the hamlet of Bulbourne are the old BWB workshops where to this day traditional wooden lockgate-making is carried out by a small team of craftsmen. Just to the west the old Wendover Arm joins the canal, constantly feeding water into the summit level. This arm no longer goes to Wendover, but it is still navigable for small boats as far as Little Tring and the Tringford pumping station—the stop plank may be removed for access to this arm. Back at Bulbourne Junction, the first of the Marsworth locks begin to wind down the hill past the reservoirs; at the bottom of the flight, where there are two good pubs, is an interesting double-arched bridge, a sight often repeated between here and Stoke Bruerne 33 miles to the north. This type of bridge was built by the Grand Junction Canal Company in the expectation that the locks would later be paired—a programme that was never completed. 100yds north of the double bridge is Marsworth Junction, dominated by the BWB workshops where concrete piles were made for the protection of canal banks. At the junction the main line bears round to the north east, while the Aylesbury Arm starts its fall west through the first 8 narrow locks towards Aylesbury.

Marsworth
Bucks. P.O. Tel. Stores, garage. A quiet scattered village centred around the Grand Union Canal and the Aylesbury Arm. The Icknield Way, a Roman road, passes the village. Dunstable Downs rise to the south east, gliders are a common sight and occasionally a hot air balloon may be seen floating along in the sky.

Tringford Pumping Station At present terminus of Wendover Arm. Built by the Grand Junction Canal Company to pump water up from the three reservoirs just down the hill, and from the 100-acre Wilstone reservoir over to the west. This water, plus the supply from springs in Wendover was—and still is—fed down the arm into the Tring summit level. Originally the pumping station housed big beam engines, but these were replaced in the 20thC by heavy diesels. Now quiet, smooth, electric motors perform this vital task, lifting some 4 million gallons of water each day. The system was recently overhauled, having been in constant use since 1929.

Tring Reservoirs South of Startop's End (bridge 132) and beside Marsworth locks. 4 reservoirs with many wildfowl and waterside birds, notably the Black Tern and the Great Crested Grebe. Also abundant marsh and water plants. National nature reserve, managed by the Nature Conservancy, 20 Belgrave Square, London SW1. Public access is permitted along waymarked pathways.

Bulbourne
Herts. Tel. Canalside settlement around the BWB workshops which are a well-preserved example of early 19thC canal architecture, with characteristic fanlights. To the north east is the long railway cutting built by Robert Stephenson in 1834–38, an engineering feat of the age.

Aldbury
Herts. P.O. Tel. Stores. A charming village pond and stocks are sheltered below the hillside which rises to the east towards Ashridge. Note the quaint cottages along Stocks Road and to the north east and west of the Church of St John the Baptist, which dates from the 13thC. The monument to the third Duke of Bridgewater (an urn and a Greek Doric column) was erected on the brow of the hill beyond Stocks Road in 1832 to commemorate his pioneering work for the English canals.

Aldbury Common 1½ miles east of bridge 135 past Tring station. Acres of open land which adjoin Berkhamsted Common, Ashridge Park and Ivinghoe Common.

BOATYARDS

BWB Bulbourne Workshops Bulbourne (Tring 2261). Home of the maintenance yard and the lock-gate making team.

PUBS

🍺✕ **Red Lion** Marsworth, near bridge 130.
🍺 **White Lion** Marsworth. Canalside, at bridge 132. Food $\boxed{R}\,\boxed{W}$
🍺 **Grand Junction Arms** Bulbourne. Canalside, at bridge 133. Food $\boxed{R}$.
🍺 **Queens Head** Marsworth, near bridge 132.
🍺✕ **Royal Hotel** Tring station. Lunches and dinners daily in this elegant, isolated residential hotel.

The tranquil Aylesbury Arm. *David Perrott*

Puttenham

The Aylesbury Arm continues to fall to the
west. Totally isolated and remote, it is one of
the most peaceful stretches of canal in the
country, passing through modest farmland with
good views of the Chiltern Hills over to the east
and, in the distance to the west, of tall new
buildings in Aylesbury. The locks are only 7ft
wide, and the bridges too are extremely narrow.
This canal was once semi-derelict, but an
energetic programme of dredging and lock
repairing restored it to a good navigable
condition.

Wilstone
Herts. P.O. Tel. Stores. Quiet village running
away from the canal to Wilstone reservoir, a
national nature reserve.

PUBS
- **Prince of Wales** North of bridge 15.
- **Bell Inn** Aston Clinton. 1 mile south east
of bridge 9. Famous restaurant in attractive old
inn with 20 rooms. Excellent menu and wine
list.
- **Oak** Aston Clinton.
- **Partridge** Aston Clinton.
- **Buckingham Arms** Wilstone.
- **Half Moon** Wilstone.

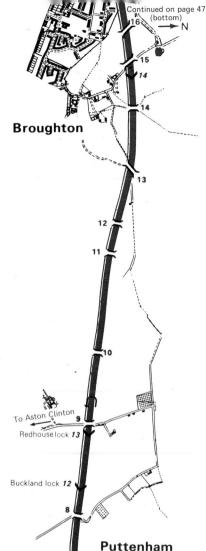

Continued on page 47
(bottom)

N

16
15
14
14

Broughton

13

12

11

10

To Aston Clinton
9
Redhouse lock *13*

Buckland lock *12*

8

Puttenham

4¼M   5L
Aylesbury

Marsworth
2M   11L

7

10 & 11
Puttenham locks

6

Wilstone

5   *9* Wilstone lock

4

3 Wilstone bridge
8

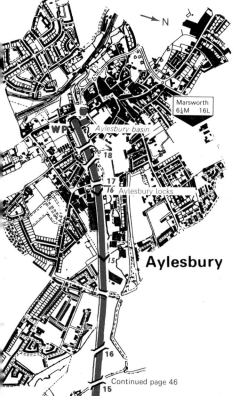

Marsworth

The main line heads north east and continues its descent through Marsworth locks before entering the remote countryside beyond Ivinghoe.

PUBS

🍺 **Red Lion** Marsworth, near bridge 130.
🍺 **White Lion** Marsworth. Canalside at bridge 132. Food Ⓡ Ⓦ.
🍺 **Grand Junction Arms** Bulbourne. Canalside at bridge 133. Food Ⓡ.

Grand Union
Aylesbury Arm

Aylesbury

The canal now runs under the Aylesbury ring road and drops down through the last 2 locks into the town; it is not a very glamorous entrance into this flourishing county town. Boatmen should be aware of the iron girder bridge 18; it is extremely narrow. Aylesbury basin itself is spacious and full of boats, although there is no longer a boatyard as such. However, there are moorings, water, fuels and a pub nearby, and all the amenities of the town centre are a mere 3-minute walk away.

Aylesbury
Bucks. EC Thur. MD Wed/Sat. P.O. Tel. Stores, garage, station, cinema. The county town of Buckinghamshire. Still a busy market town, but there are expanding engineering and printing industries. However, the 20thC has not taken over completely; the centre of Aylesbury is made up of a number of attractive squares, and the 13thC church lies hidden in its secluded churchyard a short distance away. There are some interesting Georgian buildings too. 'The King's Head', dating from the 15thC, has outstanding windows, gateway and courtyard, and Oliver Cromwell's chair in the bar.
Buckinghamshire County Museum Church St, Aylesbury. (Aylesbury 2158). Illustrates county archaeology, geology and history, local crafts, costume, natural history. Also small collection of prints and paintings. *Closed Sun.*
Hartwell House
1½ miles south west of Aylesbury. Jacobean house with a grand staircase and decorations, largely remodelled in the 18thC. The ruined early Gothic revival church of 1755 is by Henry Keene. Now a finishing school for rich young ladies. *Open May-Jul Weds & Spring B. Hol weekend. (Garden open only Sep Weds).*

BOATYARDS

Aylesbury Canal Society Aylesbury Basin (Aylesbury 5322). Ⓦ Ⓔ

PUBS

🍺✕ **Bell Hotel** Market Square, Aylesbury. Restaurant, reductions for children.
🍺 **Ship** Aylesbury Basin. Canalside.
🍺✕ **Kings Head** Market Square, Aylesbury. Restaurant, owned by the National Trust.

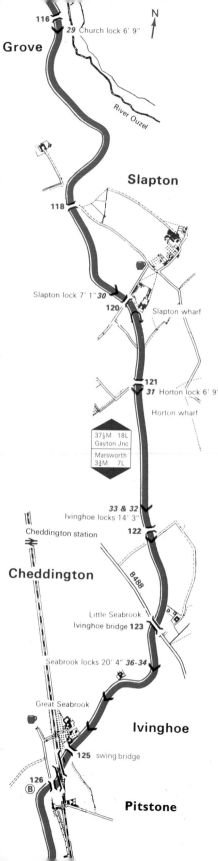

Ivinghoe

Northwards from Marsworth the canal falls
steadily away from Dunstable Downs and the
Chilterns, leaving the hills as a backdrop to the
west. As the hills give way to open grasslands,
the canal becomes more remote, a quiet, empty
section that terminates in the peace of Church
Lock. Villages are set back from the canal, only
Slapton being under 1 mile away. The main
feature of the section is the locks, carrying the
canal down from the Chilterns toward Leighton
Buzzard and the Ouzel valley; these occur
frequently, often in remote and attractive
settings. The railway and the B488 run parallel
to the canal to the west; there is a station at
Cheddington.

Grove
Bucks. An attractive group formed by the
bridge, lock, lock cottage and the tiny church, a
14thC chapel with a later bell turret.
Slapton
Bucks. EC Thur. P.O. Tel. Stores. Compact
residential village; the Perpendicular church
contains several brasses of the 15th and 16thC.
Cheddington
*Bucks. EC Thur. P.O. Tel, stores, garage,
station.* 1 mile north of bridge 126. A residential
area spread around the station, clearly a
commuter development. The church contains a
richly carved Jacobean pulpit. On the hills
south of the village are the remains of a
medieval field cultivation.
Mentmore House 1½ miles west of Horton
lock. A Tudor-style stone mansion built in the
1850s by Sir Joseph Paxton for the Rothschild
family. Large plate glass windows, central
heating and fresh air ventilation made the house
advanced for its time, reflecting the ingenuity
of the architect.
Whipsnade White Lion On Dunstable Downs,
visible from the canal from around Slapton and
Cheddington. The lion was cut in 1935 and is
over 480ft long.
Ivinghoe
Bucks. EC Wed. P.O. Tel. Stores, garage. 1 mile
east of bridge 123 or 126. An attractive
although greatly expanded village, which
centres round the large 13th and 14thC church,
notable for its crossing tower and Jacobean
pulpit. The main street, leading west from the
church, contains the old town hall, partly
16thC. ¼ mile south of the village is Pitstone
Green Mill, a post mill scheduled as an ancient
monument.
Iron Age Hill Fort 1 mile north east of
Ivinghoe, on top of Beacon Hill. The triangular
hill fort encloses 6 acres: within this area stands
a bowl barrow thought to date from the Bronze
Age. There is a tumulus to the south and
another to the east of Beacon Hill.

BOATYARDS

Ⓑ **Grebe Canal Cruisers** Pitstone Wharf.
(Cheddington 661920). Ⓦ Ⓔ Hire craft, shop,
repairs, mooring.

BOAT TRIPS

Grebe Canal Cruises Pitstone Wharf.
(Cheddington 661920).

PUBS

☖ **Carpenters Arms** Slapton.
☖✕ **Kings Head** Ivinghoe. Restaurant.
☖ **Old Swan** High St. Cheddington.
☖ **Three Horseshoes** Cheddington.
☖ **Bell Inn** Pitstone.
☖ **Duke of Wellington** 100yds south of bridge
126.

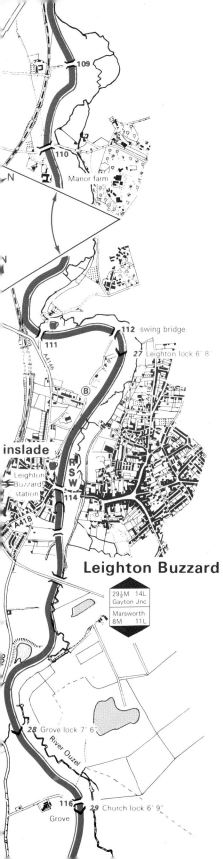

Leighton Buzzard

The canal now runs parallel to the river Ouzel to the east and, leaving the open fields behind, passes through the joined towns of Linslade and Leighton Buzzard, effective acting as a boundary between them. Leighton Buzzard station is actually in Linslade. The A418 crosses the canal in the town centre. Leaving these towns, the canal enters the valley of the Ouzel and meanders sharply, following the river. Steep hills rise to the east and west, thickly wooded to the east. A low towpath hedge allows fine views of this beautiful valley. This section contains a good mixture of canal townscape and landscape. Grove and Leighton locks both having attractive and well-kept lock-houses. The railway and the B488 continue to follow the canal to the west.

Leighton Buzzard
Beds. EC Thur. P.O. Tel. Stores, station, garage, cinema. A picturesque market town with a superlative church. 17th and 18thC houses and half-timbered cottages are to be found in the streets leading to the Market Cross, which has stood for some 600 years in the centre of the town. There are also some fine 19thC buildings; note particularly Barclay's Bank. In North Street stand the almshouses founded by Edward Wilkes in 1633 on condition that the bounds of the parish be beaten every Rogation Monday. The custom is still maintained, and on May 23rd a choir boy stands upon his head in front of the almshouses while the appropriate extracts from the donor's will are read.
All Saint's Parish Church Dates from 1288 and is notable for its 191ft tower and spire and the 15thC wooden roof. It retains its ancient sanctus bell, 13thC font, misericordes, brasses and a medieval lectern. The medieval graffiti are interesting and include a depiction of Simon and Nellie arguing about whether the Mothering Sunday Sim-nel cake should be boiled or baked.
Linslade
Bucks. P.O. Tel. Stores, garage, station. Linslade is virtually a residential extension of Leighton Buzzard. Traces of the old village can just be found to the north, especially the church, near the canal, easily recognised by its battlements; the front and parts of the structure date from the 12thC. West of the church is a railway tunnel with an extraordinary neo-Gothic portal in grey brick, looking delightfully incongruous.
Ascott House 2 miles to the west, along the A418 from Linslade. (Wing 242) Attractive, irregular timber-framed house built in 1606, with extensive additions made in 1874 and 1938. Collection of paintings, French and Chippendale furniture, oriental porcelain. 12 acres of grounds and gardens containing rare trees.

BOATYARDS

Ⓑ **The Wyvern Shipping Company** Rothschild Rd, Linslade (Leighton Buzzard 372355). Ⓦ Ⓓ Ⓔ Pump-out, gas, boat hire, dry dock, boat building, mooring, toilets, trip boat for charter.

PUBS

🍺 **Globe Inn** Globe Lane. Linslade. Canalside, near bridge 111. Food.
🍺 **Black Lion** High St, Leighton Buzzard.
🍺 **White Horse** near the station in Linslade.
🍺✕ **Locks Bar** 24 Leighton Rd, Linslade. (Leighton Buzzard 381156). Waterside bar with a restaurant above. Ⓔ

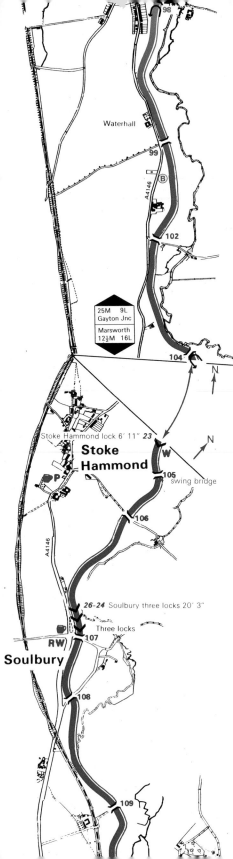

Soulbury

The canal meanders along the Ouzel valley to the north west through beautiful scenery. The hills rising steeply to the west and the natural woods to the east make the canal seem like a river, which is rare on the Grand Union. As the valley widens, the canal continues its steady fall towards Bletchley, following the Ouzel closely. Flat meadows reaching to the west precede the approach to Bletchley. All the locks, the Soulbury flight of three, and one at Stoke Hammond, form an attractive canalscape, the double-arched bridges showing where the locks were once doubled. Remains of the supplementary locks can still be seen at Soulbury alongside the small pumping station that returns water back up the flight whenever necessary. The railway and the B488 run closely to the west of the canal.

Stoke Hammond
Bucks. EC Sat. P.O. Tel. Stores, garage. Set above the canal to the west, the village overlooks the valley as it spreads untidily along the B488. The church, weighted down by its squat central tower, contains a decorative 14thC font.

Soulbury
Bucks. 1 mile west of the Three Locks. P.O. Tel. Stores. The church contains a monument in white marble by Grinling Gibbons, 1690. To the south is Liscombe House, a rambling 17thC brick mansion with a fine Gothic facade of 1774, set in a large landscaped park.

BOATYARDS

Ⓑ **Willowbridge Marina** Stoke Rd, Bletchley (Milton Keynes 643242). Ⓡ Ⓢ Ⓦ Ⓟ Ⓓ Ⓔ Pump-out, gas, repairs, mooring, slipway. By bridge 99.

PUBS

🍺 **Dolphin** Stoke Hammond. Food.
🍺✕ **Three Locks** Stoke Hammond. Ⓦ Ⓡ Canalside. Lunches, afternoon teas, garden.

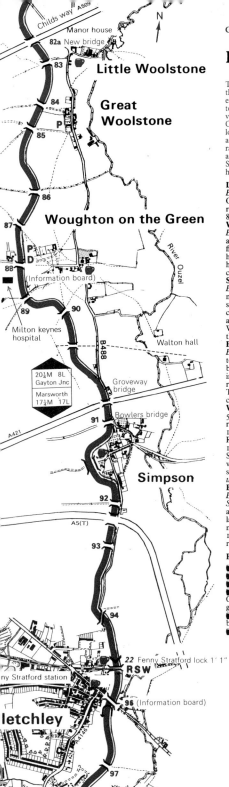

Bletchley

The canal runs through open country, but to the south lie the suburbs of the rapidly expanding town of Bletchley. Once north of the town the canal again meanders gently through villages, still following the course of the River Ouzel as far as Woolstone. There is only one lock on this section, but the old arched accommodation bridges abound. The main railway leaves the canal south of Bletchley, but another line, to Bedford, crosses at Fenny Stratford. There is a station close to the canal here.

Little Woolstone
Bucks. A tiny hamlet with a pub and a garage. Great Woolstone is even smaller. Willen Lake recreation area is best approached from bridge 83.

Woughton on the Green
Bucks. P.O. Tel. Stores. The village is attractively scattered round a huge green flanked by the canal to the west. There are houses of all periods, mixed in a random but harmonious manner and presided over by the church built on a mound to the east.

Simpson
Bucks. P.O. Tel. Stores. A main-road village, much redeveloped as a suburb of Bletchley, but still retaining elements of independence. The church is mainly 14thC, note the wooden roof and a monument by John Bacon, 1789. Beyond Woughton Park to the north is Walton Hall, the Open University.

Fenny Stratford
Bucks. P.O. Tel. Stores, garage, station. The town is now merged into Bletchley. The building of the red-brick church, 1724–30, was inspired by Browne Willis, the antiquarian, as a result it is an early example of Gothic revival. The old pump house is now a gift shop and cafeteria, run by handicapped youth.

Woburn Abbey
5 miles east of Fenny Stratford. 18thC mansion rebuilt by Flitcroft 1747 and Henry Holland 1802. Set in 3000-acre park landscaped by Repton. State apartments, French and English 18thC furniture, silver. English, Dutch, Spanish, Italian paintings. Forest with 11 varieties of deer, wild animal park, bird sanctuary, antique market. *Open daily throughout the year.*

Bletchley
Bucks. EC Wed. MD Thur/Sat. P.O. Tel. Stores, garage, station, cinema. This formerly agricultural and lace-making town is now a large, modern place that has swallowed up its neighbour, Fenny Stratford. A small part of the 12thC St Mary's Church remains; much restoration and alteration has been done.

PUBS

- **Barge Inn** Little Woolstone. Food.
- **Old Swan** Woughton on the Green. Food.
- **Plough** Simpson.
- **Red Lion** Fenny Stratford Lock. Bletchley. Canalside. Food, garden for children, camping, groceries. R W
- **Bridge** Fenny Stratford. Canalside, at A5 bridge. Food. E
- **Plough** West of bridge 98.

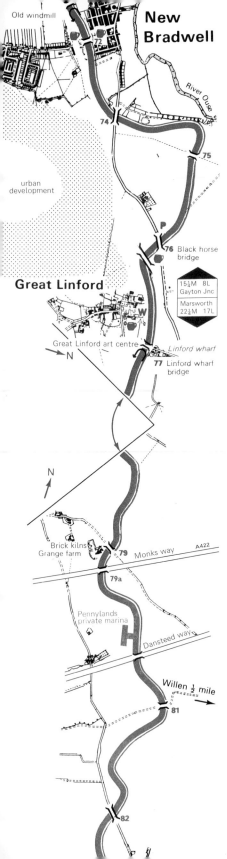

Milton Keynes

Continuing north west, and then at Great
Linford turning sharply to the west, the canal
runs through attractive, lightly wooded scenery
that gradually gives way to hills and follows the
Ouse valley, clinging to the south side. To the
south, where once were open fields, the new
town of Milton Keynes has been built. Willen
and Great Linford are well worth visiting.
There are no locks, but a variety of bridges. At
Great Linford Wharf there is a winding hole
that marks the junction with the Newport
Pagnell branch, closed many years ago. After
Great Linford, the A422 follows the canal,
crossing it in 2 places.

New Bradwell
Bucks. P.O. Tel. Stores. A Victorian railway
town, built on a grid of extreme monotony and
regularity. The church, by Street, 1858, is of
interest, especially for its Victorian stained
glass. The bird observatory here is manned
during the migration season. The 19thC
Bradwell Windmill is now restored. Access
from bridge 72.

Great Linford
Bucks. P.O. Tel. Stores. Great Linford is
magnificent: a traditional village street running
away from the canal, and then by the canal a
marvellous group formed by church, manor,
farm and almshouses, all in rich golden
stone—an unchanged 18thC scene. The 14thC
church right alongside the canal contains
Georgian box pews and pulpit, and fine 19thC
stained glass. The almshouses are 17thC with
strong Dutch gables. The manor, symmetrical,
dignified and elegant in a totally 18thC way,
completes the picture.

Milton Keynes
*Bucks. All services and a major shopping centre
accessible by bus from bridge 82a.* An exciting
new town development encompassing Bletchley
and the scattered villages to the north. Work on
the 22,000-acre area began in the early 1970s
and the original population of 40,000 has grown
to around 100,000. Strategically placed
between Birmingham and the capital, close to
the M1 and the main railway line (Milton
Keynes Central Station opened in 1982), the
Development Corporation has been successful
in attracting many companies to the area,
including Volkswagon, GEC-Marconi, General
Motors and Minolta. The housing schemes are
imaginative, and well endowed with green
space and trees. Great emphasis is placed on the
social and recreational needs of the population
and in this respect the new town makes good
use of the canal.

Willen
Bucks. 1/2 mile east of bridge 81. P.O. box. Tel. A
hamlet wholly dominated by the Wren church,
which is well worth a visit. Built in 1679 by
Robert Hooke, it is a city church placed
dramatically in the middle of empty fields.
Built of brick and stone, the tall nave and tower
rule over the surrounding landscape. All the
interior fittings are original, and the plaster
work, pews, organ case and front should be
seen. The 170-acre lake is a watersports centre,
with sailing, canoeing etc.

BOAT TRIPS

Canal Waterbuses
Every Sun from Jun to Aug, scheduled services.
From bridge 68 to Great Linford Arts Centre,
calling at bridges 71, 72, 76—ring for details:
Milton Keynes 563377.
From bridge 96 to bridge 83, calling at lock 22
and bridges 91, 88—details Marlow 72500.

PUBS

🍺 **New Inn** New Bradwell, near bridge 72.
Food.
🍺✕ **Black Horse** Black Horse Bridge, Great
Linford. Canalside. Food.
🍺 **Nag's Head** Great Linford.
🍺 **Foresters** New Bradwell. Just north of
bridge 73.

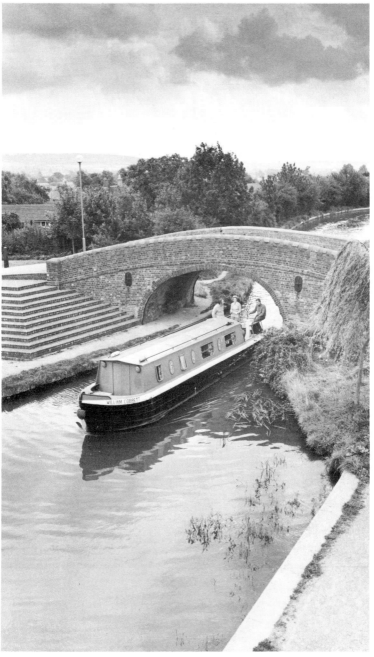

Milton Keynes: a new town that really appreciates it's canal. *Derek Pratt*

Cosgrove

The canal continues westwards past industrial
Wolverton, and then turns north west prior to
crossing the Ouse valley by means of an
embankment and aqueduct. Hills now begin to
dominate the landscape to the west as the canal
follows the course of the river Tove, an
indication of the climb ahead up to Stoke
Bruerne. After Wolverton the canal becomes
more remote, with only Cosgrove exploiting it.
The railway 1 mile to the east provides the only
intrusion. There is plenty of canalscape;
Wolverton aqueduct, Cosgrove Lock ending
the 11-mile Fenny Stratford Pound, Cosgrove
Bridge and the disused and long abandoned
Buckingham Arm branching away to the west.
(Part is now a nature reserve, and a nature trail
follows the disused canal). After Cosgrove and
the old junction, the A508 runs parallel to the
West.

Castlethorpe
Bucks. P.O. Tel. Stores. A quiet village,
thatched houses around a green, 1 mile north
east of Castlethorpe Wharf. The main railway
running in a cutting below the village is the
only disturbance. Parts of the church date back
to 1200, although the tower was built in 1729.
North of the church is the site of an extensive
castle.

Cosgrove
Northants. EC Wed. P.O. Tel. Stores. The
village climbs west away from the canal, its
spread visually terminated by the wooded
church. The best parts are by the canal: a range
of warehouses, a curious pedestrian tunnel
under the canal, and a splendid stone bridge
charmingly decorated in the Gothic taste, built
in 1800. Its style is unique among canal
bridges, and there is no obvious reason for its
solitary splendour. The Georgian house that
dominates the west bank by the lock is
Cosgrove Hall; in 1958 a Roman bathhouse was
discovered in front of the hall.

Wolverton
*Bucks. EC Wed. MD Fri. P.O. Tel. Stores,
garage, station.* Ignore the regularity of New
Wolverton, and continue further west where
the remains of the old village still survive
among the trees. The Norman-style church was
built in 1815, its large size perhaps anticipating
the coming of the railway! By the church is the
rectory with a handsome portal, built in 1729.
Several other houses from 16th to 18thC can be
found.

Great Ouse Aqueduct North of Old Wolverton
the canal crosses the Ouse via an iron trunk
aqueduct, a square cast-iron trough carried on
stone pillars. Built in 1811, it replaced a brick
structure that collapsed in 1808. This in turn
had replaced 9 locks that enabled the Ouse to
be crossed on the level, a system abandoned
because of the danger of floods.

BOATYARDS

Ⓑ **Cosgrove Marina** The Lock House,
Cosgrove (Milton Keynes 562467). Ⓡ Ⓢ Ⓦ Gas,
mooring, crane, slipway close by. Mobile
breakdown service.
Ⓑ **Wharfside Boatbuilders** by bridge 68
(Milton Keynes 317321). Ⓦ Ⓓ Boat repairs,
chandlery, souvenirs.

BOAT TRIPS

Linda Day Cruises Cosgrove Lock (Milton
Keynes 563377). Cruises from Cosgrove Wharf
to Stoke Bruerne etc, for private parties. Ⓔ

PUBS

🍺 **Navigation Inn** Castlethorpe Wharf,
Cosgrove. Canalside.
🍺✕ **Barley Mow** Cosgrove, by bridge 65.
Mann's beer, snacks, large garden with swings
and a slide, mooring.
🍺 **Galleon Inn** Wolverton. Canalside at bridge
68.

Yardley Gobion

The canal leaves the low hills to the west and
passes through open fields to Grafton Regis,
where the hills reappear. A quiet, rural stretch,
with only the noise of the railway. The villages
lie set back to the west, but are easily
approached. Accommodation bridges occur
with even regularity, mostly old brick arches.
After Grafton Regis the River Tove joins the
canal and then branches away to the west after
¾ mile; there is a winding hole by this
junction. At once the canal starts the 7-lock
climb to Stoke Bruerne, via single wide locks.
The A508 crosses after the second lock.

Stoke Park Approached via Stoke Bruerne, or
along a footpath that leaves the canal at lock
20. The park is then ½ mile west of the canal.
Built 1629–35 by Inigo Jones for Sir Francis
Crane, head of the Mortlake Tapestry Works,
the symmetrical facade with its flanking
pavilions and colonnade made Stoke Park
House (now demolished) one of the earliest
Palladian or classical buildings in England. The
exterior only, and the gardens may be visited.
Open Jul–Aug, Sat & Sun only.
Grafton Regis
Northants. EC Sat. P.O. Tel. Stores. A quiet
stone village that runs gently westwards from
the canal, it still preserves a strong manorial
feeling. The large church, near the canal, is
mostly 13th and 14thC, but contains a Norman
font. There is also a fine Neo-classical
monument by Flaxman, 1808.
Yardley Gobion
Northants. EC Wed. P.O. Tel. Stores. A small
thatch and stone village, set on a slope to the
west of the canal. The village is cut in half by
the A508, which has prompted much
redevelopment. The church that overlooks the
road was built in 1864.

BOATYARDS

Ⓑ **Yardley Wharf** Yardley Gobion (542454).
Ⓢ Ⓦ Ⓓ Ⓔ Pump-out, gas, laundry, baths,
B&B. Marine engineers.

PUBS

🍺 **White Hart** Grafton Regis. On A508 west of
canal from bridge 57. Food.
🍺 **Coffee Pot** Yardley Gobion. Food. South of
bridge 60.

Stoke Bruerne

Now the hills become more dominant, especially to the west and north west, anticipating Blisworth Tunnel. After the tunnel and the thickly wooded approach cutting, the hills recede to the west, and the canal, becoming wider but shallow at the edges, reaches Gayton Junction through open fields. The villages are very much on top of the canal, partly because of the landscape, and partly because of their importance to the canal; Stoke Bruerne is an ideal canal village. After Stoke Bruerne top lock the level remains unchanged for several miles. A deep cutting leads to Blisworth tunnel, the second longest in Britain still navigable. (Dudley Tunnel is the longest, at 3154yds). The Waterways Museum at Stoke Bruerne makes this altogether an exciting stretch. The A43 crosses in the middle of Blisworth, but Blisworth station is closed.

Blisworth
Northants. P.O. Tel. Stores, garage. A large brown stone village built around the A43, it climbs up steeply from the canal, which passes through in a cutting shortly after leaving the tunnel. The church, mostly 14thC, is just to the east of the canal, but appears to sit astride it. There are houses of all periods, the most striking built of local stone in the 18thC. Blisworth stone was quarried extensively. On the road that runs above the tunnel, marked by the regular grey caps of the air vents, are several elegant stone houses, one, now a farm, is handsomely titled in carved lettering, 'Blisworth Stone Works'.

Blisworth Tunnel At 3057yds long, Blisworth is the second longest navigable canal tunnel in Britain. No towpath, but the channel is wide enough to allow the passing of two 7ft boats, so keep to the right. *Boats over 7ft beam must give advance notice to the section inspector at Gayton (Tel: Northampton 858233) or to the lock keeper or the manager at the Waterways Museum, Stoke Bruerne (Roade 862229) so that boats can be prevented from entering the tunnel at the opposite end.*
The Grand Junction Canal was completed and opened in 1800 with the exception of this tunnel. The first attempt at excavation failed, and so a tramway was built over Blisworth Hill, linking the 2 termini Boats arriving at either end had to be unloaded onto horse-drawn waggons, which were then pulled over the hill, and reloaded on to boats. A second attempt at the tunnel was more successful, and it opened on 25th March, 1805. Originally boats were legged through. (Note the leggers' hut at the south end.) 1984 saw the completion of BWB's £4.3 million restoration project.

Stoke Bruerne
Northants. EC Sat. P.O. Tel. Stores. Perhaps the best example of a canal village in this country. Built mostly of local Blisworth stone, the houses flank the canal, clearly viewing it as a blessing. To the west the hilly landscape warns of the approaching tunnel under Blisworth Hill. The Perpendicular church with its Norman tower overlooks the village, while the warehouses and cottages along the wharf have become a canal centre, greatly encouraged by the presence of the Waterways Museum. As a canalscape Stoke Bruerne has everything: a pub, locks, boat scales, a double-arched bridge, museum and canal shops and a nearby tunnel. (During *summer,* pleasure trips to tunnel mouth).

Waterways Museum Stoke Bruerne. (Roade 862229). Housed in a fine old stone warehouse, a unique collection brings to life the rich history of over 200 years of canals. Exhibits include a traditional narrow boat, boat weighing scales, a reconstructed butty boat cabin, steam and diesel engines, and extensive displays of clothing, cabinware, brasses, signs, models, paintings, photographs, and documents. Museum shop selling canal literature, maps, postcards, souvenirs and other ephemera. *Open daily (except Christmas, Boxing Day and winter Mons).*

BOATYARDS

Ⓑ **D. Blagrove** Wharf Cottage, Stoke Bruerne (Roade 862174). Ⓦ Ⓓ Ⓔ Canal carriers. B & B.
Ⓑ **BWB Gayton Yard** Blisworth. (Blisworth 858233). Ⓡ Ⓢ Ⓦ Ⓓ Moorings, slipway, toilets.
Ⓑ **Blisworth Tunnel Boats** Gayton Rd, Blisworth. (Blisworth 858868). Ⓡ Ⓢ Ⓦ Ⓟ Ⓔ Pump-out (*not winter weekends*), boat hire, gas repairs, mooring, books & maps, souvenirs, toilets.

PUBS

🍺 **Royal Oak** Blisworth. Food, garden for children.
🍺 **Boat Inn** Stoke Bruerne. (Roade 862428). Canalside. Food, skittles. Can get very crowded.
✗🍷 **Butty** Stoke Bruerne. Italian food. Popular, so reservation is advised—ring Roade 863654.

The north entrance to Blisworth Tunnel. *Derek Pratt*

Milton Malsor

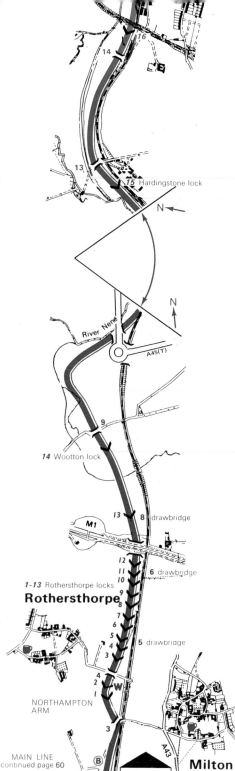

At Gayton Junction the Northampton Arm of the Grand Union branches away to the north east. It falls steeply through 5 miles of open country to Northampton where it connects with the navigable River Nene and thus with Peterborough, the Fens and ultimately the Wash. There are no villages on the canal, and the main feature of interest is the flight of 17 locks down to Northampton. Most of the long flight is visible from the top, as is Northampton in the distance. Several traditional drawbridges cross the canal, which look very pretty but are hard work to operate. Only the M1 bridge, a long concrete tunnel, interferes with the unchanged feeling of the arm. A guide sheet is obtainable from the box at Gayton Junction, and those who navigate the arm can obtain a plaque and certificate from R. Hardwick, 11 Newton Road, New Dunston, Northampton (584919).

Rothersthorpe
Northants. EC Sat. P.O. Tel. Stores. A comfortable mixture of brick and stone built round a large square. The church contains a Tudor pulpit. To the west of the village is a large circular dovecot with 900 nesting places.

Milton Malsor
Northants. P.O. Tel. Stores. Attractive, meandering brick stone village, spreading east towards the 14thC church. Around the church are several elegant stone houses of the 17th and 18thC, making an exploration on foot worth while. New houses have been well incorporated with the old.

BOATYARDS

Ⓑ **Freshwater Marine**. Blisworth Arm, Blisworth. (Blisworth 858685). 400yds up the Northampton Arm. Ⓡ Ⓢ Ⓦ Ⓓ Pump-out, gas, hire fleet, moorings, chandlery, craneage, repairs, licences.

PUBS

🍺 **Chequers** Rothersthorpe. Food.
🍺 **Greyhound** Milton Malsor. Food.
🍺 **Compass** Milton Malsor.

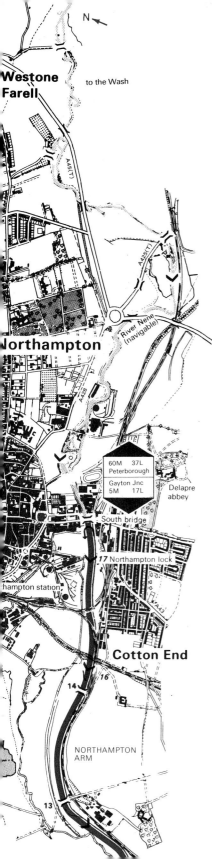

Northampton

Continuing north east and then swinging east
after Hunsbury Hill, the canal leaves the open
country behind as it approaches Northampton.
Housing estates fringing the canal soon appear.
The entry into the town passes factories,
disused wharves and railway junctions before
reaching Cotton End Wharf. Anyone
considering stopping in Northampton is
advised to pass through the bottom lock and
into the Nene Navigation, where surroundings
are more inviting.

Navigational note
The River Nene is a fully navigable river from
Northampton down to the Wash. At
Peterborough, which is 60 miles and 37 locks
away, the river becomes tidal. Boats using the
river need ordinary Grand Union-sized 1¼in
windlasses, and also a set of special lock keys.
Information and permission to navigate the
river should be sought from the Welland &
Nene River Authority. North St. Oundle.
Peterborough (Oundle 73701).
Northampton
*Northants. EC Thur. MD Wed, Sat. P.O. Tel.
Stores, garage, station, cinema, theatre.* The
centre of the town was destroyed by fire in
1675, and so little remains of Northampton's
famous history. Today it is a centre of the shoe
industry. Only an archway of the 12thC castle
remains, one of the best-known Norman
castles. Thomas à Becket was tried here in
1164. There are several churches of interest,
including a rare round Norman one of c1110.
The richly decorated Town Hall was built
during the 19thC in the Glothic style.
Abington Museum Abington Park. Period
rooms, toys, bygones, Northampton lace,
ceramics, natural history exhibited in a manor
castle. *Closed Sun in winter.*
Central Museum and Art Gallery Guildhall
Rd. Archaeology, antiquities, paintings,
furniture and the finest collection of historical
footwear in Europe, including Queen Victoria's
wedding shoes and ballet shoes of Nijinsky.
Delapre Abbey London Rd (A50). ½ mile
south of canal. A former Cluniac nunnery,
founded in 1145, the Abbey underwent major
alterations in the 16th and 17thC. *Open Thur &
Sat afternoons.* South of the Abbey park is
Eleanor Cross, one of 3 surviving crosses set up
by Edward I in 1290 to mark the last resting
places of Queen Eleanor on her way to burial in
Westminster Abbey from Harby in
Leicestershire where she had died.
Battle of Northampton 10th July, 1460 ½ mile
south of Northampton Lock, between Delapre
Abbey and Hunsbury Hill. A significant battle
in the Wars of the Roses in which the
Lancastrian King Henry was defeated by
Edward of York. Beaumont, Shrewsbury,
Egremont and Buckingham were slain and
many bodies floated in the River Nene. In
London the Lords agreed to make York
Protector and heir apparent during Henry's
lifetime. Most of the battle was fought by the
river, the keenest fighting taking place in Nunn
Mills road by the Avon cosmetics factory.

PUBS

🍺✕ **Plough Hotel** Bridge St, Northampton.
Food (except weekends), accommodation.
🍺 **Saddlers Arms** Bridge St, Northampton. ½
mile north of South Bridge. Not easy to find: if
you get to the church, you have missed it!

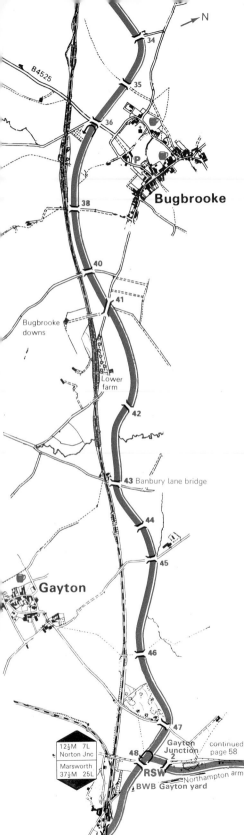

Gayton Junction

Continuing north west after Gayton Junction, the canal enters a relatively empty stretch of agricultural, open fields falling away to the north and steep hills to the south through which the railway cuts its way parallel to the canal. At Banbury Lane bridge there is an attractive group of buildings—once the Anchor pub and wharf. As it approaches Bugbrooke, the only village on this stretch, it begins to meander as the hills become more dominant. There are no locks, but a large number of old brick arched bridges provide some interest. The canal is accompanied by the A5 and M1, both in the distance, while the B4525 crosses at Bugbrooke.

Bugbrooke
Northants. EC Sat. P.O. Tel. Stores, garage.
Although much rebuilding has taken place in the north, there are still fine 18thC houses to the south and a pretty Baptist church of 1808. The parish church is set by itself in parkland and is mainly 14thC incorporating a 12thC chapel. A well proportioned building of golden stone, it was sensitively restored in 1921. Look for the plaque in the belltower, which warns, in rhyme, against improperly dressed bellringers. One of the great pleasures of this manorial village is the well marked footpaths and bridleways.

Gayton
Northants. P.O. Tel. Stores. Set on a hill to the west of the canal junction, the village seems to be composed of large, handsome stone houses, ranging in style from the 16thC to the 19thC; trees among the houses increase the rural grandeur. The large church with its ornamented tower maintains the unity of the village.

PUBS
🍺 **Bakers Arms** High St, Bugbrooke. Garden.
🍺 **Five Bells** 14 Church Lane, Bugbrooke. Very fine old pub opposite the church serving lunchtime food (*not Sun*) and Mann's real ale. The garden is shaded by willows and the tables are well spaced. Swings, a climbing frame and pet rabbits will amuse the children. The stocks in front of the pub recall less tolerant times.
🍺 **Eykn Arms** Gayton.
🍺✕ **Queen Victoria Inn** Gayton. Restaurant, reductions for children.

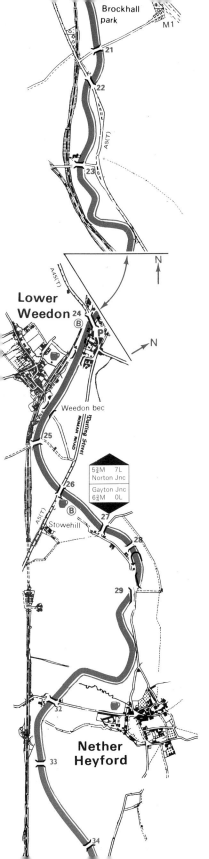

Weedon

The canal begins to meander sharply because of
the hills encroaching to the west; at the same
time the landscape becomes more dramatic as
the valley steepens on both sides of the canal.
Weedon is passed on a long embankment that
dominates the village, and then a quiet open
stretch follows which gives way to the
landscaped woods of Brockhall Park. The canal
avoids most villages, passing directly only
through Weedon, where there is much of
interest: aqueducts over a road and the River
Nene, an embankment, the old wharf (private)
and the elegant barracks. There are good
moorings above the church. Several transport
routes merge now to produce a strange picture
of 3 totally different means of transport
running parallel: the old Roman road, Watling
Street (A5), keeping as straight a course as
possible through the hills; the canal, its junior
by 1800 years, now looking more outdated than
the Roman road; the London–Midland railway
line and the 20thC motorway complete the set
of contrasts. Of all the thousands of travellers
passing through this area every hour, it must
surely be those who travel on the canal who
enjoy it the most as they compare the canal's
dignity and quiet progress to the noise and rush
of the roads and the railway.

Weedon
Northants. EC Thur. P.O. Tel. Stores, garage.
The canal passes much of Weedon via an
embankment, and so the village seems to be set
in a valley. Sandwiched curiously between
railway and canal embankments is the Victorian
church with a Norman tower. Upper Weedon
runs west from the canal, a long L-shaped
street flanked by fine houses of all periods. To
the north are the remains of Weedon barracks,
begun in 1803; at one time very extensive,
including a Royal Pavilion to be used by George
III in case of invasion, the barracks were built
here because it was the furthest point from any
coast! Many buildings survive, although the
canal arm cut to serve the barracks was closed
when the railway was electrified.

Nether Heyford
Northants. P.O. Tel. Stores. A small residential
village dwarfed by pylons on all sides. The
canal skirts the village. A large Roman building
was discovered to the east of the village in 1699.

BOATYARDS

Ⓑ **Concoform Marine** The Boatyard, High St,
Weedon. (40739). W P D Pump-out, gas,
moorings, hire fleet, slipway. *Open Tues–Sat
summer, closed winter weekends.*
Ⓑ **Waterways Holidays** Stowe Hill Wharf,
Weedon. (42300). R S W D Pump-out, gas,
repairs, narrow boat hire, toilets, provisions.
Trip boat 'Saucy Sue'. *Closed Sun.*
Ⓑ **Stowe Hill Marine** Stow Hill Wharf,
Weedon. (41365). D Gas, boat building and
repairs, dry dock, long term mooring.

PUBS

🍺 **New Inn** Weedon, near bridge 24.
🍺✕ **Crossroads Hotel** Weedon. Real ale,
children welcome.
🍺 **Narrow Boat** Weedon. Charles Wells ales. A
popular venue.
🍺 **Globe** Weedon. Near bridge 24.

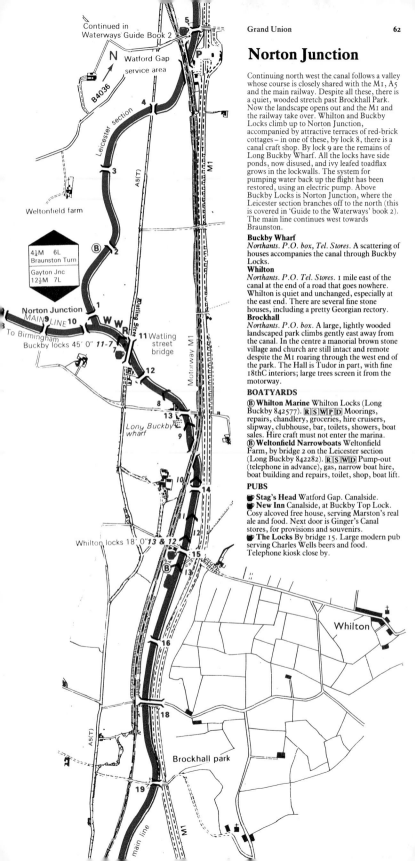

Norton Junction

Continuing north west the canal follows a valley whose course is closely shared with the M1, A5 and the main railway. Despite all these, there is a quiet, wooded stretch past Brockhall Park. Now the landscape opens out and the M1 and the railway take over. Whilton and Buckby Locks climb up to Norton Junction, accompanied by attractive terraces of red-brick cottages – in one of these, by lock 8, there is a canal craft shop. By lock 9 are the remains of Long Buckby Wharf. All the locks have side ponds, now disused, and ivy leafed toadflax grows in the lockwalls. The system for pumping water back up the flight has been restored, using an electric pump. Above Buckby Locks is Norton Junction, where the Leicester section branches off to the north (this is covered in 'Guide to the Waterways' book 2). The main line continues west towards Braunston.

Buckby Wharf
Northants. P.O. box, Tel. Stores. A scattering of houses accompanies the canal through Buckby Locks.

Whilton
Northants. P.O. Tel. Stores. 1 mile east of the canal at the end of a road that goes nowhere. Whilton is quiet and unchanged, especially at the east end. There are several fine stone houses, including a pretty Georgian rectory.

Brockhall
Northants. P.O. box. A large, lightly wooded landscaped park climbs gently east away from the canal. In the centre a manorial brown stone village and church are still intact and remote despite the M1 roaring through the west end of the park. The Hall is Tudor in part, with fine 18thC interiors; large trees screen it from the motorway.

BOATYARDS

Ⓑ **Whilton Marine** Whilton Locks (Long Buckby 842577). Ⓡ Ⓢ Ⓦ Ⓟ Ⓓ Moorings, repairs, chandlery, groceries, hire cruisers, slipway, clubhouse, bar, toilets, showers, boat sales. Hire craft must not enter the marina.
Ⓑ **Weltonfield Narrowboats** Weltonfield Farm, by bridge 2 on the Leicester section (Long Buckby 842282). Ⓡ Ⓢ Ⓦ Ⓓ Pump-out (telephone in advance), gas, narrow boat hire, boat building and repairs, toilet, shop, boat lift.

PUBS

🍺 **Stag's Head** Watford Gap. Canalside.
🍺 **New Inn** Canalside, at Buckby Top Lock. Cosy alcoved free house, serving Marston's real ale and food. Next door is Ginger's Canal stores, for provisions and souvenirs.
🍺 **The Locks** By bridge 15. Large modern pub serving Charles Wells beers and food. Telephone kiosk close by.

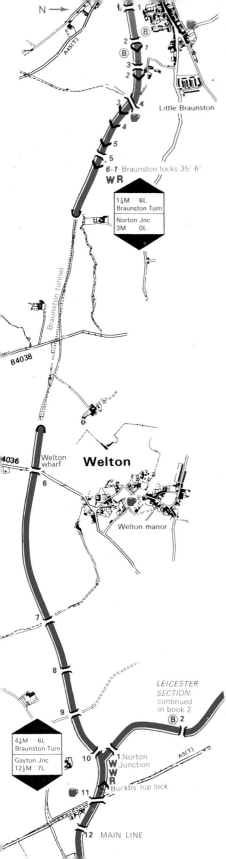

Welton

From Norton Junction to Braunston the canal
turns westward through hills and wooded
country. At first there are good views to the
north and north east, with the embankment
carrying the Leicester line branching away to
the north. The canal then runs into a wooded
cutting which leads to Braunston tunnel.
Before Welton Wharf, the feeder from the
Daventry Reservoir, built 1804, is reached; the
Welton feeder enters by bridge 6 and the
Drayton feeder enters the canal at the east end
of Braunston tunnel. A similar cutting follows
the tunnel, and then the landscape opens out
although the hills stay present on either side.
The flight of 6 wide locks takes the canal down
towards Braunston, a big canal centre. A canal
shop by Braunston Bottom Lock stocks fresh
fruit and veg, milk, bread, crafts and
chandlery.

Braunston Tunnel Opened in 1796, to bore
through the Northamptonshire heights, the
tunnel is 2042yds long. Its construction was
hindered by quicksands, and a mistake in
direction has given it a slight 'S' bend.
*Two boats of 7ft beam can pass in this tunnel, but
wide beam boats must get permission from the lock
keepers at Buckby (Long Buckby 842234) or
Braunston (Rugby 890259) to enter the tunnel.
They will then give a clear passage.*
Welton
Northants. P.O. Tel. Stores. The village climbs
up the side of a steep, winding hill, which
makes it compact and attractive, especially
round the church.

BOATYARDS

Ⓑ **Weltonfield Narrowboats** Weltonfield
Farm, by bridge 2 on the Leicester Section
(Long Buckby 842282). Ⓢ Ⓦ Ⓓ Pump-out
(telephone in advance) narrow boat hire, gas,
boat buildings and repairs, toilet, shop, boat
lift.

PUBS

🍺 **Admiral Nelson** Little Braunston.
Canalside, at lock 3. Manns beer, bar food (*not
Thur eve or Sun*).
🍺 **White Horse** Welton. Food, skittles.
🍺 **New Inn** Buckby Top Lock. Canalside.

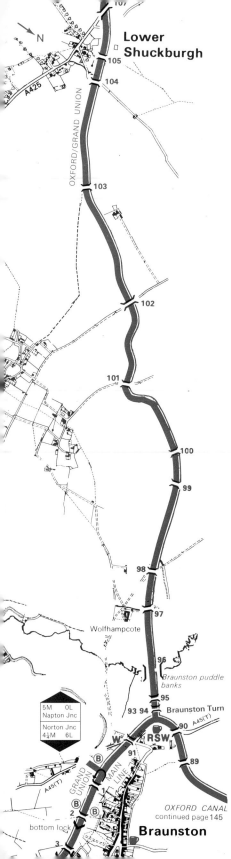

Braunston

Long rows of moored craft, including many
narrow boats, flank the canal at Braunston and
there is a fine selection of old buildings. A large
marina situated on an arm to the south meets
most boating needs; note also the iron
side-bridge and the 18thC dry dock. The arm in
fact was part of the old route of the Oxford
Canal before it was shortened by building a
large embankment (Braunston Puddle Banks)
across the Leam valley to Braunston Turn. The
entrance to this arm was thus the original
Braunston Junction. Leaving Braunston, the
canal runs south west towards Napton
Junction. This stretch of the Oxford Canal was
used jointly by the Grand Junction Company,
and as a result the Oxford charged excessive toll
rates in an attempt to get even with their rival,
whose more direct route to London had
attracted most of the traffic. Flowing through
open country with a background of hills to the
south, the canal is curiously quiet and empty
after the activity around Braunston. The land is
agricultural, with few houses in sight. There
are no locks, no villages and few bridges,
making this a very pleasant rural stretch of
canal, although the state of the towpath,
nonexistent in many places, will be a great
disappointment to walkers. The A425 crosses
through Lower Shuckburgh.

Lower Shuckburgh
Warwicks. P.O. box. A tiny village along the
main road. The church, built 1864, is attractive
in a Victorian way, with great use of contrasting
brickwork inside. The farm, west of bridge
104, sells eggs.
Braunston
Northants. P.O. Tel. Stores, Launderette. Set up
on a hill to the north of the canal, so that the
spire of Braunston church dominates the valley
for miles around. The village is really a long
main street, with houses of all periods that give
the feeling of a spacious market town. The
village is a very well known canal centre, and as
such is no less significant today than when the
Oxford and Grand Junction Canals were first
connected here.

BOATYARDS

ⓑ **Ladyline Braunston Marina** Braunston
(Rugby 890325). Ⓡ Ⓢ Ⓦ Ⓟ Ⓓ Gas, moorings,
chandlery, boat sales and repairs, toilets,
showers. Hotel boats operate from here.
ⓑ **Braunston Boats** Bottom Lock, Braunston
(Rugby 891079). Ⓦ Ⓓ Pump-out, gas, slipway,
chandlery, boat building and repairs. Narrow
boat hire.
ⓑ **Union Canal Carriers** Canalside, Braunston
(Rugby 890784). Ⓦ Ⓓ Hire craft, camping
boats, fitting out and repairs, dry dock.

PUBS

▯✕ **The Boatman** Braunston. Once the Rose
and Castle, now a comfortable and friendly
modern hotel/restaurant/pub. Watney and
Manns real ale, bar meals (vast helpings) and
candlelit dinners. Children's room, canalside
garden with swings and overnight moorings for
patrons.
▯ **Old Plough** Braunston. Imposing 17thC pub
serving Ansells real ale. Children's room, bar
food and garden.

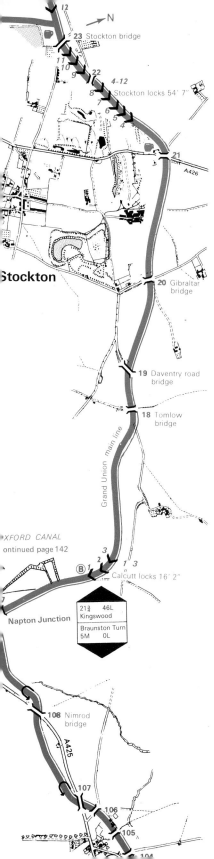

Napton Junction

Continuing west from Lower Shuckburgh, the
canal flows through wide open fields to Napton
Junction, where the Oxford Canal continues to
the south and the Grand Union branches north
towards Birmingham. The empty landscape
rolls on, broken by Calcutt Locks, towards
Stockton where there is a sudden change. Hills
come close to the canal, broken by the quarries
and thick woods along the south bank. The
quarries produce Blue Lias, a local stone, and
cement. This industrial belt contrasts with the
open landscape that precedes and follows it.
Stockton Locks continue the fall towards
Warwick, the B4100 crosses before Stockton
locks.

Stockton
Warwicks. EC Sat. P.O. Tel. Stores, garage.
Stockton is a largely Victorian village in an area
dominated by the smoking chimneys of the
cement works to the west. The church is built
of Blue Lias, quarried near Stockton Locks.

BOATYARDS
Ⓑ **Calcutt Boats** Calcutt Top Lock, Stockton,
Rugby (Southam 3757). ⑤ Ⓦ Ⓓ Pump-out, gas,
slipway, narrow boat hire and building, repairs,
mooring, chandlery, toilets and provisions.
Charter and hotel boats.

PUBS
🍺 **Boat** Stockton. Canalside at bridge 21.
🍺 **Blue Lias** Stockton. Canalside, at bridge 23.
Food, fine selection of malt whiskies. Garden
contains an assortment of animals.
🍺 **Barley Mow** School St, Stockton.
🍺 **Crown** High Street, Stockton.
🍺✕ **Napton Bridge** ¾ mile west of Napton
Junction on the Oxford Canal, by bridge 111.
(Southam 2466). Good canalside pub with
garden. Worth a walk from the junction.

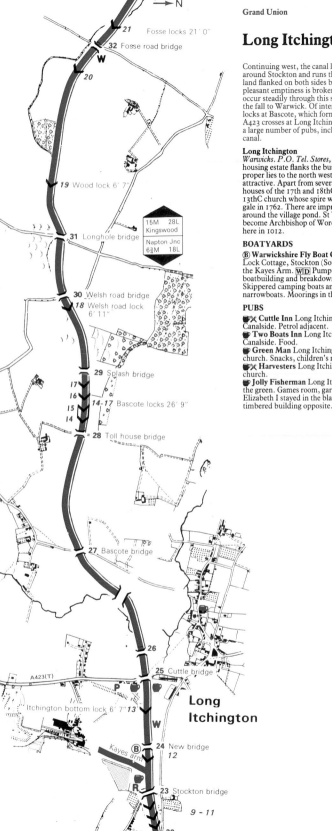

→ N

22

21   Fosse locks 21' 0"

32   Fosse road bridge

W

20

19   Wood lock 6' 7"

31   Longhole bridge

15M	28L
Kingswood	
Napton Jnc	
6¾M	18L

30   Welsh road bridge

18   Welsh road lock 6' 11"

29   Splash bridge

17
16
15
14

14–17   Bascote locks 26' 9"

28   Toll house bridge

27   Bascote bridge

26

25   Cuttle bridge

A423(T)

P

Itchington bottom lock 6' 7"   13

Long Itchington

W

24   New bridge
12

Kayes arm   B

23   Stockton bridge

9 – 11

22

Long Itchington

Continuing west, the canal leaves the industry around Stockton and runs through open arable land flanked on both sides by hills. The pleasant emptiness is broken by the locks that occur steadily through this section, continuing the fall to Warwick. Of interest are the top 2 locks at Bascote, which form a staircase. The A423 crosses at Long Itchington, a village with a large number of pubs, including 2 on the canal.

Long Itchington
Warwicks. P.O. Tel. Stores, garage A large housing estate flanks the busy A423; the village proper lies to the north west, and is very attractive. Apart from several pubs there are houses of the 17th and 18thC, and a largely 13thC church whose spire was blown down in a gale in 1762. There are impressive poplars around the village pond. St Wulfstan, who later become Archbishop of Worcester, was born here in 1012.

BOATYARDS
Ⓑ **Warwickshire Fly Boat Company** Shop Lock Cottage, Stockton (Southam 2093). By the Kayes Arm. Ⓦ Ⓓ Pump-out, gas, shop, boatbuilding and breakdown service, dry dock. Skippered camping boats and 12-berth narrowboats. Moorings in the Kayes Arm.

PUBS
Ⓟ✕ **Cuttle Inn** Long Itchington. Bridge 25. Canalside. Petrol adjacent.
Ⓟ **Two Boats Inn** Long Itchington. Bridge 25. Canalside. Food.
Ⓟ **Green Man** Long Itchington. Past the church. Snacks, children's room.
Ⓟ✕ **Harvesters** Long Itchington, near the church.
Ⓟ **Jolly Fisherman** Long Itchington, opposite the green. Games room, garden. Queen Elizabeth I stayed in the black and white timbered building opposite.

Royal Leamington Spa

After Fosse Locks the canal continues west
through attractive and isolated country to
Radford Semele, where there is a fine wooded
cutting. Emerging, the canal joins the A425 and
then carves its private course straight through
Leamington. Midway through the town the
canal enters a deep cutting that hides it from
the adjacent main road and railway. The A425
accompanies the canal through Leamington.
There are good moorings and shops by bridge
40.

Royal Leamington Spa
*Warwicks. EC Mon/Thur. P.O. Tel. Stores, by
bridge 40, garage, station, cinema.* During the
19thC the population of Leamington increased
rapidly, due to the late 18th and 19thC fashion
for spas generally. As a result the town is
largely mid-Victorian, and a number of
Victorian churches and hotels dominate the
town, several designed by J. Cundall, a local
architect of some note who also built the brick
and stone town hall. The long rows of villas,
elegant houses in their own grounds spreading
out from the centre, all express the Victorian
love of exotic styles—Gothic, Classical,
Jacobean, Renaissance, French and Greek are
all mixed here with bold abandon. Since the
Victorian era, however, much industrialisation
has taken place.

Art Gallery & Museum
Avenue Rd. British,
Dutch and Flemish paintings of the 16th and
17thC. Also a collection of modern art, pottery
and porcelain through the ages and a specialist
series of 18thC English drinking glasses.
Victorian costume and objects. *Open Mon–Sat
and Sun afternoons.*

All Saints' Church
Bath St. Begun in 1843 to
the design of J. C. Jackson, the church is of
Gothic style, not always correct in detail. The
north transept has a rose window patterned on
Rouen Cathedral; the west window is by
Kempe.

Jephson Gardens
Alongside Newbold Terrace,
north of bridge 40. Beautiful ornamental
gardens named after Dr Jephson (1798–1878),
the local practitioner who was largely
responsible for the spa's high medical
reputation.

Radford Semele
Warwicks. EC Thur, P.O. Tel. Stores, garage. A
main road suburb of Leamington, Radford
Semele takes no notice of the canal that runs
below the village, alongside the River Leam
and the closed railway line to Rugby. Among
the bungalows are some fine large houses,
including Radford Hall, a reconstructed
Jacobean building. The Victorian church is set
curiously by itself, seemingly in the middle of a
field.

Offchurch
Warwicks. P.O. Tel. Stores, garage. A scattered
residential village reflecting the proximity of
Leamington. It takes its name from Offa, the
Saxon King of Mercia, reputedly buried near
here. The church, with its tall grey stone tower,
contains some Norman work. To the west lies
Offchurch Bury, whose park runs almost to the
canal. Originally this was a 17thC house, but it
has since been entirely rebuilt. The façade is
now early 19thC Gothic.

PUBS
- **Emscote Tavern** Canalside at bridge 46.
- **Royal Exchange** Tachbrook Rd,
  Leamington Spa. 100yds north of bridge 41.
- **Queens Head** Canalside at bridge 40.
- **George** High St, Leamington Spa. ¼ mile
  north of bridge 40.
- **Stags Head** Offchurch. Popular thatched
  pub with garden, snacks.
- **White Lion Inn** Southam Rd, Radford
  Semele. Smart village pub, once a coaching inn,
  built in 1622. Garden.

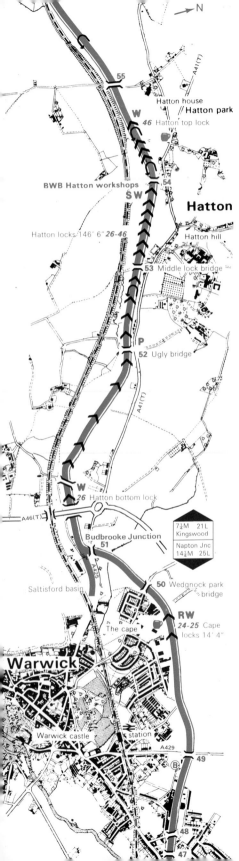

Warwick

After leaving Leamington the canal swings
north west under the A425 and then crosses the
railway and the River Avon on aqueducts.
Warwick is best approached from bridge 46, as
the canal skirts round the town to the north.
After climbing the 2 Cape locks, it swings south
to Budbrooke Junction, where the old Warwick
and Napton Canal joined the Warwick and
Birmingham. Turn to the west, pass under 2
large road bridges, and then the first of the 21
locks of the Hatton flight appears, with the
distinctive paddle gear and gates stretching up
the hill ahead, a daunting sight for even the
toughest boatman. Consolation is offered by the
fine view of the spires of Warwick as you climb
the flight. On reaching the top, the canal turns
to the west, passing the wooded hills that
conceal Hatton village and Hatton Park. The
A41 follows the canal to the north, the railway
to the south; there is a station at Hatton.

Hatton
Warwicks. This heavily wooded village is
scattered around the top of the Hatton locks.
The church, set by itself, is partly
Perpendicular, partly Victorian. North of
Hatton, and seemingly inseparable from it, is
Haseley, also surrounded by woods; its small
church is pretty and relatively unrestored, still
retaining its box pews. Parts of it date from the
13thC.
Warwick
Warwicks. EC Thur. MD Wed/Sat. An historic
town which still contains many medieval
buildings.
Church of St Mary's Of Norman origin, it
contains a large 12thC crypt. Unfortunately
much of the building was burnt down in 1694
and only the 14thC chancel and the Beauchamp
chapel were left. The most striking feature of
the rebuilt church is its pseudo-Gothic tower.
Warwick County Museum Market Place.
Mainly local natural history, geology,
archaeology and the history of Warwickshire.
Includes the Sheldon tapestry map of
Warwickshire which dates from 1588. *Closed
Fri and Sun morning.*
Doll Museum Oken's House, Castle St. *Closed
Sun morning.*
Court House Jury St. The present building,
which dates from 1725, was built on the site of a
16thC civic building. The ball room is
decorated in Regency style.
Lord Leycester Hospital High St. The
hospital was founded by the Earl of Leycester
in 1571 in the buildings of the guilds. It is now
a hospital for retired or disabled servicemen.
Warwick Castle Castle Hill. The exterior is a
famous example of a 14thC fortification. Inside
are pictures by Rubens, Van Dyck and
Velasquez. The castle overlooks pleasant
grounds laid out by Capability Brown. *Open
Good Fri–mid Sep daily.*

BOATYARDS

BWB Hatton Workshops near the top of
Hatton locks. (Warwick 492192). Ⓢ Ⓦ
Drydock available for hire, also crane for boats
up to 2 tons.
Ⓑ **Kate Boats Warwick** The Boatyard, Nelson
Lane, Warwick (492968). Ⓢ Ⓦ Ⓓ Pump-out,
gas, narrow boat hire, provisions, chandlery,
books.

PUBS

 New Inn Hatton. Lunches and dinners
(*except Sun*).
 Dun Cow Saltisford. ¼ mile east of bridge
51.
 Cape of Good Hope Cape Locks, Warwick.
Canalside. Food.
 Lord Leycester Hotel Jury St, Warwick.
Restaurant.
 Westgate Arms Bowling Green St,
Warwick.
 Gold Cup Castle St, Warwick. Snacks and
meals.

Looking down Hatton Locks towards Warwick. Note the distinctive caps on the ground paddle mechanism. *Derek Pratt*

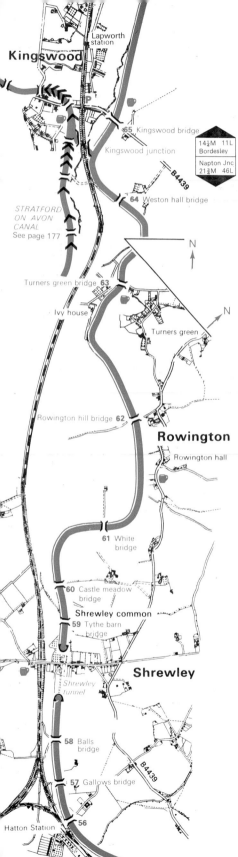

Kingswood

The canal now enters the wooded cutting that precedes Shrewley Tunnel. After the tunnel the hills surround the canal on all sides as it travels through steep wooded folds. A tall embankment carries it to Rowington, and then this gives way to wooded meadows that continue to Kingswood and the junction with the Stratford-on-Avon Canal, the southern part of which was restored by volunteers in 1964, owned by the National Trust until 1982 and now run by the newly-formed Stratford Canal Trust. There are no locks, a relief after the exhausting Hatton flight; instead the curious tunnel and the junction provide canal interest. The villages on this stretch tend to be scattered and shapeless, but there are plenty of facilities near at hand, and Packwood House is worth a visit. The railway continues to flank the canal to the west, occasionally interrupting the peaceful landscape: there is a station at Lapworth (Kingswood). The B4439 follows the canal to the east. The Stratford-on-Avon Canal is covered on pages 171 to 180.

Packwood House Hockley Heath 2 miles west of bridge 66. (Lapworth 2024). Timber-framed Tudor house, enlarged in the 17thC. Collection of tapestry, needlework and furniture. Park with formal grounds and 17thC yew garden laid out to represent the Sermon on the Mount, the trees taking the place of Jesus and his followers. *Open afternoons except Mon and Fri from Apr-Sep. Oct-Mar open Wed, Sat, Sun and B. Hols.* National Trust property.

Kingswood
Warwicks. P.O. Tel. Stores, garage, station. The village is scattered over a wide area from the Grand Union canal to the Stratford-on-Avon canal. The centre is 1 mile to the west, around the ambitious 15thC church, and the area immediately around the canal is residential, its character determined by the railway station. The main feature of interest is the canal junction with the Stratford-on-Avon canal and resulting basin. Note particularly the iron turnover bridge by the lock at the junction, which is split to allow the towing rope to pass through without being unhitched from the horse. Such bridges are a feature of the Stratford-on-Avon canal.

Wroxall
Warwicks. 1½ miles north east of Rowington. Little remains of the Benedictine Abbey founded in c1135; the 14thC nave and 17thC tower of its church, and fragments of the buildings around the cloisters survive. The mansion, a gloomy Victorian pile set in wooded parkland, replaced a Tudor house bought by Sir Christopher Wren for his son in 1713.

Rowington
Warwicks. P.O. Tel. Stores. A residential village of Tudor-style houses, handsome but suburban. Hidden among them are occasional 17thC and 18thC buildings, while near the canal the 13thC church retains some furnishings and a fine peal of bells.

Shrewley
Warwicks. P.O. Tel. Stores, garage. Runs in an untidy line along a minor road crossing the north end of the tunnel. Most of the village is recent ribbon development—useful as a source of supplies.

Shrewley Tunnel 433yds long, the tunnel was opened in 1799 with the completion of the Warwick and Birmingham canal. It is remarkable for the very clearly defined path over the top of the hill that a towing horse would use while its boat was 'legged' through the tunnel. This horsepath in fact goes through its own miniature tunnel for 40yds and emerges at the north west end above and beside the canal tunnel.
This tunnel allows two 7ft boats to pass: keep to the right.

PUBS

🍺 **Navigation** Kingswood. Canalside. Food.
🍺 **Tom o' the Wood** Finwood Rd, Rowington. Fine canalside pub serving Whitbread and Flowers real ale, food. Garden.
🍺 **Cock Horse** Rowington. Food.
🍺 **Durham Ox** Shrewley. Food, large garden.

About to ascend Knowle Locks. Only one gate need be opened for narrow craft. *Derek Pratt*

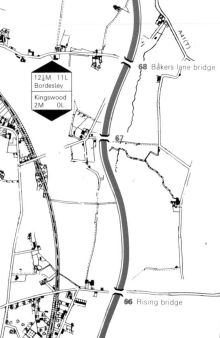

Knowle

After Kingswood the canal moves north, passing through a long straight stretch where the flat landscape is temporarily overshadowed by electricity pylons; Knowle Locks introduce more hilly countryside again, and this green and pleasant land continues right through to Solihull, concealing the nearness of Birmingham. The flight of 5 wide locks at Knowle used to be 6 narrow ones, until the 1930s: the remains of the old ones can still be seen alongside the new, together with the side ponds (originally built to save water). The locks are comparatively deep, and very hard work, but they are well maintained and beautifully painted up. They are also the northernmost wide locks for many miles now, since all the Birmingham canals have narrow locks. Both Baddesley Clinton and Knowle are set back from the canal (Knowle station is fully 2 miles away), but both warrant a visit.

Knowle
W. Midlands. EC Wed. P.O. Tel. Stores, garage, station. Despite its proximity to Birmingham, Knowle still survives as a village, albeit rather self-consciously. It is blighted by the A41, which roars through the middle, threatening to destroy the number of old buildings that remain. These date from the Middle Ages and include such gems as Chester House, which illustrates the advances in timber frame construction from the 13th to the 15thC. The church, consecrated in 1402, is large, formal and elegant, and battlemented all round. Just to the west is the timber-framed Guildhouse. ½ mile north of the village is Grimshaw Hall, a gabled 16thC house noted for its decorative brickwork. There are good views of it from the canal.

Baddesley Clinton
Warwicks. P.O. Tel. Stores. The village is a mile from the canal at bridge 66, but nearer are the church and the hall, set amid parkland. The church is mostly 16th and 17thC, but the hall is earlier—a typical late medieval manor built in a mixture of brick and stone. Much of the brickwork dates from the Queen Anne period, the stables and parkland completing the feeling of unity.

PUBS
🍺 **Wilsons Arms** High St, Knowle. Modernised pub dating from 16thC. Lunchtime snacks.

🍺 **Black Boy** Knowle. Canalside, at bridge 69. Food.

🍺 **Orange Tree** Chadwick End, Baddesley Clinton. Lunchtime snacks, garden.

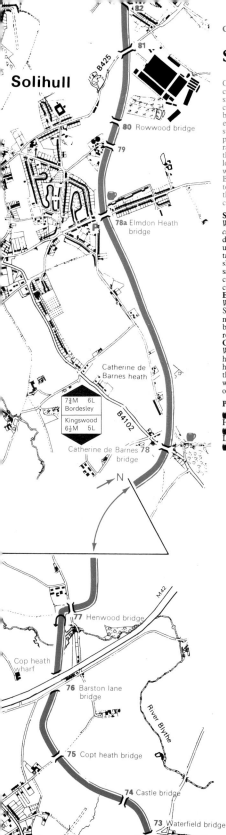

Solihull

Solihull

Continuing north west through wooded country, the canal crosses the river Blyth on a small aqueduct and enters the long wooded cutting that carries it all the way to Olton bridge. This attractive screen conceals the expanding suburban areas. The presence of suburbia means that supplies are available in plenty, but the embankment makes access rather difficult. Catherine de Barnes Heath is the last village easily approached. There are no locks, and the bridges tend to be high above the water. Traffic noise and the presence of Birmingham city airport, 2 miles to the north, tend to disturb the illusion of peace created by the cutting. The B4102 and the B425 cross the canal, while the A41 bisects Solihull.

Solihull
W. Midlands EC Wed. P.O. Tel. Stores, garage, cinema, station. A modern commuter development, with fine public buildings. What used to be the town centre, dominated by the tall spire of the parish church, is now a shopping area. The church, built of red sandstone, is almost all 14thC. The interior contains work of all periods. 17thC pulpit and communion rail, 19thC stained glass.

Elmdon Heath
W. Midlands. EC Thur. P.O. Tel. Stores, garage Suburb of Solihull. The athletic navigator in need of supplies can climb up the embankment by bridge 79 and find all he needs—but the return journey can be difficult if laden.

Catherine de Barnes
W. Midlands. Tel. Stores, garage. A higgledy-piggledy village in an area of isolation hospitals, far from the romanticism implied by the name. However, a convenient supply centre with easy access from the canal before the bulk of Birmingham.

PUBS

🍺 **Greville Arms** Damson Lane, Elmdon Heath. Lunchtime food and garden.
🍺 **Red Horse** Hermitage Rd, Solihull. Lunchtime snacks and garden.
🍺 **Boat Inn** Catherine de Barnes. Food.

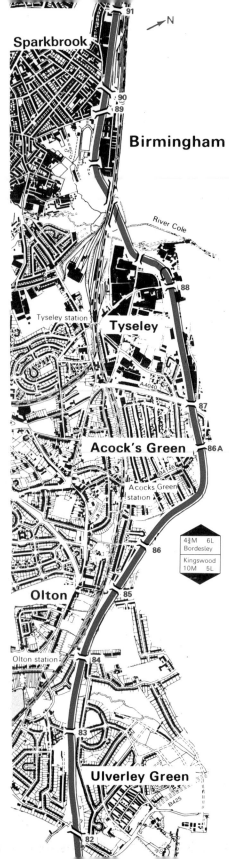

Tyseley

Continuing north west into Birmingham, the wooded cutting ends abruptly at Olton Bridge. From this point on, housing estates and disused wharves accompany the canal. The boatman should be wary of rubbish in the canal as he approaches the city. Factories flank the canal, and presently these give way to a short stretch of open wasteland to which Tyseley goods yard forms a suitable backdrop. Then the factories take over again, and access to and from the canal becomes increasingly difficult. Camp Hill Locks and all the succeeding locks are narrow: only boats of 7ft beam or less can pass. After passing through subterranean vaults formed by the criss-crossing of railway viaducts, Camp Hill Bottom Lock and Bordesley Junction are reached.

Tyseley Goods Yard ¼ mile south west of bridge 88. Here the Standard Gauge Steam Trust has a large depot for maintaining, storing and running private steam railway engines. *Open to visitors weekends Apr-Oct* (there is usually at least one locomotive in steam every Sunday) and on 2 big open days every summer.

Birmingham

The former Birmingham and Warwick
Junction Canal runs north from Bordesley
Junction to join the Birmingham & Fazeley and
Tame Valley Canals at Salford Junction. It was
opened in 1844 to by-pass the heavily-locked
stretches of the B & F at Ashted and Aston.
The 2¾-mile cut runs through industrial
surrounds. The 5 Garrison locks carry the canal
down to the Erdington level, where there is a
stop lock. The area of the junction itself is
completely covered by elevated motorways,
which join here in a huge multi-level
interchange; this provides an awe-inspiring
contrast between the old and the new forms of
transport. Beyond Bordesley Junction the canal
continues towards the Birmingham Canal Main
Line, passing Digbeth Basin, and climbing the
6 Ashted Locks and 13 Farmer's Bridge Locks
to join the Birmingham and Fazeley Canal at
Farmer's Bridge Junction.

Navigational note
There is a risk of vandalism here; moor only at
recognised sites in the city, such as Gas Street,
Cambrian Wharf or boatyards (by
arrangement).

Tame Valley canal
See book 2

Birmingham & Fazeley canal

M6

Salford Junction
See book 2

Nechells
shallow lock 6"

Saltley canal

Aston

Birmingham & Fazeley canal

11 Aston locks
70'0"

1¾M   11L
Salford Jnc

Farmer's Br
1¾M   13L

Aston Junction

6 Ashted locks   5 Garrison locks 34'5" **59-63**
35'1"

Digbeth branch

13 Farmers Bridge
locks 81'0"

Digbeth Basin
95

Bordesley Junction

Bordesley

Farmers Bridge
Junction
Cambrian
Wharf

New Street
Station

Gas Street
Basin

1¼M   6L
Aston Jnc

Kingswood
14¾M   11L

94

Camp Hill locks
52-57   41'8"
93

92

91A

BWB
Sampson
road
depot

Worcester & Birmingham canal
Continued on page 194

Grand Union Canal
Continued from
previous page
91

Birmingham

W. Midlands. EC Wed. MD Thur. P.O. Tel. Stores, garage, station, cinema, theatre, university.
It is strange to think that the medieval town that centred round the parish church and the moated manor originally stood on the site of the present Smithfield market. The Bull Ring, a modern shopping centre, used to be the village green. Industrial and commercial development continued with such speed during the 19thC that Birmingham began to be considered as the trade centre of the Midlands. The town is famous for such men as John Baskerville, William Murdoch, Joseph Priestley, Matthew Boulton and James Watt.

Farmer's Bridge A canalside development at Cambrian Wharf in which four skyscrapers, a canal pub and a restored 18thC street complete with gaslights are grouped beside a canal basin. The pub is totally canal-orientated, sporting much canal paraphernalia and a bar in a genuine floating narrow boat.

Saltley Reservoir Joins the Saltley Canal below Garrison Locks. A rare wildlife haven in the city.

Information Bureau 110 Colmore Row, Birmingham 3. (021-235 3411).

BOATYARDS

ⓑ **Brummagem Boats** Sherborne St Wharf, Oozell's Street loop west of Farmer's Bridge Junction. (021-643 8397). ⓡ ⓢ ⓦ ⓔ Pump-out, gas, boat hire, boat building and repairs, chandlery, toilets. Safe overnight mooring. *Closed Sun in winter.*

PUBS

Moor safely at Gas Street or Cambrian Wharf, the following are all fairly close by.

🍺 **Australian Bar** Bromsgrove St, ½ mile south east of Gas St Basin. Lunchtime snacks.

🍺 **White Lion** Horse Fair, ½ mile south east of Gas St Basin.

🍺 **St Pauls Tavern** Ludgate Hill, in the jewellery quarter. Near Farmers Bridge Locks.

🍺 **Long Boat** Farmers Bridge top lock, Kingston Row, Birmingham 1. Canalside. Food.

🍺 **Prince of Wales** Cambridge St. Past the Long Boat, turn left and the pub is on the right.

🍺 **Crown** Broad St, 200yds west of Gas St Basin. Out back is the old Butler's Brewery, used before he became part of Mitchells and Butler in 1898.

Camp Hill Locks. The wear caused by the ropes of many horse drawn boats can be seen on the cast iron bridge in the foreground. *Derek Pratt*

KENNET & AVON

Maximum dimensions

Reading to Bath, junction with River Avon
Length: 72'   70'
Beam: at 7'   or   at 13' 9"
Headroom: 7' 6"
Bath to Hanham Lock
Length: 75'
Beam: 16'
Headroom: 8' 9"

Mileage

READING to
Aldermaston Wharf: 10
Tile Mill Lock: 8
Aldermaston Wharf: 10
Newbury Lock: 18½
Kintbury: 24½
Hungerford: 27½
Crofton Top Lock: 35
Pewsey Wharf: 41½
Devizes Top Lock: 53½
Bradford-on-Avon: 65½
Dundas Aqueduct: 70
Bath, junction with River Avon: 75¼
HANHAM Lock (start of tidal section): 86½
Bristol Docks: 93
AVONMOUTH entrance to Severn
Estuary: 100¾

Locks: 105

The Kennet & Avon Canal is one of the most splendid lengths of artificial waterway in Britain, a fitting memorial to the canal age as a whole. It is a broad canal, cutting across southern England from Reading to Bristol. Its generous dimensions and handsome architecture blend well with the rolling downs and open plains that it passes through, and are a good reminder of the instinctive feeling for scale that characterised most 18th and early 19thC civil engineering.

The canal was built in three sections. The first two were river navigations, the Kennet from Reading to Newbury, and the Avon from Bath to Bristol, both being canalised. Among early 18thC river navigations the Kennet was one of the most ambitious, owing to the steep fall of the river. Between Reading and Newbury 18 locks were necessary in as many miles, as the difference in level is 138 feet. John Hore was the engineer for the Kennet Navigation, which was built between 1718 and 1723 and included 11 miles of new cut. Subsequently Hore was in charge of the Bristol Avon Navigation, carried out between 1725 and 1727. These river navigations were interesting in many ways, often because of the varied nature of the country they

passed through. The steep-sided Avon Gorge meant that a fast-flowing river had to be brought under control. Elsewhere the engineering was unusual: for example the turf-sided locks on the Kennet, now being replaced with brick structures.

For the third, linking stage a canal from Newbury to Bath was authorised in 1794. Rennie was appointed engineer, and after a long struggle the canal was opened in 1810, completing a through route from London to Bristol. The canal is 57 miles long, and included 79 broad locks, a summit level at Savernake 474ft above sea level and one short tunnel, also at Savernake. Rennie was both engineer and architect, anticipating the role played by Brunel in the creation of the Great Western Railway; in some ways his architecture is the more noteworthy aspect of his work. The architectural quality of the whole canal is exceptional, from the straightforward stone bridges to the magnificent neo-classical aqueducts at Avoncliffe and Limpley Stoke. Rennie's engineering, however, left something to be desired; the summit level was too short, and so pumping stations had to be installed at Crofton and Claverton to maintain the water level and feed the locks; in other places the canal bed was built over porous rock, and so leaked constantly, necessitating further regular pumping.

Nevertheless the canal as a whole was a striking achievement. At Devizes the canal descends Caen Hill in a straight flight of 29 locks, the longest flight of broad locks anywhere in Britain. The many swing bridges were designed to run on ball bearings, one of the first applications of the principle. The bold entry of the canal into Bath, a sweeping descent round the south of the city, is a firm expression of the belief that major engineering works should contribute to the landscape, whether urban or rural, instead of imposing themselves upon it as often happens nowadays.

Later the Kennet and Avon Canal Company took over the two river navigations, thus gaining control of the whole through route. However traffic was never as heavy as the promoters had expected, and so the canal declined steadily throughout the 19thC. It suffered from early railway competition as the Great Western Railway duplicated its route, and was eventually bought by that railway company. Maintenance standards slipped, and this, combined with a rapidly declining traffic, meant that navigation was difficult in places by the end of the 1914–18 war. The last regular traffic left the canal in the 1930s, but still it remained open, and the last through passage was made in 1951 by n.b. 'Queen', with the West Country artist P. Ballance on board. Subsequently the canal was closed, and for a long time its future was in jeopardy. However, great interest in the canal had resulted in the formation of a Canal Association shortly after the 1939–45 war, to fight for restoration. In 1962 the Kennet & Avon Canal Trust was formed out of the Association, and practical steps towards restoration were under way. Using volunteer labour, funds raised from all sources, and with steadily increasing help from BWB, the Trust have reopened a great deal of the navigation, and it seems certain that this remarkable through route will re-open entirely during the 1980s.

Natural history

This canal forms a unique series of freshwater habitats which vary along its length according to depth of water, aspect, height of the banks and the time of year.

The stonework of bridges, locks and aqueducts provides additional habitats for shallow-rooting plants. The three ferns, hartstongue, wall-rue and black spleenwort are of special interest. Where the lock walls are capped with limestone, lime-loving plants such as fairy flax and quaking-grass are found.

For much of its length the canal is bordered on one or both banks by trees, including several species of willow, and bushes, predominantly hawthorn. A detailed survey in 1972 showed that plants along the towpath vary little, growing in profusion along its length. There are many kinds of grasses; other frequent species are white deadnettle, hogweed, meadow cranesbill, ground ivy and fine specimens of the ratstail plantain. Apart from the marsh marigold, the yellow iris and the greater pond sedge, there are few flowers at the water's edge and on the canal bank until after mid-summer when purple loosestrife, the three-petalled arrowhead and flowering rush, together with the clusters of small creamy-white flowers of meadowsweet and pink-tinged angelica, contrast with the tall reed-grass and reedmace (often mistakenly called 'bulrush'). Rooting just in the water, the commonest plant is the branched burreed. It has a profusion of leaves but the green, spherical, prickly-looking flowers are often sparse. Large tufts of tussock sedge, clumps of water dock and short stretches of common reed, having all the leaves on the tall stems turning to face away from the wind, can be found at the water's edge. Of all the marginal plants, perhaps the most handsome is the flowering rush, which is commonest near Bath. Deeper water supports such plants as yellow water-lily, water crowfoot and several pondweeds that root in the mud but hold their leaves and flowers above the water surface. A few plants are entirely submerged, the commonest being hornwort, which grows in long bushy, brittle tassels.

In the summer and autumn much of the water surface is covered with small floating plants that are moved by the wind. There are four species of duckweed and a water fern, azolla, accidentally introduced from North America, which turns the canal red in autumn. It has become a problem near Seend where, with the duckweeds and blanket weed, it forms a blanket 4ins thick, eliminating light and air from the water surface. In hot weather this causes hundreds of fish to suffocate. The weed is only killed by a hard frost, when it sinks to the bottom and decays.

A botanist has recorded 190 different species of plants associated with the presence of the canal along a 4-mile stretch near Melksham. The different plant zones make not only for numerical and visual diversity but also for the diversity of animals dependent on them. Mute swans, coots and moorhens nest and take refuge in the dense vegetation at the water's edge, water voles feed on it and use rushes and grass to line their nests. These are four of the canal's largest animals but they, like all wildlife, are part of the food chains that depend on the oxygen in the water and the light that filters into it. Amongst the tangle of submerged green plants and their roots lives a host of small animals, many visible only under a microscope. Some of the water snails, the large swan mussels (8ins long), fresh-water shrimps and flatworms feed on decaying plant matter, while others such as water beetles, water spiders, water boatmen, dragonfly nymphs and the strange water stick insects, represent the hunting predators, actively seeking out their quarry, which is often much larger than themselves. Many of these freshwater creatures are found only in the comparatively still water of canals and ponds, for they would be swept away in the streams and rivers. They provide food for water shrews, fish, frogs and, occasionally, grass snakes, which can be seen on sunny days curled up on the towpath or swimming across the canal in a few regular haunts.

The shy little grebe, with its trilling call, has spread from Wilton Water and now nests, on platforms made by willow branches dipping into the water, as far west as Devizes. Kingfishers have returned to the localities they frequented prior to the severe winters of the early 1960s and single herons are regular fishermen along the canal, though their diet also includes frogs, etc. The abundance of newly-emerged insects attracts many small birds to the canal. In spring, the bushes are sometimes full of chiff-chaffs and willow warblers, eagerly feeding after their long flight from their winter quarters. Later, sedge and reed warblers arrive, take up their territories along the canal, sometimes singing all day and night, and build their nests in rushes and reeds. Swallows and house martins leave their nesting sites in the villages on summer evenings to feed over the canal, skimming low to pick up insects off the surface of the water. In late summer brambles growing on the banks are in flower, attracting butterflies to feed on them. The commonest are meadow brown, speckled wood, small tortoiseshell, peacock, brimstone and the quaintly-named gatekeeper. In autumn, pied wagtails converge on the canal pounds near Devizes at dusk to roost in the rushes. By December they number around 300.

The canal offers a wealth of interest and for students of all ages it can serve as an open-air natural history laboratory. If restoration work succeeds in producing the healthy ecological balance that has emerged near Bath, then naturalists, anglers and all other users will benefit.

The Kennet & Avon Canal Trust, The Wharf, Couch Lane, Devizes, Wilts. Tel: Devizes 71279, *mornings only*.

The Caen Hill flight at Devizes, one of the last major obstacles to restoration on the Kennet & Avon currently being re-gated. *Derek Pratt*

Reading

The River Kennet leaves the Thames east of
Reading. The mouth of the river is marked by
gasometers and the main railway, which runs
parallel to the south bank of the Thames. The
Kennet leads south west towards the centre of
Reading, passing Blake's Lock, the only lock
maintained by the Thames Conservancy that is
not actually on the Thames. The Kennet
through Reading is narrow, shallow and
fast-flowing, being a river navigation; also there
are several sharp blind bends in the town so
great care in navigation is needed. Keep a sharp
lookout for other boats and remember to allow
for the flow of the river. The river cuts across
the middle of the town, and so access to all
facilities is easy. Rows of riverside cottages and
a surprising variety of bridges decorate the
Kennet in Reading, High Bridge being the
most central access point. The Kennet passes
over a weir with County Lock adjoining. The
weirs are a feature of river navigation that
should be treated with respect, as the current
they create can often affect the course of a boat,
especially when making a slow approach to a
lock. The river gradually leaves the town,
passing through Fobney Meadow to Fobney
Lock.

Navigational note
The Kennet & Avon Canal locks require
windlasses of an intermediate gauge—1⅛in
instead of the normal 1in or 1¼in. Such
windlasses may be bought or hired from the
Reading Marine Company or from the BWB at
Padworth.

Reading
Berks. EC Mon/Wed. MD Mon. The town lies
at the extremity of the Berkshire Downs and
the Chiltern Hills, where the Thames becomes
a major river. It is the Victorian architecture
that makes this town interesting, as the
university buildings are not to everyone's taste.
Canal walkers in Reading will find there is no
towing path in the centre of town; however
west of Reading the whole canal is a public
right of way. (Because of the risk of vandalism
only recognised mooring sites should be used.)
Abbey Ruins Fragmentary remains of this
12thC abbey built by Henry I lie on the edge of
Forbury Park. The 13thC gatehouse, altered by
Scott in 1869, still stands.
The Gaol Forbury Rd. Designed by Scott and
Moffat in 1842–44 in the Scottish Baronial
style. Oscar Wilde wrote his 'Ballad of Reading
Gaol' while imprisoned here.
Museum of English Rural Life White Knights
Park. A fascinating collection of relics of old
English agriculture, and a small display of
painted canal ware with a set of tools used for
making narrow boats. *Closed Sun, Mon, B.
Hols.*
Museum & Art Gallery Friar St. Has an
exceptional natural history and local
archaeology collection. Also prehistoric
collection. *Open weekdays.*
Information Centre Central Library, Belgrave
St, Reading (55911).

BOATYARDS

Ⓑ **Kennet Mouth Boatyard** Kennetside.
Reading. (Reading 67742). Ⓦ Ⓓ Pump-out,
gas, boat hire, slipway, boat building and
repairs, overnight mooring, provisions. *Open
summer only.*
Ⓑ **Reading Marine Co.** Crane Wharf. Kings
Rd. Reading. (Reading 53917). Ⓡ Ⓦ Ⓓ
Pump-out, gas, boat hire, slipway, boat and
engine repairs, mooring, chandlery, toilets.
Open summer only.

BOAT TRIPS

K & A Canal Trust Trips in n.b. 'Lancing'.
Details: Reading 81115/598247.

PUBS

🍺 **Horn** St Mary's Butts, Reading. North of
Bridge St Bridge.
🍺 **Cap and Gown** King's Rd, Reading.
🍺 **Fisherman's Cottage** Kennetside, Reading.
Canalside. Food.
🍺 **Jolly Anglers** Kennetside, Reading.
Canalside. Food, water.
🍺 **Kennet Arms** By Berkeley Ave Bridge.

The map shows:
N
5' 3" Southcote lock *104*
Milkmaid's Footpath
105 Fobney lock 7' 8"
Reading
River Kennet
Berkeley avenue bridge
New ring road bridge
County lock *106*
Bear Free Wharf
Bridge street bridge
Traffic light controls
High bridge
Ⓑ
Watlington street bridge
Kings road bridge
Reading General station
Blake's lock 3' 4"
18½M 21L Newbury
Brentford 60M 21L
Ⓑ
Kennet mouth
A329
A4
River Thames

County Lock and Weir, Reading. There are several blind corners downstream. *Derek Pratt*

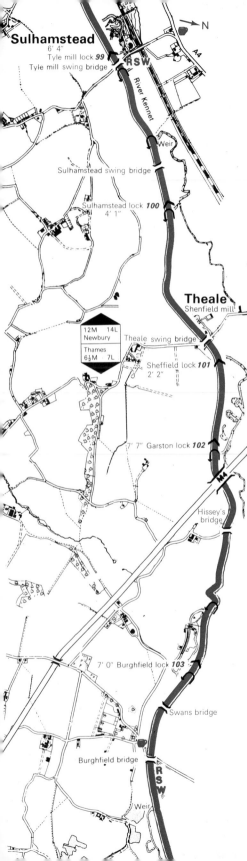

Theale

Continuing west, the canal passes Burghfield Bridge, a handsome stone arch. Burghfield Lock is turf-sided, one of several that survive from the early Kennet navigation, now under threat of 'improvement'. This old style lock makes getting on and off the boat slightly more difficult. The Kennet winds through water meadows, the straight stretches marking the canal sections. The new M4 motorway and the railway inevitably affect the peace and quiet of this stretch, although the country to the south of the Kennet improves steadily as it progresses westwards. Berkshire is well-known as orchard country. At Theale there is the first of the swing bridges that occur along the Kennet & Avon. Fortunately, since the completion of the M4, this bridge has reverted to carrying relatively infrequent road vehicles, so the passage of a boat no longer causes a major traffic hold-up. Opening the bridge is hard work, but there are instructions to help you. Make sure that you close the traffic barriers first of all and open them behind you. Theale village is ½ mile north of the bridge. After Theale, the Kennet flows steadily through wooded fields towards Sulhamstead and reaches Tyle Mill after a pleasant tree-lined straight cut. The moorings here are administered by the BWB section inspector (*see below*).

Sulhamstead
Berks. P.O. Tel. Stores. A scattered village ¼ mile south east of Tyle Mill, but with no real centre. There are several large houses standing in their own grounds; the most impressive is Folly Farm, built by Lutyens in 1906 in a William and Mary style. In 1912 Lutyens extended the house, this time using a Tudor style. The mixture of the two periods is most successful. The house is *private*.

Theale
Berks. EC Wed. P.O. Tel. Stores, garage, bank, station. ¾ mile north west of Sheffield Lock. Although largely a Reading suburb, Theale has been given a new lease of life by the opening of the bypass and the M4 motorway. The main street is now quiet and relatively traffic-free, and the Georgian terraces can be enjoyed. The large church with its tall tower is interesting. It was designed by E. W. Garbett and built 1820–32 in a style based entirely on Salisbury Cathedral. Theale station is half-way between the town and Theale swing bridge.

BOATYARDS
Ⓑ **BWB** Burghfield Bridge. (Enquiries to BWB Section Inspector, Lower Wharf, Padworth, Reading, Woolhampton 2277). Ⓡ Ⓢ Ⓦ Moorings.

PUBS
🍺 **Three Kings Jacks Booth** Bath Rd. Sulhamstead, ½ mile north of Tyle Mill.
🍺 **Falcon** High St, Theale.
🍺 **Lamb** Church St, Theale.
🍺✕ **Cunning Man** Burghfield Bridge. Canalside. Food (hot lunches).
✕🍷 **Knight's Farm Restaurant** Burghfield (Reading 52366). ½ mile south of Burghfield Bridge. New cuisine and whole food in a Queen Anne House. *Closed Sun D and all Mon.*

This section is navigable

Woolhampton

Leaving Tyle Mill the canal continues south west, constantly joining and leaving the River Kennet. Swing bridges are very common, often carrying busy roads. The A4 runs parallel for many miles, but always keeps its distance; the Great Western Railway also runs parallel but much closer. There are attractive stations at Aldermaston and Woolhampton.

Woolhampton
Berks. P.O. Tel. Stores, garage, station. A village on the A4 that owes its existence to the days of mail coaches on the old Bath road. There is a good mixture of buildings in the main street, several pubs and hotels, and to the south, a charming GWR station, still resplendent in brown and cream. Up on the hill to the north of the village are the Victorian church, the Georgian buildings of Woolhampton Park and Douai abbey and school, the latter a fine group of 19thC buildings with more recent additions.

Aldermaston
Berks. P.O. Tel. Stores. Attractively placed at the foot of a wooded hill, 1½ miles to the south of Aldermaston Wharf (along a minor road), the village is particularly fine. Mellow brick houses of all periods face each other across the sloping main street, which has survived the inroads of traffic. At the top of the street is the pebble-dashed church, and Aldermaston Court, a private house containing magnificent 17thC woodwork.

Aldermaston Wharf
Berks. P.O. Tel. Stores, station. A small canalside settlement bisected by the busy A340. The old swing bridge has been replaced with a hydraulic lift bridge, push-button operated with the aid of a BWB key. It cost the local council £250,000 to build.

Ufton Green
Berks. A lush, peaceful hamlet built round a small triangular green. All that remains of the church is one flint wall, standing proudly in the middle of a field, and capped with a marvellous mantle of ivy.

BOATYARDS

BWB Padworth Yard near Aldermaston Wharf. (Woolhampton 2277). Information about the canal, and moorings on the navigable sections. Special K & A-sized windlasses for sale.

PUBS

Row Barge Woolhampton. Canalside. Lunches daily, dinners at 12 hours notice.
Angel Hotel Woolhampton. Lunches, snacks and dinners. Also bed & breakfast.
Falmouth Arms Woolhampton
Butt Inn Aldermaston Wharf. Food.
Hinds Head Aldermaston. Food.

Limit of navigation Reading to Aldermaston. Padworth swing bridge should be operational June 1985; Aldermaston lift bridge is subject to rush-hour restrictions; Padworth and Aldermaston Locks will be in use in 1985.

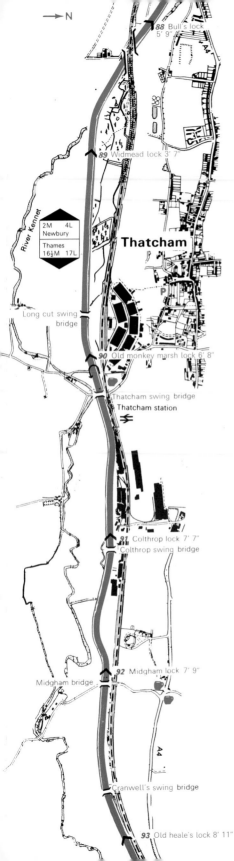

Thatcham

The canal leaves Midgham Park to the north
and continues due west through
water-meadows, the woods and hills receding to
the south. At Colthrop a large industrial estate
appears unexpectedly beside the canal; much of
it consists of paper mills. Thatcham station is
conveniently beside the canal; an hotel is
nearby. The village itself is a mile to the north
west. The canal now flows very straight
through isolated water-meadows under a
railway bridge to Bull's Lock.

Thatcham
*Berks. EC Wed. P.O. Tel. Stores, garage,
station.* The main square of this expanding
village is set back from the A4, and so it
manages to retain some peace. The church is
mostly Victorian, but at the end of the main
street there is a 14thC chapel, now used as a
school.

PUBS
- **Swan Hotel** near Thatcham station.
- **Broadway Restaurant** Thatcham.
- **Cricketers** High St, Thatcham.
- **Kings Head** The Broadway, Thatcham.
- **Coach and Horses** ½ mile north of
Midgham Bridge. Food.

Limit of navigation West from Widmead Lock
(89) to Crofton pumping station, except in very
dry conditions.

Map labels:

N

88 Bull's lock
5' 9"

A4

89 Widmead lock 3' 7"

River Kennet

2M   4L
Newbury
Thames
16½M 17L

Thatcham

Long cut swing bridge

P

90 Old monkey marsh lock 6' 8"

Thatcham swing bridge

Thatcham station

91 Colthrop lock 7' 7"
Colthrop swing bridge

92 Midgham lock 7' 9"

Midgham bridge

A4

Cranwell's swing bridge

93 Old heale's lock 8' 11"

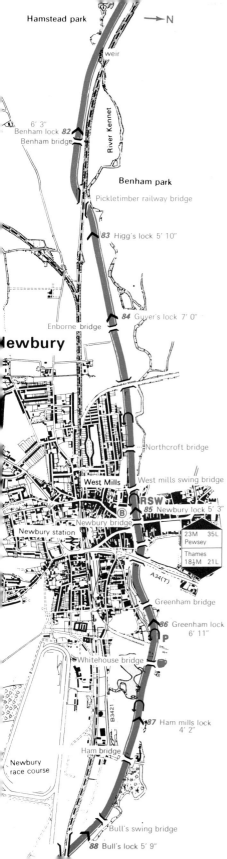

Newbury

The navigation enters Newbury under a
handsome new road bridge. Just beside this
bridge is Newbury Wharf, where there is a
stone building used by the K & A Canal Trust
as an information centre and museum, and old
warehouses, which have been ingeniously
converted into bus station buildings. This large
wharf used to be the terminus of the Kennet
Navigation from Reading, before the Kennet &
Avon Canal Company extended it to link up
with the Avon at Bath. West of the wharf the
channel gets narrower and faster until it reaches
a splendid stone balustraded bridge. Just
beyond is Newbury Lock, where there is a
mooring site. The river cuts right through the
town, and the town makes the most of it. West
of the lock is the delightful, quiet West Mills
area, where rows of terraced houses face the
navigation. West of Newbury, the navigation
again passes through extensive water-meadows
before the wooded hills of Hamstead Park close
in from the south.

Newbury
Berks. EC Wed. MD Tue. Newbury developed
in the Middle Ages as a cloth town of
considerable wealth, its stature indicated by the
size of the church. Although the cloth trade has
long vanished, the town has managed to retain
much of its period charm. It is a busy shopping
centre, and the shop fronts in the main streets
have buried many 17th and 18thC houses.
Elsewhere in the town the 18thC is well in
evidence, especially in the West Mills area.
There are fine almshouses, and a pretty,
ornamental stone bridge over the navigation.
There are also signs of the agricultural
importance of Newbury: the 19thC Italianate
Corn Exchange, for example.
St Nicolas Church West Mills. Borders the
canal on the south bank. A large Perpendicular
church, built c1500 at the height of Newbury's
prosperity as a wool town. Its 17thC pulpit is
most unusual.
St Nicolas School Enborne Rd. By
Butterfield, 1859.
Borough Museum Wharf Rd. Originally built
in 1626 as a cloth-weaving workshop to give
employment to the poor, this is one of the most
interesting buildings in Newbury. Adjoining is
the corn store, once on the edge of the Kennet
Wharf. The museum collection illustrates the
prehistoric and Saxon history of the region, as
well as the medieval and modern. Also a natural
history section with an excellent display of
moths and butterflies. Models illustrate the
Battles of Newbury. *Closed Sun. EC Wed.*
Round Barrow Cemetery Wash Common, near
the site of the 1st Battle of Newbury in 1643.
Memorial stones to the victims surmount the
two smaller mounds.
Newbury Fair Northcroft Lane, Northcroft.
Leave canal at Kennet Bridge. Annual
Michaelmas fair held since 1215. *Thur following
11 Oct.*
1st Battle of Newbury, 20 Sept 1643 Site of
Wash Farm off A343. 1¾ miles south of
Guyer's Lock. The Royalists were defeated by
the Parliamentarians in one of the bloodiest
onslaughts of the Civil War. Guyer's and Higg's
Locks are named after troop commanders in
the battle.
2nd Battle of Newbury, 28 Oct 1644
Donnington Castle, Donnington. 1½ miles
north of Newbury Lock off the A34. The
Royalists were in possession of Donnington
Castle when the Parliamentarians attacked.
Charles' army withdrew to Oxford, but a week
later they returned and relieved the castle.
There is a reconstruction model of the battle in
Newbury Museum.

This section is navigable.

BOATYARDS

Ⓑ **Newbury Boat Co** Greenham. (Newbury
30306) Ⓡ Ⓢ Ⓦ Ⓓ Slipway, gas, boat and engine
repairs, mooring. Working boats for hire.
Mon–Fri.

BOAT TRIPS

Kennet Horse Boat Co 32 West Mills,
Newbury, Berks. (Newbury 44154).
Horse-drawn and motor barge. Mostly private
charter. *Easter–end Sep.* Public trips on the
motor barge *Sun, B. Hols, some weekdays Aug.*
Must book.

PUBS

🍺✗ **Queen's Hotel** Market Place. Newbury.
Restaurant.
🍺 **Bacon Arms** Oxford St. North of West Mills
Bridge.
🍺 **Catherine Wheel** Cheap St. South of West
Mills Bridge.
🍺 **Globe** Bartholomew St. South of West Mills
Bridge.

The elegant and sturdy Newbury Bridge. *Derek Pratt*

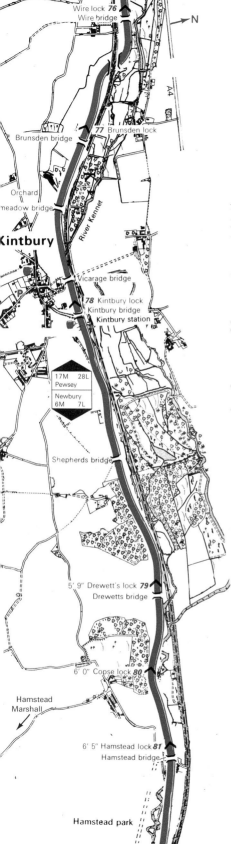

Kintbury

Passing the beautiful woods of Hamstead Park, the canal reaches Hamstead, Copse, Drewett's and Kintbury Locks. Wooded rolling hills flank the canal to the south as it climbs up the locks towards Kintbury, making this a particularly attractive stretch. The canal enters the village beside the railway, passing the splendid station, and the Dundas Arms, which overlooks the lock. The centre of Kintbury is up on the hill to the south of the lock. Leaving the wharf, the canal follows the railway, passing the Victorian Gothic vicarage, and then continues westwards through pleasing open countryside.

Kintbury
Berks. P.O. Tel. Stores, station. A quiet village with attractive buildings by the canal, including a watermill and canalside pub. The church is originally 13thC, but was restored in 1859; the railway lends excitement, and noise, to the situation.

Hamstead Park A very fine park bordered by the canal. There used to be a castle here and several interesting buildings adjoin the church on the side of the hill. There is an old watermill by the lock. The hamlet of Hamstead Marshall lies to the south, 1½ miles from Hamstead Lock.

PUBS

🍺 **Crossways Inn** Inkpen Rd, Kintbury.
🍺✕ **Dundas Arms** Kintbury. The River Kennet and the canal flow on either side of this pub, which was named after the Lord Dundas who opened the canal in 1810, giving his name also to the aqueduct at Limpley Stoke. The restaurant has a good French menu. *Open D Tue–Sat. Closed Royal Ascot week.*
🍺✕ **White Hart** Hamstead Marshall. Restaurant in an old country pub. 1 mile south of Hamstead Lock.
🍺 **Red House** Marsh Benham. ¼ mile north east of Hamstead Lock. Pub in a thatched estate village near Benham Park.

This section is navigable.

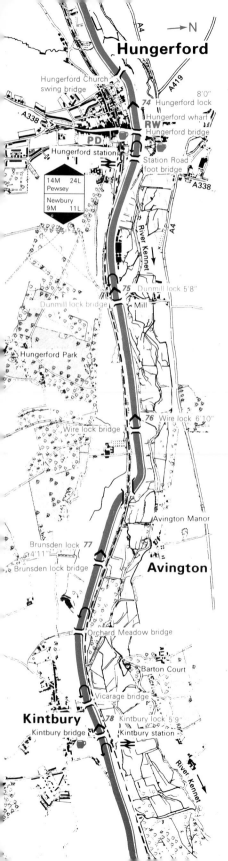

Hungerford

The canal continues westwards through open countryside. The railway and the River Kennet are constantly present, the river leaving the canal for the last time west of Kintbury. Locks 77 and 76 carry the canal past Avington, with its Norman church visible among the trees. Pretty woods accompany the canal to the south as it approaches Hungerford, while to the north river and canal run side by side through water-meadows, separated only by a narrow ridge carrying the towpath. By lock 75 the towpath turns over to the south bank. From the bridge there is a good view of Denford Mill. As the canal enters Hungerford, the Kennet swings away to the north, feeding the trout farm that lies between canal and river. Gardens flank the canal as it comes into the centre of the town. Access to Hungerford is easy by the town bridge, which leads directly to the handsome main street.

Hungerford
Berks. EC Thur. P.O. Tel. Stores, garage, bank, station. Hungerford is built along the A338, which runs through the town southwards from the junction with A4. The pleasant 18th and 19thC buildings are set back from the road, giving the spacious feeling of a traditional market town. None of the buildings is remarkable, but many are individually pretty. Note the decorative ironwork of the house by the canal bridge. The manor was given to John of Gaunt in 1366, and any monarch passing through the town is given a red rose, the Lancastrian emblem, as a token rent.
Hocktide Ceremonies On the second Tuesday after Easter, 99 commoners (those living within the original borough who have the rights of the common and the fishing) are called to the Town Hall by the blowing of a horn. Two Tuttimen are appointed, who have to visit the houses of the commoners to collect a 'head penny' from the men and a kiss from the women: they give oranges in return. All new commoners are then shod by having a nail driven into their shoes. This ceremony dates from the medieval period.
Avington
Berks. The village is best approached along the track that runs east from lock 76, although the more adventurous can go directly across the water-meadows, crossing the Kennet on a small footbridge. The little church is still wholly Norman, and contains a variety of original work; the chancel arch, the corbels and the font are particularly interesting.

BOAT TRIPS
K & A Canal Trust Cruises *weekends and B. Hols.* Ring Hungerford 3396/2144.

PUBS
🍺 **John of Gaunt** Hungerford. 16thC. Food. B&B.
🍺 **Three Swans** Hungerford. Food. B&B.
🍺 **Bear** Charnham St. 13thC.

This section is navigable.

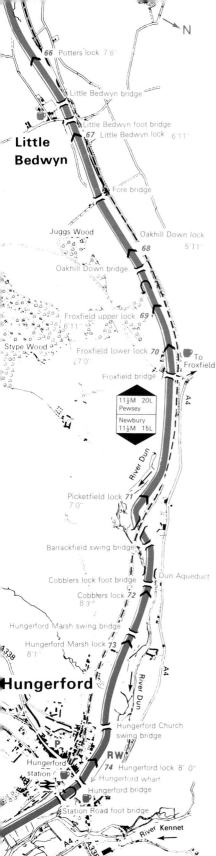

Froxfield

Leaving Hungerford, the canal passes the old wharf. An original stone warehouse survives, but much of the wharf area has now been built on. West of the wooded 19thC church, with its pleasantly overgrown churchyard, the canal suddenly enters an open landscape. Water-meadows and pasture land, rich in buttercups, flank the waterway, which seems to be more river than canal. The railway is in a cutting to the south, and the quiet browsing cattle give a feeling of 18thC rural serenity. The canal is then carried on to an embankment as the wooded hills reappear on both banks, crossing the River Dun on a small brick aqueduct. The railway crosses the canal west of the aqueduct, and now hugs the north bank for several miles. The roar of the frequent diesel expresses to and from the West Country is the only interruption in the natural peace and solitude of the canal. Froxfield lies to the north, flanking the A4. The best access is from the new bridge. This was rebuilt in 1972 during a road improvement scheme using traditional methods and materials, even to the correct colour of brick. Three locks carry the canal past Froxfield, and then the spire of Little Bedwyn Church comes into view, half-hidden by trees on the north bank. The village is cut in half by the canal and the railway. In the centre the lock continues the climb towards the summit.

Little Bedwyn
Wilts. P.O. Tel. Divided by the canal, the village falls into two distinct parts. North is the estate village, pretty 19thC terraces of patterned brick running eastwards to the church, half-hidden among ancient yew trees. To the south is the older farming village, handsome 18thC buildings climbing the hill away from the canal.

Froxfield
Wilts. P.O. Tel. Stores. The village is ranged along the A4, which has obviously affected its development. The main feature of the village is the Somerset Hospital, a range of almshouses founded by the Duchess of Somerset in 1694, extended in 1775 and again in 1813. Facing onto the road, the hospital is built round a courtyard, which is entered by a Gothic-style gateway, part of the 1813 extension.
Littlecote 1½ miles north of Froxfield. A Tudor building of the 16thC. Littlecote is the most important brick mansion in Wiltshire. The formal front overlooks the gardens that run down to the Kennet. Inside, the Great Hall, the armoury and Long Gallery are particularly notable. *Open: Apr–mid Oct. Tue, Wed, Sat, Sun afternoons. Winter opening by appointment.*

PUBS
🍺 **Harrow** Little Bedwyn. In the southern half of the village.
🍺 **Pelican** Froxfield. On A4. ¼ mile north of the new bridge.

This section is navigable.

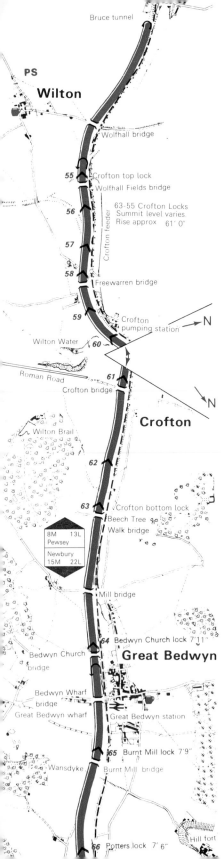

Crofton

Leaving Little Bedwyn, the canal continues
through a rolling landscape towards its summit,
closely accompanied by the railway. To the
north is a hill fort, overlooking ridges that
break up the farmland. The canal stays on the
south side of the valley, a shallow side-cutting
carrying it into Great Bedwyn. The village is
ranged over the hillside to the north of the
canal, newer houses spilling downwards
towards the canal and railway station. The
canal leaves the village past the church, and
enters a wooded stretch that takes it up towards
Crofton. The hills encroach more sharply as the
summit draws nearer. Crofton appears as the
canal starts a wide swing to the north west. The
engine house stands on a rise above the canal,
its blunt, iron-bound chimney making its
purpose unmistakable. To the south lies the
long expanse of Wilton Water, a natural lake
from which the Crofton pumps draw their
supplies. After Crofton the country opens out
for a while as the flight of locks continue the
final climb to the summit. Then, as the land
rises steeply on both banks, it prepares itself for
the short Bruce Tunnel. A wooded cutting
leads towards the tunnel, taking the canal
through the fringes of the Old Savernake
Forest. To the north are the extensive
parklands of Tottenham House, and Savernake
Forest itself. The towpath climbs over the top
of the tunnel.

Wilton
Wilts. P.O. Tel. Stores. A compact village at the
southern end of Wilton Water, with a pretty
duck pond in the centre.
Crofton
Wilts. The scattered village is dominated by the
brick pumping house with its separate
chimney. It houses two 19thC steam engines,
one built in 1812 by Boulton and Watt, the
oldest working beam engine in the world, the
other in 1845 by Harveys of Hayle, Cornwall.
Both have been restored to working order, and
are steamed on several weekends in the year.
The pumping house and the engines are open
for viewing *every summer Sun*. For details of
'steaming' weekends, ring Marlborough
810575.
Great Bedwyn
Wilts. P.O. Tel. Stores, garage, station. The
main street climbs gently away from the canal
and the railway. It is wide, with generous grass
verges; attractive houses of all periods line the
street. At the top is the pub. The large church,
with its well-balanced crossing tower, is mostly
12th and 13thC; inside are some interesting
monuments. The road running westwards to
the church passes the Bedwyn Stone Museum,
an amazing establishment.
Bedwyn Stone Museum A collection of stone
work of all types, showing the work of seven
generations of stone masons. There are statues,
tombstones, casts, even the fossilised footprint
of a dinosaur. *Open daily.*

BOAT TRIPS
K & A Canal Trust Cruises from Crofton Top
Lock. Details from Winterslow 862155.

PUBS
 Swan Inn Wilton. ½ mile south of lock 61,
on road running beside Wilton Water.
 Three Tuns Great Bedwyn.

Limit of navigation East from Crofton
pumping station to Widmead Lock, 89
(Thatcham), except in very dry conditions.
West from Crofton Top Lock to Devizes.

Wootton Rivers

The canal emerges from the western portal of Bruce Tunnel into a deep cutting. Woods line both banks, hiding the railway, which is now on the south bank having crossed over the tunnel. The towpath passes under the railway and descends steeply to the canal. The cutting continues westwards to the high brick bridge that carries the A346, and then the landscape opens out: the rolling hills still follow the canal, but recede slightly. Immediately after the bridge is Burbage Wharf; several of the original brick canal buildings still stand, attractively converted to domestic use, and a restored wooden wharf crane hangs over the water. Pasture and arable land flank the canal on its course to the first of the four Wootton locks. This flight ends the short summit, and starts the long descent towards Bath. By the first lock there is a pretty cottage and garden, while the second is in the middle of Brimslade farm, whose attractive tile-hung buildings date from the 17thC. The last two locks take the canal to Wootton Rivers; the houses stretch northwards away from the canal, which is overlooked by the church. As the country undulates, the canal maintains its level, moving alternately from low cutting to low embankment. Woods break up the hills, giving fine views to the south. New Mill is a small hamlet south of the canal with a convenient pub; there is also a small wharf. At the end of this section the railway moves away to the south to pass through Pewsey, leaving the canal in peace at last.

New Mill
Wilts. A pretty hamlet scattered below the canal. The mill that gave it its name is now a house, with a fine garden.
Wootton Rivers
Wilts. P.O. Tel. Stores. A particularly pretty village composed almost entirely of timber-framed thatched houses, climbing gently up the hill away from the canal. Even the walls by the canal are thatched. All the houses are attractive, including the large manor by the canal. The little church with its wooden bell turret is set among trees; it was extensively rebuilt in the 19thC.
Bruce Tunnel Named in honour of Thomas Bruce, Earl of Ailesbury. 502yds with chains on the walls, with which to pull boats through.
Savernake Forest
Wilts. A small village grew up in the 19thC around the hotel and the two railway stations, to cater for an early holiday trade. Today the stations have vanished, but the hotel still thrives, on the hill above Bruce Tunnel. Timber from the forest was used to restore the handsome crane at Burbage Wharf.

PUBS

Liddiard Arms New Mill. Bar billiards.
Royal Oak Wootton Rivers. Bar billiards. Very attractive pub in the main street.
Savernake Forest Hotel Savernake Forest. Restaurant. The hotel has fishing rights on the canal.
Three Horse Shoes Stibbs Green.

This section is navigable.

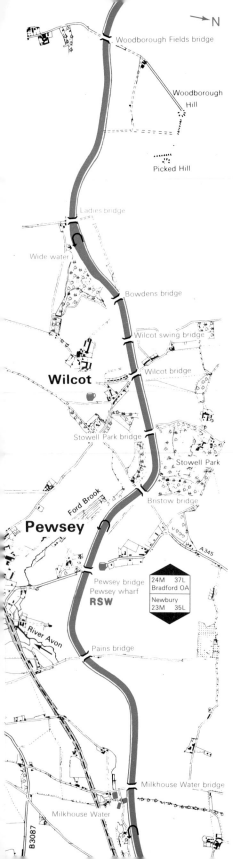

Pewsey

This 15-mile-long pound continues westwards towards Devizes through rolling hills. To the north, hills descend to the water's edge, and to the south the land opens out, giving fine views over the Vale of Pewsey. The canal crosses this landscape with a mixture of cutting and embankment, passing through woods from time to time. The railway lies to the south, and is now out of sight. The canal turns towards Pewsey, but still passes well outside the town, which fills the Vale to the south. Pewsey Wharf is ½ mile from the town centre, and so has developed as a separate canalside settlement, with a pub, cottages, and warehouse buildings. The canal leaves Pewsey in a low wooded cutting, swinging back to its usual westerly course. The woods continue past Stowell Park, whose landscaped grounds extend to the north. The house built early in the 19thC, can be seen clearly from the canal. A miniature suspension bridge carries a private footpath from the park across the canal. A straight stretch leads to the first cottages of Wilcot; the rest of the village is to the south. The steep bare mound of Picked Hill dominates the canal as it passes Wilcot and enters the wooded Wide Water, a natural pond incorporated into the canal. This is terminated by the unusual Ladies Bridge: dated 1808, and attributed to Rennie, this decorative stone bridge is rich in Neo-classical ornament. It is a unique bridge on the canal, for such splendour was usually reserved for major engineering works. The canal skirts Picked Hill, giving a good view of the field terracing that is a relic of Celtic and medieval cultivation. The equally dominant Woodborough Hill now fills the north bank, while to the south open country leads to the village of Woodborough.

Wilcot
Wilts. P.O. Tel. Stores. A pretty village scattered round the green; there are several thatched houses, a little village school with a prominent bell, and a blacksmith. Parts of the church date from the 12thC, but it was mostly rebuilt in 1876 after a fire.
Pewsey
Wilts. EC Wed. P.O. Tel. Stores, garage, bank, station (but very few trains stop). The little town is set compactly in the Vale of Pewsey. At its centre, overlooking the young River Avon is a fine statue of King Alfred, erected in 1911. From this all the roads radiate. There is the usual mixture of buildings; but while many are attractive, none is noteworthy. The church is mostly 13th and 15thC, but parts of the nave are late Norman: the altar rails were made from timbers of the 'San Josef' captured by Nelson in 1797.
Pewsey White Horse 1½ miles south of the town. Dating from the 18thC, the horse was re-cut in 1937 to celebrate the coronation of George VI. It is 66ft long.

PUBS

🍴 **Golden Swan** Wilcot. At the far end of the village, overlooking the green. Food. B&B.
🍺 **French Horn** Pewsey. Canalside, on A345 by wharf.
🍺 **Royal Oak** Pewsey. In town centre. Food. B&B.
🍺 **Phoenix** Pewsey. In town centre. B&B.
🍺 **Coopers Arms.** Pewsey.
🍺 **Greyhound** Pewsey.

This section is navigable.

Honey Street

Leaving Woodborough Hill behind, the long pound continues westwards towards Devizes. To the south the land falls away, while to the north the tower of Alton Priors Church comes into view. Beyond the village can be seen the white horse, cut into the hill in 1812, a copy of the one at Cherhill. The canal passes Honey Street Wharf, one of the best-preserved on the canal, with a fine collection of original buildings, and a canalside pub. The canal now begins to meander through the open countryside, roughly following a contour line to maintain its level. Its progress is marked by a succession of shallow cuttings and low embankments. Several villages are near the canal, all visible and easily accessible from the many bridges, but none actually approach the waterside. Their interests lie rather in the rich agricultural lands that flank the canal. Leaving Allington the canal curves round the Knoll, a major feature of the landscape to the north.

Allington
Wilts. Tel. A small agricultural village scattered round a Victorian church. East of the village is All Cannings Cross, a large Iron Age settlement.

All Cannings
Wilts. P.O. Tel. Stores. An attractive village built round a square, with houses of all periods. To the south there is a large green, overlooked by the church with its tall central tower. Although the church is mostly 14thC, its most interesting feature is the ornamental High Victorian chancel, added in 1867.

Stanton St Bernard
Wilts. P.O. Tel. Stores. Built in a curve of the hills, the village has one main street, flanked by pretty gardens. The best building is the 19thC manor, which incorporates relics of an earlier house. The battlemented church is Victorian.

Honey Street
Wilts. A traditional canalside village. There are brick cottages, a warehouse, and some pretty weatherboarded buildings.

Alton Barnes
Wilts. P.O. Tel. Stores, garage. The village runs along the road northwards from Honey Street. The best part is clustered round the church. Fine farm buildings and an 18thC rectory are half-hidden among the trees. The church is essentially Anglo-Saxon, but has been heavily restored; everything is in miniature, the tiny gallery, pulpit, and pews emphasising the compact scale of the whole building.

Alton Priors
Wilts. Tel. Approached along a footpath from Alton Barnes churchyard, the isolated church is the best feature of this scattered hamlet. This pretty Perpendicular building with its wide, well-lit nave contains a most interesting monument, a big box tomb is surmounted with a large engraved Dutch brass plate, dated 1590, rich in extravagant symbolism. To the east of the village the Ridgeway runs southwards towards Salisbury; this Bronze Age drover's road swings north-east along the downs for 50 miles, finally joining the Thames valley at Streatley. The path is not clearly defined here, but 5 miles to the north, by the A4 crossing, it becomes a wide unmistakable track, which continues unbroken to the Thames.

PUBS

🍺 **Kings Arms** All Cannings. ¼ mile south of Woodway Bridge.
🍺 **Barge** Honey Street. Canalside. Food. B&B. Caravan hire.

This section is navigable.

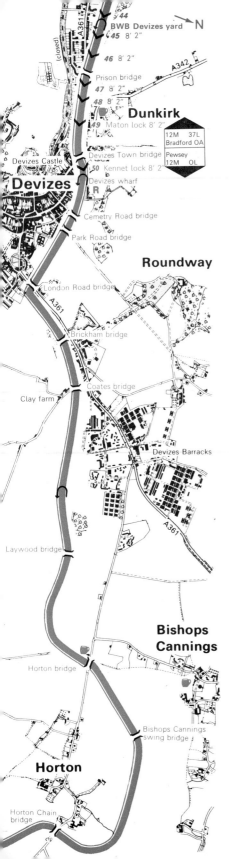

Devizes

Leaving Horton, the long pound continues westwards towards Devizes. Following the contour of the land, it swings in a wide arc towards Bishops Cannings. The rolling hills climb fairly steeply to the north, while the pasture land falls away to the south. After a low cutting, the tower of Bishops Cannings Church comes into view, half-hidden by trees: a footpath from the swing bridge is the quickest way to the village. At Horton bridge, where there is a convenient canalside pub, the canal enters another short cutting. The landscape opens out again, to allow a view of the handsome Victorian barracks outside Devizes. The canal passes the barrack buildings, which are partly hidden by trees, and then enters the long wooded cutting that carries it through Devizes. Houses appear, their gardens overlooking the cutting, and the traffic noise on the busy A361 marks the return to civilisation. Several very elegant large stone bridges (many listed as ancient monuments) span the cutting. Access to the town is easy at all the bridges. At Cemetery Road Bridge the towpath turns over to the north bank for a short stretch, returning to the south at the next bridge. Between these two bridges is Devizes Wharf, where the K & A Canal Trust have a museum and shop in a converted warehouse. Beyond the wharf, and the gas works that follow it, the long pound ends at the first lock of the famous Caen Hill flight, preceded by the generous stone bridge with its separate towpath archway. Locks now come at regular intervals, preparing the canal for the dramatic descent down Caen Hill.

Devizes
Wilts. EC Wed. MD Thur and Sat. P.O. Tel. Stores, garage, bank, cinema. Despite the effects of traffic, Devizes still retains the atmosphere of an old country market town. Originally the town grew up around the castle, but as this lost its significance the large marketplace became the focal point. Handsome 18thC buildings now command the square, while the market cross records the sad story of Ruth Pierce. Elsewhere there are timbered buildings from the 16thC. The two fine churches, one built for the castle and the other for the parish, tend to dominate the town, and hold it well together. Only the mount and related earthworks survive of the original Norman castle; the present building is an extravagant Victorian folly.
St John's Church Built by Bishop Roger of Sarum, who was also responsible for the castle, this 12thC church with its massive crossing tower is still largely original. There are 15thC and 19thC additions, but they do not affect the Norman feeling of the whole.
St Mary's Church Dating from the same time as St John's, this church was more extensively rebuilt in the 15thC; plenty of Norman work still survives, however.
Wiltshire Archaeological and Natural History Museum Long Street. The collections include finds from the Neolithic, Bronze and Iron Age sites in Wiltshire, the most famous being the Stourhead collection of relics excavated from burial mounds on Salisbury Plain. There are also Roman exhibits. *Open daily.*
Tourist Information The Wharf, Devizes. (Devizes 71279).
Battle of Roundway Down, 13 July 1643 Devizes was held by a Royalist army that had already tested the Roundhead forces, who were tired, dispirited and short of supplies after their defeat at Lansdown Hill, near Bath. A Royalist cavalry charge took the Roundheads by surprise, and most of the confused and battle-weary Roundheads were killed or captured. The battlefield, off the A361 north east of Devizes, is still largely intact, and can easily be explored on foot.
Coate
Wilts. P.O. Tel. A nondescript farming village built round a square; there is an interesting pub, the New Inn.

Limit of navigation East from Kennet Lock, Devizes to Crofton Top Lock.

Wiltshire Regiment Museum Le Marchant Barracks, 1½ miles east of Devizes on A361; also accessible from the canal. The history of the regiment from its foundation in 1756 to the present day. *Open weekdays.*

Devizes to Westminster Canoe Race The toughest and longest canoe race in the world takes place every Easter. The course, from Park Road Bridge, Devizes, to County Hall Steps, Westminster, includes 54 miles of the Kennet & Avon, and 71 miles of the Thames, the last 17 of which are tidal. There are 77 locks. The race grew from a background of local rivalry in Pewsey and Devizes to find the quickest way to the sea by boat; in 1948 the target was 100 hours. In 1950 the first regular annual race over the course took place; three years later the junior class was introduced. The number of entries increases every year, and is now well above 300. Anyone may enter for the race, but they would have difficulty in beating the highly-trained army and navy teams from Britain and Europe.

Bishops Cannings
Wilts. P.O. Tel. Stores. Apart from one or two old cottages, the main feature of this village is the very grand church. This cruciform building, with its central tower and spire, is almost entirely Early English in style; its magnificence is unexpected in so small a village. Traces of the earlier Norman building survive. Inside is a 17thC penitential seat, surmounted by a giant hand painted on the wall with suitable inscriptions about sin and death.

BOAT TRIPS

Charlotte Dundas II This boat, operated by the Kennet & Avon Canal Trust, runs pleasure trips on the long pound, between Devizes and Pewsey. Details from Devizes 71279.

PUBS

Black Horse by lock 48. Snacks.
Bear Market Place, Devizes. This coaching inn dates from 1559.
Grapevine 13 High St, Devizes. Wine bar serving good food. Garden. *Closed Mon.*
Black Swan Market Place, Devizes.
Three Crowns Maryport St, Devizes.
New Inn Coate. Beer garden, with a small aviary of exotic birds.
Crown Bishops Cannings.
Bridge Inn Horton. Canalside, by Horton Bridge. B&B.

Charlotte Dundas II moored at Devizes Wharf. The small amount of traffic results in a blanket of duckweed on the canal. *Derek Perrott*

Sells Green

Leaving Devizes, the canal continues westwards. Ahead the landscape falls away, giving advance warning of the steep descent at Caen Hill. Locks occur at regular intervals west of Devizes, each separated by a long, wide pound. These were designed to hold sufficient water while permitting the locks to be close together to follow the slope. The towpath is in very good condition; apart from the attraction to visitors of the Caen Hill flight, the whole area is obviously used for recreation by the people of Devizes. To the south the busy A361 accompanies the canal down the hill, but it is out of sight for most of the way. At lock 44 the major flight starts; wide lock follows wide lock down the hill, each with an enormous side pound. The scale of the whole flight is most impressive. At lock 29 the Caen Hill flight ends, but the locks continue the descent, now separated once again by longer pounds. The canal passes under the B3101 road bridge, and then at lock 22 reaches the end of the long fall—29 locks in two miles. By this last lock the towpath turns over to the north bank, and the canal is joined by the old railway, which follows it closely. The railway bridge has been removed. Water-meadows accompany the canal to the south, with views of the hills that rise in the distance. The canal turns past Sells Green in a low cutting that hides most of the village, and then strides along the valley. The hills to the south climb steeply up to the village of Seend, and to the north flat pastureland stretches away. After 2 swing bridges the canal reaches the first of the 5 Seend locks; this is the best point for access to the village. By the third lock there is a pub, and a lane leading to Seend Cleeve village.

Seend Cleeve
Wilts. Tel. An agricultural village built on the steep slopes of the hills that overlook the canal. Some new development has merged well with the existing houses.
Seend
Wilts. P.O. Tel. Stores, garage. Although the main road cuts the village in half, Seend is still attractive. Elegant 18thC houses flank the road, and conceal the lane that leads to the battlemented Perpendicular church.
Sells Green
Wilts. P.O. Tel. Garage. A scattered main road village, the houses doing their best to hide from the traffic behind decorative gardens.

BOATYARDS
BWB Devizes Yard Devizes 2859.

PUBS
🍺 **Brewery Inn** Seend Cleeve. ¼ mile from lock 19.
🍺 **Bell Inn** Seend. On A361. ½ mile from lock 21.
🍺 **Barge Inn** Seend. Canalside, by lock 19. Bar billiards. P.O.
🍺 **Three Magpies** Sells Green. On A365. ¼ mile from Martinslade Bridge.

Limit of navigation Controlled navigation west from lock 22, Caen Hill bottom.

Semington

Leaving Seend locks behind, the canal
continues its western course, maintaining a
fairly straight line through open country. The
steep hills around Seend are left behind, giving
way to rolling farmland extending into the
distance on both banks. This is a quiet and
secluded stretch with no villages beside the
canal; however, farms occur regularly along the
bank, each generally with its own swing
accommodation bridge. In the distance to the
north the embankment of the disused railway
follows the course of the canal. The two
Semington Locks continue the descent towards
Bath with an attractive lock house by lock 15,
Just beyond the lock the canal is crossed by the
A350; this is the best access point for
Semington. A close examination of the north
bank just before the bridge will reveal a
bricked-up side bridge; this marks the site of
the junction with the long abandoned Wiltshire
& Berkshire Canal, which used to go to
Abingdon. Beyond the bridge the canal curves
round past Semington on an embankment,
crossing the Semington Brook on a small stone
aqueduct. A long straight stretch now leads
towards Hilperton, while to the south the hills
return to follow the canal. To the north the
River Avon draws gradually nearer, and the
two waterways begin to share the same valley.

Semington
Wilts. P.O. Tel. Stores, garage. Despite the
main road, Semington is a pretty village. Large
handsome houses with fine gardens run beside
the road. Several date from the 18thC. The
little stone church, crowned with a bellcote, is
at the end of a lane to the east of the village.
The old village school is beside the church,
built in the same style.
The Wiltshire & Berkshire Canal
Opened in 1810, the canal wound in a
meandering course for 51 miles between
Semington on the Kennet & Avon and
Abingdon on the River Thames. A branch was
opened in 1819 from Swindon to connect with
Latton on the Thames & Severn Canal.
Although the carriage of Somerset coal was the
inspiration for the canal, its eventual role was
agricultural. Profits were never high, partly
because the wandering line of the canal and its
45 locks made travel very slow, and so it
suffered early from railway competition. By the
1870s, moves were afoot to close the canal, and
despite various efforts to give it a new lease of
life, the situation had become hopeless by the
turn of the century. Traffic finally stopped in
1906, and the canal was formally abandoned in
1914. Little remains of it now, but its course
can be traced with difficulty.

PUBS

🍺 **Somerset Arms** Semington. ¼ mile south of
Semington Bridge.

Limit of navigation West from lock 15, and
controlled navigation to lock 22, Caen Hill
bottom.

Bradford on Avon

Continuing its westerly course, the canal passes
through open pastureland: the wide Avon
valley, which the canal now follows, begins
gradually to narrow as the hills encroach to the
north and the south. The canal curves round
below Hilperton; although the main village is a
mile to the south, there is a convenient pub,
post office and stores by the road bridge and
wharf. West of Hilperton the canal passes the
grounds of Wyke House, whose Jacobean-style
towers stand among the trees; then the land to
the north falls away as the canal returns to its
original course on a sweeping curve. Canal and
river now converge as the canal swings on a
huge embankment towards the Avon, crossing
the railway and the River Biss on two stone
aqueducts. The classical arch over the river is
particularly handsome; it is necessary to walk
down the side of the embankment in order to
see it properly. The view northwards across the
Avon valley is very fine. For a while river and
canal run side by side, the river down in the
valley, the canal high above in a side cutting,
shielded by trees, and then they part again to
make their separate entries into Bradford. The
canal stays high above the town, which fills the
steep-sided valley, while the river cuts the town
in two. Bradford basin appears suddenly,
followed by the lock, and then the canal turns
to pass to the south of the town. It rejoins the
course of the river, and now the two run closely
together all the way to Bath. West of Bradford
the canal passes through beautiful woods on the
steep southern slope of the valley. From this
point there are fine views of the town, spread
out beyond the Tithe Barn, which is right
beside the canal. The Avon rushes along the
valley and beyond it the railway appears and
disappears among the trees on the far side,
while high above the canal pursues its more
sedate course towards Bath. The thick woods
often give the canal user a feeling of total
seclusion. The elegant stone arches of the
Avoncliff aqueduct carry the canal high above
the fast flowing river and the railway. The canal
then turns west again to continue its wooded
course. The towpath crosses back to the south
side by the aqueduct.

Avoncliff
Wilts. Station. A hamlet clustered in the woods
beside the canal. Originally it was a centre of
weaving, and many traces of the old industry
can be seen: weavers' cottages, and the old mills
on the Avon, which falls noisily over a weir at
this point. The hamlet is dominated by
Rennie's aqueduct, built in 1804 to take the
canal across the valley to the north side. A
classical stone structure, the aqueduct suffered
from casual repair work and patching in brick
when owned by the GWR.

Bradford on Avon
*Wilts. EC Wed. P.O. Tel. Stores, garage, bank,
station.* Set in the steeply wooded Avon valley,
Bradford is one of the beauty spots of
Wiltshire, and one of the highlights of the
canal. Rather like a miniature Bath, the town is
composed of fine stone terraces rising sharply
away from the river, which cuts through the
centre of the town. Until the 19thC it was a
prosperous centre for weaving, but a depression
killed the industry and drove most of the
workers away. Bradford is rich in architectural
treasures from the Saxon period to the 19thC,
while the abundance of fine 18thC houses make
an exploration of the town a positive pleasure.
The centre is very compact, and so the walk
down the hill from the canal wharf lays most of
it open to inspection, including the town
bridge, Holy Trinity Church, the Victorian
town hall, and the fine Gothic revival factory
that dominates the riverside. There is also a
swimming pool near the canal.

This section is navigable

Bradford Wharf The canal wharf is particularly attractive. There is a small dock with some of the original buildings still standing, plenty of mooring space, and an old canal pub beside the lock.

Town Bridge The 9-arched bridge is unusual in having a chapel in the middle, one of the few still surviving in Britain. Parts of the bridge, including the chapel, are medieval, but much dates from a 17thC rebuilding. During the 17th and 18thC the chapel fell out of use, and was turned into a small prison, serving as the town lock up.

Holy Trinity Church Basically a 12thC building with additions dating over the next 3 centuries. Inside are some medieval wall paintings, and fine 18thC monuments.

Saxon Church of St Lawrence Founded in 705, this tiny church was enlarged in the 10thC. Since then it has survived essentially unchanged, having been at various times a school, a cottage and a slaughterhouse. The true origins and purpose of the building were only rediscovered in the 19thC, and so it remains one of the best-preserved Saxon churches in England.

Great Tithe Barn Standing below the canal embankment, this great stone building is one of the finest tithe barns in England. It was built in the 14thC by the Abbess of Shaftesbury. Its great length (168ft) is broken by two porches, with massive doors that open to reveal the beamed roof. Maintained by the Department of the Environment the barn now contains a collection of old agricultural implements, and is *open to the public at all reasonable times.*

Westwood Manor
1 mile south west of Bradford. This 15thC

stone manor house contains much original Jacobean plaster and woodwork, although much was lost when the manor became a farm in the 18thC. Skilful restoration by the National Trust has returned the manor to its former glory. *Open: Wed afternoons Apr–Sep..*

Staverton
Wilts. Tel. Stores. The village lies north of the canal, spreading down to the banks of the Avon, where there is a small Nestlés factory. A small isolated part of the Avon is navigable here, and is used by a few pleasure boats. In the village are terraces of weavers' cottages, a sign of what was once the staple trade of the area.

Hilperton
Wilts. P.O. Tel. Stores, garage. A scattered village that stretches away from the settlement by the canal wharf. Wyke House stands to the west of the village, this very ornate Jacobean mansion was in fact built in 1865, a replica of the original house. House *not open to the public.*

BOATYARDS

ⓑ **Kennet & Avon Navigation Company** Hilperton (Keevil 870614). W D Trip boats, mooring, slipway.

PUBS

🍺 **Cross Guns** Avoncliff. 17thC gabled inn by south side of aqueduct.
🍺✕ **Barge Inn** Bradford. Canalside, by wharf. Food, B&B.
🍺 **Canal Tavern** Bradford. Canalside.
🍺 **The Beehive** Widbrook Bridge, Snacks.
🍺 **Old Bear Inn** Staverton. ¼ mile north west of canal, on B3105.
🍺 **Kings Arms** Hilperton. 100yds south of Hilperton Wharf.
🍺 **Lion & Fiddle** Hilperton village.

Avoncliff Aqueduct, where the Kennet & Avon crosses over the Bristol Avon.

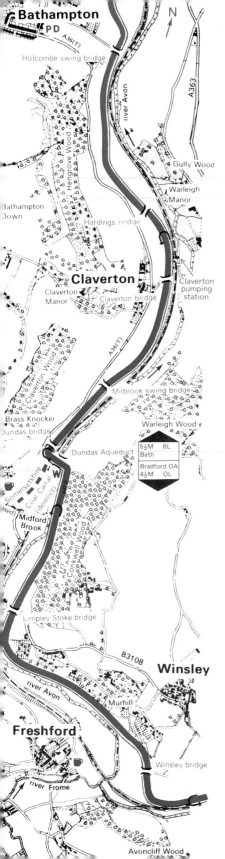

Claverton

Leaving the Avoncliff aqueduct, the canal continues westwards through the woods above the river Avon. The valley gets steeper and narrower as it approaches Bath and thick woods cover both sides as the river and canal run side by side. The canal passes Limpley Stoke, scattered over the southern valley side. The country opens out slightly, to allow views across the valley as the canal approaches the Dundas aqueduct, perhaps the best known feature of the Kennet & Avon. Emerging from the woods, the canal turns suddenly onto the aqueduct, which carries it across the Avon valley and the railway to the south side. At the southern end of the aqueduct is a small wharf and basin, with an old crane standing over the water. Here was the junction with the Somersetshire Coal Canal, which, until its closure in 1904, ran south from the Kennet & Avon Canal towards Paulton. Beyond the basin the towpath turns over to the north bank, where it remains until Bath is reached. The canal enters another thickly wooded stretch, a side cutting taking it towards Claverton. The woods soon give way to allow fine views to the north, across rolling country and the railway and River Avon in the valley below. Claverton flanks the canal, but it is hidden by the folds of the land to the south. Access is easy, and both the village and Claverton Manor are worth a visit. Claverton Ram, a water-powered pump which lifts water up from the Avon to feed the canal has been restored by the Kennet & Avon Canal Trust, with help from engineering students from Bath University. The more open country continues, allowing views across the valley to Warleigh Manor, now a college, and to Bathford Church. The canal follows the contours of the land as it turns towards Bath, maintaining the level of the 9-mile pound that runs from Bradford to Bath Top Lock.

Claverton
Somerset. Tel. Although devoid of all facilities, Claverton is well worth a visit. It is a manorial village of stone houses, surrounding the 17thC farm, and in early days clearly dependent upon Claverton Manor. The main road misses the village, increasing the peace and seclusion.
Claverton Manor The American Museum in Britain. The manor was built in 1820 by Sir Jeffry Wyatville in the Greek revival style. It now houses a museum of American decorative arts from the late 17th to the mid-19thC. *Open: Apr-Oct, Tue-Sun afternoons.*
Claverton Pump The waterwheel pump at Claverton is the only one of its kind on British canals. Designed by John Rennie, the pump was built to feed the 9-mile Bradford–Bath pound, and started operating in 1813. The 2 undershot breast wheels, each 15ft in diameter and 11ft wide, then powered the pumping machinery until a major breakdown in 1952 prompted its closure, and replacement by a temporary diesel pump. The original machinery has now been restored, and 'pumping weekends' are organised—details Bristol 515954. New electric pumps now do the day-to-day work, raising water from the Avon 47ft below.
Dundas Aqueduct
Built in 1804, this 3-arch classical stone aqueduct is justifiably one of the most well-known features of the canal, and stands as a fitting monument to the architectural and engineering skill of John Rennie. It is necessary to leave the canal and walk down into the valley below to appreciate the beauty of the aqueduct, and see it in the context of the narrow Avon valley into which it fits so well.
Somersetshire Coal Canal Opened in 1805, this narrow canal was sponsored by the Somerset Coal owners, who wanted a more efficient means of moving their coal to Bath, Bristol and the rest of England. Originally surveyed by Rennie in 1793, the canal was to run from Limpley Stoke to Paulton, with a branch to Radstock. There were steep gradients to overcome at Midford and Combe Hay, and these plagued the canal throughout its life. The

This section is navigable.

Radstock Arm was never completed and tramroads were built over the difficult stretches. The canal was never profitable, and was sold to the Somerset & Dorset Railway in 1871. The main line was completed throughout, but not before some remarkable solutions to the problems of the Combe Hay gradient had been tried out. First there was Robert Weldon's caisson lock; a watertight caisson, large enough to hold a narrow boat and crew, was pulled up and down an 88ft-deep water-filled cistern by means of a rack and pinion. This terrifying device was soon replaced by an inclined plane, which in turn was replaced by a conventional flight of locks. Once open, the canal carried a large tonnage of coal throughout the 19thC: it served 30 colleries more directly than the railway. However, by the end of the century the inevitable competition was taking away the traffic, which finally stopped in 1898. The canal was officially abandoned in 1904. It is hoped that the first ¼ mile may be restored for use as a mooring basin in the not-too-distant future.

Limpley Stoke
Avon. P.O. Tel. Stores. Built on the side of the valley overlooking the river, Limpley Stoke is a quiet village, a residential outpost of Bath. The little church includes work of all periods, from Norman to the 20thC: inside is a collection of carved coffin lids.

Freshford
Somerset. P.O. Tel. Stores, garage. Although not on the canal, Freshford is well worth the ½-mile walk south from Limpley Stoke. It is a particularly attractive village, set on the side of the steep hill that flanks the confluence of the Rivers Avon and Frome. At the top of the hill is the church, and terraces of handsome stone houses fall away in both directions, filling the valley below, and crowding the narrow streets. At the bottom of the hill is the river, crossed by the medieval bridge.

PUBS

Viaduct Hotel Claverton, on Bath Road 200yds south of Dundas Aqueduct. B&B. Restaurant.

Danielle Limpley Stoke Bridge (3150). French provincial menu. *D and Sun L. Book.*

Hop Pole Limpley Stoke.

Rose & Crown Limpley Stoke.

Cleveland House, standing over the canal in Sydney Gardens, Bath. *Derek Pratt*

Widcombe flight

7 Bath lower lock 9' 3"
  Bath
  deep lock 19' 5"
10 Wash House lock 8' 6"   6 Weston
11 Abbey View lock 9' 0"   lock
12 Pulteney lock 9' 5"   9' 3"
13 Bath top lock 9' 0"

W

Weir

Weston cut

Dolphin bridge

A431

A4

River Avon

Royal Victoria
Park

11M   6L
Hanham

Bradford OA
10M   6L

A36

Crescent
Gardens

Churchill road bridge

Bath

Abbey
Bath station
Dolmead bridge

Baptist chapel bridge
Widcombe flight
Bath deep lock

Henrietta
Park

A4

10
11 Horse shoe bridge
12 13

R

Sydney Wharf bridge

Sydney Gardens foot bridge

Cleveland house tunnel

river Avon

Sydney Gardens
(No. 2 tunnel)

A36(T)

Folly Foot swing bridge

Bathampton Down

Golf Course

Candy's bridge

Bathampton

P D

A36

Bathampton bridge

R

river Avon   B

Holcombe swing bridge

Bath

Following the course of the River Avon, the canal turns west towards Bath, leaving behind Bathford Church on the opposite side of the valley. Groups of houses appear more frequently scattered among the trees of the Avon valley; these form the outposts of Bath, whose suburbs are now visible to the west. The canal passes through Bathampton, on a low embankment above the school and church, and then continues on a straight course, closely flanked by the railway, which is in a cutting below. On the south bank there are gardens running down to the water, which accompany the canal into Bath. The entry into Bath is magnificent. The canal sweeps round the south of the city, cut into the side of the hill, and so there are extensive views across Bath. From this point it is possible to pick out many of the features of the city, and the Georgian terraces can be seen spread out over the far side of the valley. As the buildings fill the valley, canal and River Avon part, to make their separate entries into Bath. The first Georgian buildings flank the canal as it reaches Sydney Gardens. A short tunnel with a fine Adamesque portal takes the canal under a road, and then it passes two pretty cast iron bridges, both dated 1800. A cutting carries the canal through this attractive part of Bath, and so the houses seem to hang over the water. Another ornamental tunnel actually carries houses over the canal, among them Cleveland House, the old canal company's headquarters. The towpath turns over briefly to the south side, returning to the north at the next bridge. The cutting then ends, once more allowing magnificent views over the city before the canal reaches lock 13, the top lock of the Widcombe flight. This flight of 6 locks takes the canal down to join the Avon. Locks 8 and 9 were merged together as part of a road-building scheme, making one new lock with a fall of over 19ft. The canal joins the Avon immediately beyond Bath Lower Lock (number 7) in the middle of the industrial quarter of Bath. The railway station is opposite the junction of canal and river, and factories and warehouses flank the Avon as it leaves Bath. The fine Georgian city surrounds the unnavigable Avon to the east. The junction is the best point of access for Bath as a whole. New roads have made the towpath of the Avon Navigation difficult to find, but after a while it establishes itself on the north bank. A long belt of industry accompanies the river out of Bath but access to the towpath is always easy. There are several footbridges across the river, some of them private, and a disused railway crosses twice as the river meanders in long, gentle curves. As the industry gradually falls away, the river divides; the right fork leads to Weston Lock, the left to a weir, as the river continues its fall to the sea.

Navigating the Bristol Avon
Pleasure boats should always give way to barges, and should let them use the locks first. In general, downstream traffic has right of way, especially through bridges. All the locks are accompanied by weirs, and so boatmen should take great care to turn into the lock cuts, and avoid the weir channel. Remember that a river always has a current, and is liable to changes in speed and level of flow. When mooring, allow enough slack on lines. Do not moor in lock cuts or near weirs. All pleasure boats should moor up at night, and show a white light. With the exception of Hanham, the locks are not manned. Remember that boats should always be held by ropes while the locks are being operated, for there is a strong flow in these large locks.

Bath
Avon. EC Thur, MD Wed. Bath was first developed by the Romans as a spa town and resort because of its natural warm springs. They started a trend of bathing and 'taking the waters' which survives today. There are extensive Roman remains to be seen in the city, not least the baths themselves. The city grew

This section is navigable—Bath Locks closed *Oct–Easter.*

further during the medieval period, when it was a centre of the wool trade; the fine abbey dates from this time. But the true splendour of Bath is the 18thC development, when the city grew as a resort and watering place that was frequented by all levels of English society, from Royalty downwards. Despite heavy bombing in the 1939–45 war, Bath is still a magnificent memorial to the 18thC and Neo-classicism generally. The terraces that adorn the steep northern slope of the Avon valley contain some of the best Georgian architecture in Britain. Much of the city was designed by John Wood the Younger, who was responsible for the great sweeping Royal Crescent. Other architects include Thomas Baldwin, who built the Guildhall, 1766–75, and the Pump Room, 1789–99, and Robert Adam, whose Pulteney Bridge carries terraces of shops across the Avon. Plagued by traffic, Bath is best seen on foot, for its glories and riches are far too numerous to list. Visitors should not fail to try the waters, which gush continuously from a fountain outside the Pump Room.

Bath Abbey Set in an attractive piazza, the abbey is a pleasingly uniform Perpendicular building, founded in 1499. Twin towers crown the west front, decorated with carved angels ascending and descending ladders. Inside, the abbey is justly famous for its fan vaulting, which covers the whole roof of the building but is not all of the same date. Inside also is a wealth of memorials of all periods, an interesting indication of the vast range of people who, over the ages, have come to die at Bath.

Holburne of Menstrie Museum Great Pulteney Street (Bath 66669). Housed in an 18thC Palladian building that was designed as part of the Sydney pleasure gardens, it contains collections of silver, ceramics and 18thC paintings and furniture. *Open Feb–Nov Tue-Sat, and B. Hols.*

Museum of Costume Assembly Rooms. (Bath 61111). Display of fashion from the 17thC to the present day; one of the largest collections of costume in the world. *Open daily.*

Bath Roman Museum Abbey Churchyard. (Bath 61111). The great bath buildings with their dependent temple were the centre of Roman Bath. Much of these survive, incorporated into the 18thC Pump Room. The museum, attached to the bath buildings,

contains finds excavated from the site. *Open daily all year.*

1 Royal Crescent A typical mid-18thC house, complete with original furniture and fittings. *Open Mar–Oct weekdays and Sun afternoons.*

Victoria Art Gallery Bridge Street. (Bath 28144). Collection of 18thC and modern paintings, prints and ceramics. Visiting exhibitions. *Open weekdays.*

Information Centre Bath 62831.

Bathampton

Avon. P.O. Tel. Stores, garage. The centre of the village surrounds the canal and is still compact and undeveloped, but new housing around the village has turned it into a suburb of Bath. The church is mostly 19thC.

BOATYARDS

Ⓑ **John Knill** Bathampton swing bridge (Bath 63603). Ⓡ Ⓢ Ⓦ Pump-out, boat and engine sales, storage.

BOAT TRIPS

John Rennie Boat Co Summer trips from Widcombe Top Lock. Details Bath 60717.
K & A Canal Trust Weekend trips from Widcombe Top Lock. Details Bath 317357.
Bristol Narrowboats Sunday trips to Claverton Pump *in summer*. Details Bath 314509.

PUBS

Plenty of good pubs in Bath, including:
🍺 **Dolphin** Dolphin Bridge.
🍺 **Golden Fleece** Lower Bristol Rd. Near Weston cut, south side.
🍺 **Windsor Castle** Upper Bristol Rd. North side, opposite gas works.
🍺 **Hop Pole** Upper Bristol Rd. Not far from Windsor Castle.
🍺 **Railway Brewery** Wells Rd. Walk south from Churchill Rd bridge.
🍺 **Crystal Palace** Abbey Green. Near the Abbey.
🍺 **George Inn** Bathampton. Canalside.
✕🍷 **Sweeney Todds** 15 Milsom St. Pizzas etc, consume here or take away.
✕🍷 **Clarets** 6–7 Kingsmead Sq. Wine bar. Food. *Closed Sun.*
✕🍷 **La Vendange** Brock St. Bath's original wine bar. Food. *Closed Sun.*

Widcombe Locks, Bath.

Saltford

The river Avon at last leaves behind the industries of Bath, and enters a wooded stretch. The railway closely follows the south bank, vanishing at one point into a tunnel. As the river continues its wide, wandering course westwards, the valley opens out, and rolling hills and pastureland flank both banks. A disused rail bridge is followed by the elegant single stone arch of New Bridge, carrying the A4. At this point the towpath crosses to the south bank, although, as on all river navigations, its position is never well-defined. After New Bridge there is a small boatyard, and a line of moored craft along the north bank. The river passes Kelston Park in a series of gentle bends, against a background of wooded hills to the north. The disused railway crosses the Avon for the fourth time, an indication of the river's winding course. The river straightens as it approaches Kelston Lock, where the stream again divides. Navigators should take the right fork to the lock, and avoid the weir on the left. Saltford can be seen among the trees on the south bank. Mooring is possible by the lock, and this is the best access point for boaters visiting the town. The towpath continues along the north bank, as the river curves towards Saltford Lock. At one time there was a horse and passenger ferry near the lock that allowed the towpath to cross to the south bank. By Saltford Lock is Saltford Sailing Club where there is a riverside pub. At Saltford the lock is on the left. The river then turns past Saltford Mead towards Swineford, passing a large factory on the low-lying land to the south. At Swineford the river again divides, the left fork leading to the particularly attractive lock, which is set against a background of trees and old mill buildings.

Swineford
Avon. P.O. Tel. Stores. Although bisected by the A431, the settlement by the river is still attractive; old mill buildings overlook the long weir.
Saltford
Avon. EC Wed. P.O. Tel. Stores, garage. Although Saltford has been developed as a large-scale dormitory suburb, the older parts by the river are still pretty and secluded.
Saltford Manor Situated by the church, the manor is one of the oldest inhabited houses in England. Much of the building is still original Norman work, but it is hidden behind a 17thC façade.

BOATYARDS

Ⓑ **Bristol Boats** by Saltford Lock. Jolly Sailor Boatyard, Mead Lane, Saltford. (Saltford 2032). Ⓦ Boat building, sales and repairs, inboard and outboard engine sales and repairs, slipway, chandlery. *Closed Sun in winter.*
Ⓑ **Saltford Marina** The Shallows, Saltford (2226). ⓇⓌⒹ Overnight mooring, engine repairs, shipway, crane.
Ⓑ **Richards Marine** above Saltford Lock (Bath 24301). Ⓦ Pump-out, mooring, food, rowing boats and cabin cruisers.

PUBS

🍺 **Swan** Swineford. Access is easy for boats, but virtually impossible for towpath walkers.
🍺 **Jolly Sailor** By Saltford Lock. Riverside garden.
🍺 **Bird in Hand** Saltford.

Keynsham

As the river passes Bitton it reaches another disused railway bridge. Low-lying pasture and arable land continue to flank the river in its meandering course towards Keynsham. After passing a vast brick and stone factory complex, dated 1881, which dominates the south bank, the river starts a long horseshoe bend that leads to Keynsham. The river divides, the right fork leading to the lock. Keynsham lies well to the south of the river, but is easily accessible. There is a small settlement round the lock, rather over-awed by the industry that surrounds it. Leaving Keynsham, on the south bank there is a huge chocolate and sweet factory, which fills the air with a heavy, sweet smell. Incongruously buried beneath the factory is the site of a Roman villa. As the valley narrows, steep wooded hills return to follow the north bank of the river as it twists and turns. After a particularly sharp bend, the southern hills approach as well, and Hanham Lock appears. Again the river divides, the left fork leading to the lock. This is lock 1, the last lock between Reading and Bristol, the end of the BWB's jurisdiction, and the beginning of the Port of Bristol Authority area. Note that the River Avon is tidal west of Hanham Lock. There is a small hamlet on the north bank, overlooking the weir, and a pub and boatyard. In summer a passenger ferry operates. From here the River Avon continues through a steeply wooded valley to Bristol; a canal takes boats through Bristol harbour and then the navigation rejoins the river which flows down to join the Severn estuary at Avonmouth, having passed the Clifton Suspension Bridge and the Avon gorge.

Navigational Note
Do not navigate in tidal waters without charts, tide-tables, anchor etc. Ensure your craft is suitable. Seek expert advice if in any doubt (the lock keepers are extremely helpful).

Keynsham
Avon. All services. Keynsham has grown steadily along the Bristol road, and so is now a vast shapeless suburb. However, the centre still retains a feeling of independence, and has many traces of Keynsham's past. An Augustinian Abbey was founded here in 1170, and there are a few surviving remains in Abbey Park. Elsewhere in the main street are a few 17th and 18thC houses, but bungalows and modern shops predominate. The main feature of interest is the large church. Originally 13thC, the interior is now attractively Victorian, after the restoration of 1861. The ornamental west tower was built in 1734, after the earlier tower was blown down in a storm. There is a fine 16thC monument to Sir Henry Bridges.
Bitton
Avon. P.O. Tel. Stores, garage. Although a main-road village, Bitton's heart survives intact south of the road. Here is a fine group formed by the church, the grange, and the 18thC vicarage, all built around the churchyard. The church is very splendid; it has a long Saxon nave with Norman details, a 14thC chancel, and a magnificently decorative late 14thC tower. On the main road is an attractive early 19thC Wesleyan chapel.

BOATYARDS
(B) **Chequers Inn** Hanham. (Bristol 674242). R W D Slipway available, overnight moorings. Small boats for hire by the hour or day.
BWB Hanham Lock Toll office. (Keynsham 2550). K & A windlasses.
(B) **Port Avon Marina** Bitton Road, Keynsham. (Keynsham 61626). R S W D Slipway, gas, dry dock, boat and engine repairs, mooring, chandlery, toilets, winter storage.

PUBS
🍺 **Old Lock & Weir** Hanham. Riverside, overlooking the lock.
🍺 **Chequers Inn** Hanham. Riverside, overlooking the lock.
🍺 **Ship** Temple St, Keynsham. Snacks. ¼ mile south west of the lock.
🍺 **White Hart** Bitton. On A431, most easily reached from the river along the disused railway.

Twyford Mill, on the Stort. Many of the mills are now private residences. *David Perrott*

LEE & STORT

Maximum dimensions

Limehouse Basin to Old Ford
Length: 87′
Beam: 19′
Headroom: 8′
Old Ford to Enfield lock
Length: 85′
Beam: 18′
Headroom: 6′ 9″
Enfield lock to Hertford
Length: 85′
Beam: 15′ 9″
Headroom: 6′ 9″
River Stort
Length: 85′
Beam: 13′ 3″
Headroom: 5′ 9″

Mileage

River Lee

LIMEHOUSE BASIN TO
Old Ford Locks: 2¾
Lea Bridge: 4¾
Pickett's Lock: 10
Enfield Lock: 13
Waltham Abbey: 14
Broxbourne: 18½
FEILDE'S WEIR (junction with River Stort):
20½
St Margaret's: 22½
Ware Bridge: 25
HERTFORD, head of navigation, 27¾

Locks: 18

River Stort

FEILDE'S WEIR (junction with River Lee) to
Roydon station: 1½
Burnt Mill: 4½
Harlow Lock: 6¾
Sawbridgeworth: 8¾
BISHOP'S STORTFORD, head of
navigation: 13¾

Locks: 15

Parts of the River Lee (often known as 'Lea': the spelling is optional) were used as navigations in Roman times, and much of the river was navigable before the reign of Elizabeth I. The first major attempt to speed up traffic by means of an artificial cut was made under the powers of an Act of 1571. In the same year an early pound lock was built at Waltham Abbey, using two sets of mitred gates, a principle that then became a standard feature of lock design. In the 17thC the Lee was established as a source of water supply for London, a role it still fulfils. The navigation was steadily improved throughout the 18th and 19thC, under the direction of various well-known engineers. During and immediately after the 1914–18 war enlargements were carried out to allow 130-ton boats to reach Enfield, and 100-ton boats to Ware and Hertford. In the 1930s further canalisation was carried out and more recently locks have been mechanised and duplicated. Timber has always been the main support of the Lee navigation, a trade that still survives today.

The River Stort has never been a very significant navigation commercially, and has not in fact carried any traffic for some years. The navigation as such dates back over 200 years, and has been owned by a series of individuals and companies, including Sir George Duckett; but it would have prospered far more if the ill-fated scheme to build a canal from Bishop's Stortford to Cambridge and the Fenland waterways had ever succeeded.

Lee Valley Park

In making the Lee Valley a regional park (the first area in Britain to be so designated) the Authority has realised the need of a rapidly increasing population for an expanse of open space where this new-found leisure can be both utilised and enjoyed. An amazing factor of the park is its sheer size; it runs from Eastway (A106) in the south to Ware in the north.

The Authority caters for all types: young, old, beginners, experts, teams and individuals. Outdoor and indoor sports, social centres, cultural activities and play centres have all been built.

This ambitious scheme has not been, of course, without its difficulties; there was serious danger of flooding, which has since been alleviated by the construction of drainage channels; massive areas of soil have had to be moved from one area to another; and natural vegetation has largely disappeared except for the woodlands north of Waltham Abbey. As one of the chief aims of the Authority is to make the Park visually pleasing, trees and other vegetation have been planted (especially in areas where pylons march conspicuously across the landscape), and buildings of historical interest within the park, many of which are mentioned in the text, have been preserved.

For more information and a brief guide, the address of the Lee Valley Park Authority is P.O. Box 88, Enfield, Middx. (Lee Valley 717711).

Bow

The River Lee is navigable from London up to Hertford. The River Stort, which joins the Lee at Feilde's Weir, is canalised as far as Bishop's Stortford. The Lee has always been a busy river but nowadays all the commercial (barge) traffic is concentrated at the south end, below Enfield, although the occasional barge goes right up to Ware. Traffic at the south end comprises mostly timber and copper. The fact of the Lee being busy with barges means of course that pleasure-boat steerers must be very careful and keep a sharp lookout. Barges are usually pulled in trains of 2, 3 or 4 by a tug, so they have limited control over their steering and swing across the river a lot, especially on bends. Incidentally it is inadvisable to tie up on the outside of bends, since you may be hit by a swinging barge at the end of the train. The rule of the river is, of course, 'keep to the right'. An awesome amount of floating rubbish, carried in by the tide, often covers the surface of the water in the vicinity of Limehouse Basin and Bow Locks. Obviously a pleasure boat crippled by this flotsam can cause acute embarrassment to tugs and barges ploughing through it, and sometimes this obstacle can be overcome only by taking a line ashore and 'bow-hauling'. Entrance to the river navigation can be made from three places:

From the Regent's Canal via the Hertford Union Canal
From the Thames via Limehouse Basin.
From the Thames direct up Bow Creek, and through Bow Locks.

The Hertford Union Canal is a short (1¼ miles) canal built in 1830 by Sir George Duckett (hence it is often referred to as 'Duckett's') as a useful junction between the Regent's Canal and the Lee Navigation. It is straight, has 3 locks, and borders the attractive Victoria Park for most of the way. The western entrance to Duckett's is difficult to find, and very easy to pass without noticing. It is just below Old Ford Locks and looks just like any of the private dock entrances that are common on the London canals.
The most direct route up into the River Lee from the Thames is through the ship lock into Limehouse Basin (1½ miles below Tower Bridge), then east through the new short cut and along the Limehouse Cut to Bow Locks and Old Ford. The ship lock is opened for 3½ hours preceding high tide. More information on opening times can be obtained from the Dock-master's office at (01) 790 3444. The other entrance to the Lee Navigation is by way of Bow Creek, whose mouth is 5 miles down the Thames from the Limehouse Basin entrance. Bow Creek is a tidal river—it is in fact the mouth of the River Lee. It is very twisting, 2 miles long and only navigable around high tide. For information on this water, ring British Waterways at Bow Locks (01-987 5661). Bow Locks, which are tidal, are at the top of the creek where it joins the Limehouse Cut. They are opened for approximately 4 hours before and 2 hours after high tide. The Three Mills at Bow still remain from the 18thC, although they were modified some years later. Nearby is the Abbey Mills Pumping House of Gothic-Byzantine style designed in 1868 by Bazalgette, who was also responsible for the Thames embankments. Hackney Marsh on the east bank of the canal is a footballer's delight: there are many pitches here by the Eastway Sports Centre.

PUBS

🍺 **Rising Sun** St Leonard St, E3.
🍺 **Queen Victoria** St Leonard St, E3. Both the above near Bow Locks, west of Three Mills Bridge.
🍺 **Ship Aground** Lea Bridge Rd (A104). Canalside. Food.
🍺 **Prince of Wales** Lea Bridge. Canalside. Food.

**THE RESERVOIRS OF
THE LEE VALLEY**

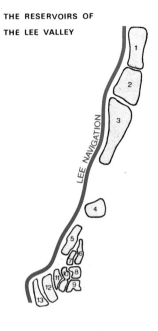

1 King George's reservoir (fishing)
2 King George's reservoir (fishing and sailing)
3 William Girling reservoir (fishing at selected spots only. Nature reserve)
4 Banbury reservoir (fishing and sailing) Banbury Sailing Centre (01-531 1129). Courses to all RYA standards
5 Lockwood reservoir (fishing and nature reserve)
6 High Maynard reservoir (fishing and nature reserve)
7 Low Maynard reservoir (nature reserve)
8 Fishing and nature reserve
9 Fishing
10 Nature reserve
11 Nature reserve
12 Warwick east reservoir (fishing and nature reserve)
13 Warwick west reservoir (fishing and nature reserve)

Tottenham

The river now begins to follow the wider
sweeping course that is typical of this
navigation. The Walthamstow Reservoirs close
in from the east, blocking off the river with
their high enbankments bordering the
navigation, while the river begins to adopt the
bleak, stark appearance that characterises it for
miles ahead. Racing 'fours' and 'eights'
emanate from the occasional rowing club, but
riverside life is sparse for the next 15 miles and
there is little to see. Flotsam is, happily, not as
common as in the Bow area, but there are
plenty of timber yards on the river and here and
there a massive baulk of wood lurks just on the
surface of the water. It is inadvisable to venture
up any of the side creeks feeding into the river;
they are usually heavily silted up. The power
station to the north of Bleak Hall Bridge is
remarkable—it generates electricity by burning
rubbish. One of the locks at Stonebridge and
Tottenham is now de-mechanised—the parallel
mechanised locks are operated by lock keepers
during usual working hours. At Walthamstow,
¼ mile north east of Springfield boatyard, is
the old Copper Mill built c1800 to process the
copper that was brought from the port of
London along the Lee. Private parties may visit
by prior arrangement with the Thames Water
Authority, Rosebery Avenue, London EC1
(01-837 3300).

Walthamstow Reservoirs Alongside the east
bank of the navigation: an important part of
London's water supply, controlled by the
Thames Water Authority. Access is allowed
only for bird-watching or fishing by permits
obtained from the Thames Water Authority,
Rosebery Avenue, London EC1 (01-837 3300),
though an extension of recreational facilities is
being considered. There is a variety of land and
water birds, including great crested grebes and
yellow wagtails, as well as 2 thriving,
long-established heronries on islands in
reservoirs 1 and 5. The stock of fish in the
reservoirs is being steadily increased and the
reservoirs where fishing is permitted may vary
each year; details can be obtained from the
T.W.A.

BOATYARDS

ⓑ **Page & Hewitt** Marsh Lane, Stonebridge
Locks, London N17 (01-808 9013). Ⓡ Ⓢ Ⓦ Ⓓ
Boat hire, slipway, gas, boat building and
repairs, mooring, toilets, showers, winter
storage. Trip boat for private charter.
ⓑ **Lea Valley Marina** Springfield Springhill,
Clapton (01-806 1717). Ⓡ Ⓢ Ⓦ Ⓜ Ⓓ Ⓔ Slipway,
gas, boat and engine repairs, mooring, toilets,
winter storage. *Closed weekend afternoons.*

PUBS

ⓧ **Cook's Ferry Inn** Edmonton. Canalside.
Food.
ⓧ **Ferry Boat Inn** Tottenham Locks,
Tottenham. Food.
 Robin Hood High Hill Ferry, Upper
Clapton. Food.
 Anchor & Hope High Hill Ferry, Upper
Clapton. Food.

Enfield

Straight as a die for over a mile, the river passes
Pickett's Lock, where the Regional Park
Authority has built a large covered leisure and
sports centre, as well as a golf course. This lock
can now be operated manually at weekends, as
can the next lock, Ponders End. The King
George & William Girling reservoirs
accompany the navigation (fishing on these
reservoirs is restricted to clubs), so do vast
power lines, which stride along as purposefully
as the river. Ponders End Locks provide canal
interest in this rather bleak area. Enfield Lock
signals the end of nearly 4 miles of reservoirs
and north of here the landscape opens out.
Near Enfield Lock there are plenty of shops
and pubs and also the Royal Small Arms
factory. This very large establishment used to
be extremely busy, especially of course during
the last war, but no manufacturing takes place
here now, only servicing and testing of
weapons. The famous Lee-Enfield rifle was
made here.

Enfield
Middx. Interesting features in this town include
the Church of St Andrew in the market place;
the chancel window is 13thC. Gentlemen's
Row, which probably dates from the early
18thC, is completely preserved from numbers 9
to 23. (Charles Lamb stayed at no. 17 in 1827).
Pickett's Lock Centre Edmonton (01-803
4756). All sorts of sports activities, including
squash, yoga, swimming, golf and many others.
Sauna, solarium. *Open daily.*
Chingford
Essex. Uninteresting town except for All Saints
Church, which is medieval. To the north of the
town, which is east of the river along the A110,
is a pole obelisk on a 300ft hill 1½ miles from
Ponders End Locks. It was erected in 1825 as a
North mark for Greenwich Observatory. 1 mile
east of the obelisk is Queen Elizabeth I's
hunting lodge—a timber-framed,
three-storeyed building from where the hunting
could be viewed, now housing a local museum.
The 10 square miles of Epping Forest lie to the
north east of Chingford: the forest is
remarkable for the large number of hornbeams
and a diminishing herd of deer.

BOATYARDS
BWB Enfield Maintenance Yard Ordnance
Rd, Enfield Lock. (Lea Valley 764626).

PUBS
🍺 **Greyhound** Enfield Lock. Canalside. Food.
🍺 **Royal Small Arms** Enfield Lock. Canalside.
Food, snooker table.
🍺 **Railway** Ponders End station.
🍺 **Granville** Northampton Rd, Ponders End.
Not far from the lock.

Waltham Abbey

Rammey Marsh Lock is the first of 5 locks in this section. Waltham Abbey is a fine old town where the ancient abbey, an architectural gem, looks down unperturbed on the traffic that flounders round it. The intermittent glinting of glasshouses around shows that this is a market gardening area. North of here the navigation runs into a massive water parkland with sailing clubs on the worked out gravel pits. The fishing on this section is famous throughout the angling world.

Cheshunt
Herts. EC Thur. P.O. Tel. Stores, station, cinema. The church of St Mary's was built in 1418–48 by the then rector of Cheshunt and is an example of the Perpendicular style. Of Cheshunt House not much remains: only one wing of a courtyard house. There is a carnival every *Jul.*

Waltham Cross
Herts. EC Thur. P.O. Tel. Stores, station, cinema. The Eleanor Cross, 1 mile west along the A121, is one of the 12 crosses (of which only 3 survive) erected by Edward I to commemorate the resting places of his dead queen, Eleanor of Castile, on her last journey from Leicestershire where she died, to Westminster Abbey. The Cross was built in 1291, but was greatly restored in Ketton stone in the 19thC.

Waltham Abbey
Essex. EC Thur. P.O. Tel. Stores, station, cinema. The history of the town goes back to before the Norman Conquest when King Harold chose it for development as a centre of learning and religious instruction. Local museum in Sun St.

Abbey Church Founded in 1030 as a collegiate church of secular canons. In 1184 it was nominated a mitred abbey and was soon one of the most prosperous and important in the country. Today's building is largely 19thC, but the Norman nave and aisles still stand. The south chapel is 14thC and the west tower, 16thC. The Jesse window at the east end is a fine example of Burne-Jones, 1861. Within the abbey grounds and just outside to the north are several interesting archaeological remains.

BOATYARDS
ⓑ **Hazelmere Marine** Highbridge St, Waltham Abbey (Lea Valley 711865). Ⓡ Ⓢ Ⓦ Slipway, repairs, mooring, toilets. *Closed weekends.*
ⓑ **Rammey Marsh CC** Rammey Marsh Lock. Ⓔ

PUBS
🍺 **Red Cow** next to Cheshunt station.
🍺 **Angel** Sun St, Waltham Abbey.
🍺 **Old English Gentleman** Waltham Town Lock. Canalside. Food.

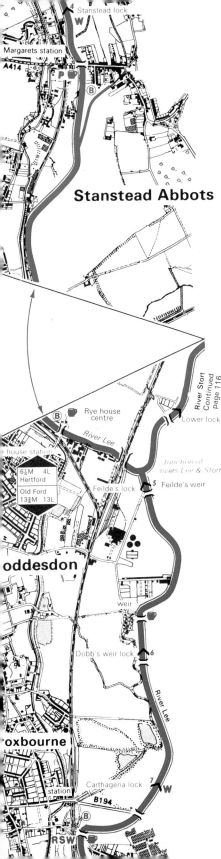

Broxbourne

At Broxbourne can be seen the first of many
holiday chalets and houseboats. Sailing and
rowing boats can be hired by the hour; this
attractive area becomes busy on a summer
weekend, with fishermen becoming more
numerous. At Feilde's Weir the beautiful River
Stort flows in from the north east and the Lee
bears round to the north west, past Rye House
and the Rye House Centre (nature reserve,
speedway, greyhound and go-kart racing) to
Stanstead Abbots, an attractive old town with
all useful facilities. Already one feels that the
character of the river is changing
dramatically—it is smaller, shallower and in
every way more attractive than further south,
and the pylons, which have relentlessly dogged
the river since the outskirts of London, at last
recede. Boaters should be careful when
ascending the Stanstead Lock: the top paddles
are, unusually, on the *gates*: the unexpected
rush of water into the lock chamber can cause
great harm to the unwary.

Stanstead Abbots
*Herts. EC Thur. P.O. Tel. Stores, garage,
station.* A picturesque village with the Church
of St James, interesting particularly because of
its 15thC open timber south porch and 16thC
brick north chancel chapel. Stanstead Bury
nearby was originally a 15thC manor house at
the west end of the village and dates from 1752.
Rye House Plot During the reign of Charles II,
Rye House (the building, not the village) was
owned by Rumbold, an ex-officer of the
Parliamentary army. It was here that he and a
group of other discontented conspirators
decided to ambush the King and his son James,
heir to the throne. The plot failed miserably
because the royal party passed by sooner than
expected, and many of the traitors were put to
death. The Rye House itself is no more, but the
nearby gatehouse, which is scheduled as an
ancient monument, has been restored by the
LVRPA as a feature of a picnic area.
Hoddesdon
*Herts. EC Thur. MD Wed. P.O. Tel. Stores,
station.* St Monica's Priory was the manor house
of Marmaduke Rawdon from 1622. A clock
tower stands in the centre of the town from
where the 2 main streets of Hoddesdon begin.
A fair is held in *Jun*.
Broxbourne
Herts. EC Wed. P.O. Tel. Stores, station. The
church is entirely 15thC and 16thC. In the
High Street there are several timber-framed
17thC Georgian brick houses. Broxbourne Lido
is a beautiful indoor heated pool, by the river.

BOATYARDS
Ⓑ **Stanstead Abbots Marina** South St,
Stanstead Abbots (Ware 870499). Ⓦ Ⓢ Ⓔ Boat
hire, chandlery, mooring, repairs.
Ⓑ **Hayes-Allen Boatyard Co** Rye House Quay,
Rye Rd. Hoddesdon (60888). Ⓡ Ⓦ Day boat
hire, slipway, mooring, chandlery, toilets,
provisions, winter storage, engine sales and
service.
Ⓑ **Broxbourne Boat Centre** Old Nazeing Rd,
Broxbourne (Hoddesdon 62085). Near
Broxbourne Station. Ⓔ Boat hire, day boat
hire, trip boat charter, slipway. *Closed winter*.

PUBS
🍺 **Jolly Fisherman** Stanstead Abbots.
Canalside. Food.
🍺✕ **Rye House** Canalside. Food.
🍺 **Fish & Eels** Dobbs Weir, Broxbourne.
Canalside. Food.
🍺 **Crown Inn** Old Nazeing Rd, Broxbourne,
Canalside. Food, garden.

Hertford

Leaving Stanstead Lock, the navigation runs dead straight for 1½ miles north west, flanked by beautiful green, uncluttered water-meadows contained by the nearby wooded hills. A lovely old branch railway line once ran from Stanstead Abbots to Buntingford—it now forms part of the 'Amwell Walkway' to Easneye Woods. The river turns west into Ware, the 'granary of London', where the river bisects this fine old town. There are some remarkable 18thC summer houses along the riverfront and Ware Lock is surrounded by beautifully maintained flower beds. Above this lock, the river wanders along one side of the valley, with water meadows on one side and wooded parkland on the other. The river enters Hertford via a deep lock, then passes a basin used for pleasure-boat moorings. A weir in the centre of the town prevents further progress.

Hertford
Herts. EC Thur. MD Mon. P.O. Tel. Stores, garage, stations. A large and mostly attractive county town with a long history. Two of its medieval parish churches still stand, and other buildings in the town bear witness to the Middle Ages. A new 'relief' road through the town has destroyed many interesting and attractive houses; but it has ensured the survival of the compact old town centre, which is now a delightful place to stroll around in. In the 9thC the area was invaded with great regularity by the Danes; they were eventually seen off by King Alfred the Great. Dane End, 3½ miles north of Hertford, marks the northern limit of their incursions into this region.
The Castle Built in 1100, the castle belonged to the Cecil family since Prince Charles, son of James I, sold it. King John of France and David Bruce of Scotland were both imprisoned here; and it was here that Bolingbroke drew up charges against Richard II that led to Richard's dethronement in 1399. A few medieval structures remain, including a 12thC curtain wall. The lawns and trees which extend to the river make an attractive setting. The 15thC gatehouse was extensively altered about 1800. Those houses in Water Lane numbered 4 to 16 are thought to have been outhouses of the castle. Several buildings in Castle Street itself are noteworthy, and also those in Fore Street, including Shire Hall, built by James Adam (brother of Robert) in the 18thC. The castle now belongs to the Council.
Hertford Museum 18 Bull Plain. Local archaeology, history, geology and natural history. *Open Mon–Sat.*
Ware
Herts. EC Thur. MD Tue. P.O. Tel. Stores, garage, station, cinema. There is much evidence of a former medieval town here, while other buildings with their projecting upper storeys show the importance of through-traffic during the coaching days.
Ware Priory Priory St. Built from the remains of a Franciscan friary founded by Thomas Wake, Lord of the Manor in 1338.
St Mary's Church Church St. Its battlemented clock tower is surmounted by a spire. There is a fascinating story connected with the oak railings enclosing the children's corner.
The New River Opposite Ware Park is the intake from the River Lee of the New River, which continues 24 miles south, terminating at Stoke Newington. It was a great feat of engineering designed by Sir Hugh Myddelton in the 17thC to bring a fresh water supply from Amwell Springs, which have since run dry, to north London to replace the polluted supply obtained from the Thames. Work started on this remarkable plan in 1609 and the original 44-mile course, including several large wooden aqueducts, was completed within 4 years. As Amwell Spring had ceased to flow by the end of the 19thC, most of the water in the New River is now drawn from the River Lee. A monument, overhung by weeping willows and a yew tree, commemorating Myddelton's great

achievement, can be seen on an island at the foot of the slope below Great Amwell church, ¼ mile west of the iron footbridge half way between Hardmead and Stanstead Locks.

BOATYARDS

ⓑ **Lea Valley Narrow Boat Co** Victoria Malting, Broadmeads, Ware (Ware 3626). W D E Pump-out, gas, narrow boat hire, boat building and repairs, chandlery. Some public trips and private charter.

PUBS

Woolpack near Mill Bridge, Hertford. Food.

Salisbury Arms Hotel Fore St. Hertford. Food.

White Hart Hotel Salisbury Square, Hertford. Food.

Old Barge Hertford Basin. Canalside. Food.

Bottles Old Cross, Hertford. Wine bar, food.

Bell & Crown 29 Cowbridge, Hertford. ¼ mile west of end of navigation.

White Horse Castle St, Hertford. ¼ mile west of end of navigation.

Spread Eagle Amwell End, Ware.

Punch House High St, Ware.

Saracen's Head Ware. Canalside. Food.

Red House London Rd. Ware.

Springtime at Feilde's Weir lock, near Broxbourne. *Derek Pratt*

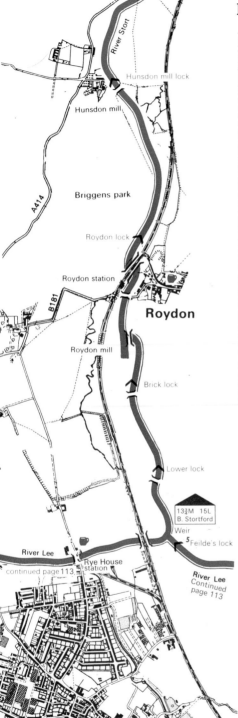

Roydon

The River Stort joins the Lee at Feilde's Weir.
It is instantly different from the Lee: narrow,
winding, totally rural along almost its entire
length, and very beautiful. There is no longer
any commercial traffic on the river, which with
its winding course, shallow draught and slightly
narrow locks (about 13ft wide), became
financially uncompetitive long ago. Water mills
are seen at many of these locks: the attendant
clapboarded buildings are a handsome feature
of this navigation. Low bridges are also
common, and when the river is swollen by
excessive rainwater, the headroom under the
bridges is even further reduced.

Starting at Feilde's Weir, the Stort follows a
line of hills past Lower Lock and Brick Lock to
Roydon. Roydon Mill is now the centre of a
large caravan site, and contains a useful
grocery. (Southbound boats should turn left
under the bridge before the mill). Roydon
village itself stretches up a hill away from the
river, which is crossed by the railway on an
extremely low bridge (about 6ft headroom) and
followed by Roydon Lock. (This lock must
always be left empty, otherwise the lock
keeper's cottage tends to get flooded). East of
Roydon the river flows through quiet
water-meadows, with Briggens Park up to the
left to Hunsdon Mill and lock—an enchanting
spot.

Roydon

Essex. EC Wed. P.O. Tel. Stores, station.
Roydon Mill is the headquarters of a large
residential and holiday caravan site. The
pleasantness of the village itself is enhanced by
the bold modern housing estate on the
waterfront. The church is small but attractive
and dates from the 13thC. Note the shield of Sir
George Jackson, later Duckett (a former owner
of the Stort Navigation) on the lock cottage.

PUBS
- **New Inn** Roydon. Food.
- **White Hart** Roydon. Food.
- **Crusader** Roydon.
- **White Horse** Roydon.

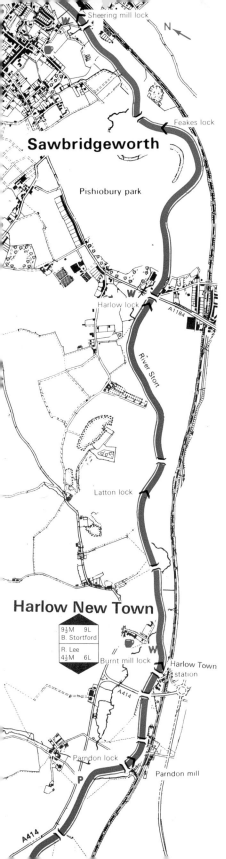

Sawbridgeworth

Leaving Eastwick to the north, the navigation passes the attractive Little Parndon Mill, then Burnt Mill; perhaps the name explains its absence. South of the railway lies Harlow New Town; it does not intrude on the navigation. Winding on north eastwards up the valley, one comes to Harlow Mill. There are usually skiffs for hire at the lock. Walkers should note that the towpath changes side at this point—do not be deceived by the path continuing up the west bank. Passing under the A11, the river continues to wind tortuously through water-meadows past Pishiobury Park. Sheering Mill Lock, with its lock cottage (the water point is at the back of the cottage) is a good point from which to enter the very attractive town of Sawbridgeworth. A little further north is Sawbridgeworth Lock and mill.

Sawbridgeworth
Herts. EC Thur/Sat. P.O. Tel. Stores, garage, station. An attractive town with houses from the 16th to the 19thC, including many white clapboarded ones. The large 14th and 15thC church is rich in monuments and brasses, and has a collection of 18thC gravestones of great elegance. The town is well shielded from the A11, but makes the most of the Stort; the group of clapboarded mill buildings are particularly pretty. There is an impressive array of maltings near the river.
Hyde Hall East of the Stort, 1 mile from town centre. Built in 1806 by Sir Jeffrey Wyatville in Tudor style, the mansion stands in a wooded park of 300 acres.
Pishiobury Castellated mansion rebuilt in 1782 by James Wyatt from earlier Tudor house. Still retains some Tudor and Jacobean work inside. Park and lake by Capability Brown. Now a school.
Harlow
Essex. EC Wed. MD Tue/Fri/Sat. P.O. Tel. Stores, garage, station, cinema. Harlow Old Town, which contains several 18thC houses, a Norman chapel at Harlowbury and the site of a Romano–Celtic temple has been swallowed up by Harlow New Town, set up in 1947 as a balanced area for London's overspilling population. Frederick Gibberd master-minded the plan, and the New Town is now well known as an important breakthrough in town planning.
Harlow Town Pets' Corner Harlow Park. Animals roaming free in the park. Also aquarium, vivarium and aviaries. *Open daily, school holidays and week-ends; afternoons during term-time.*
Parndon Mill at Parndon Lock, Harlow. A fine tall wooden watermill housing an interesting arts and crafts centre well worth a visit. A gallery exhibits and sells the pottery, etc, that is made here. *Open Sat & Sun.*

PUBS

King William IV Fairgreen, Sawbridgeworth, ¼ mile west of Sheering Mill Lock.
Old Bell Sawbridgeworth. Good food.
Churchgate Hotel Churchgate St, Harlow. Food, reductions for children.
Dusty Miller ¼ mile north of Burnt Mill Lock. Food.

Bishop's Stortford

Leaving Sawbridgeworth and its riverside malthouses, the river passes a very low railway bridge and wanders round to Tednambury Lock. Just to the north of this an arm leads off to Little Hallingbury Mill in its attractive setting at the bottom of a hill. Walbury Camp is half a mile upstream beside Spellbrook Lock, but there is little about the camp to interest the layman. Twyford House, Mill and Lock form a very attractive group in the water-meadows that flank the river, then a final sweep of the river past trees and fields brings the outskirts of Bishop's Stortford. A petrol station adjoins the towpath before the river reaches the town centre. The navigation almost reaches the middle of the town, but navigators are not advised to proceed further than the car park, where the river divides: there are only a few inches of water beyond this junction, and most boats tend immediately to get stuck.

Bishop's Stortford
Herts. EC Wed. MD Thur. P.O. Tel. Stores, garage, station, cinema. A thriving market town that has retained much of its old world atmosphere. Many of the inns are centuries old. St Michael's Church has a Norman font, which survives from an earlier church built on the same site.
Rhodes Memorial Museum South Rd. Contains a collection illustrating Cecil Rhodes' life, particularly in relation to his activities in Rhodesia. The old vicarage where Rhodes was born contains descriptive maps, pictures and documents devoted to him.
Waytemore Castle Bridge St. Only the foundations of the rectangular keep remain, and what used to be the bailey is now the pleasure gardens.
Thorley
Herts. The church retains its Norman south doorway and a west tower from the 15thC. However, extensive restoration was done in 1854 by Vulliamy. Thorley Hall nearby is a 15thC farmhouse which was modernised in the 18thC.
Little Hallingbury
Essex. P.O. Tel. Stores. The church has a Norman doorway made with Roman bricks. The south porch is of timber. Note the pretty timber-framed house behind the little pond near the church.

BOATYARDS

Ⓑ **Lee & Stort Cruises** Little Hallingbury Mill, Bishop's Stortford. (Ware [0920] 870381). Ⓦ Ⓢ Ⓔ Pump-out, gas, dry dock, boat and engine repairs, mooring, toilets. 54-seat passenger boat available for charter.

PUBS

✕ **Angela's Chophouse** 9 Northgate End, Bishop's Stortford. (Bishop's Stortford 57316). Restaurant with log fire. *Closed Mon, Sun D.*
🍺 **Three Tuns** London Rd, Bishop's Stortford. Near the station.
🍺 **Cock** Bishop's Stortford.
🍺 **Star** Bishop's Stortford.
🍺 **Old Bull's Head** London Rd, Bishop's Stortford. Food.
🍺 **Tanners Arms** Station Rd. Bishop's Stortford. Canalside. Food.

MONMOUTHSHIRE & BRECON

Maximum dimensions

Length: 45'
Beam: 7'
Headroom: 5' 7"
Draft: 'Vee' bottom boats recommended, maximum 1' 8"

Mileage
PONTYPOOL to
Goytre Wharf: 6
Llanfoist: 11½
Gilwern: 14½
Llangattock Bridge: 18
Talybont: 26½
BRECON: 33¼

Locks: 6

In 1792 the Act of Authorisation for the Monmouthshire Canal was passed. This gave permission for a canal to be cut from the estuary of the River Usk at Newport to Pontnewyndd, north of Pontypool. In addition to this 11-mile main line, there was to be an 11-mile branch from Malpas to Crumlin. The canal was designed to connect with a large network of tramways that were to be built to serve the iron ore, limestone and coal mines of the area. Thomas Dadford was appointed engineer, and the canal was opened in 1796, with many of the tramways still to be built.

The close relationship between canal and tramway from the start of the scheme was a feature of South Wales. The promoters of the canal saw these embryo railways as a means of increasing their revenue, without suspecting that they were encouraging the development of a means of transport that later was to cause the downfall of the canals.

When the Act for the Brecknock & Abergavenny Canal was passed in 1793, it was conceived in very similar terms to its southerly neighbour. The canal was planned to connect Brecon with the River Usk at Caerleon, to serve as a link between the various tramways and the Usk navigation. The directors of the Monmouthshire Canal persuaded the promoters of this rival venture to alter their plans to include a junction with their own canal, whose construction was well under way by this date. And so the Brecknock & Abergavenny Canal, with Thomas Dadford again as engineer, was cut from Brecon to Pontymoile Basin, where it joined the Monmouthshire Canal. Construction was begun in 1797. It progressed slowly because the company's first priority was the building of the tramways, a more immediate source of revenue. The canal was only to be built when all the tramways were in operation, to serve as a keystone for the whole system. After the usual delays caused by shortage of money, the Breck-

nock & Abergavenny Canal was opened throughout in 1812.

For a while the two canals were profitable, because the iron and coal cargoes justified the use of both canal and tramway. However, the greater speed and efficiency of the railways soon became apparent, and by the 1850s there were many schemes to give up the canals and rely entirely on the rail system. Some were put forward by the canal companies, in order to protect their interests as best they could. In 1865 the Monmouthshire and the Brecknock & Abergavenny Canal Companies amalgamated, becoming the Monmouthshire & Brecon Canal Company; but already it was too late for the merger to be effective. Revenues were dropping fast as the railway tentacles reached through the South Wales coalfields. Later the whole system was bought by the Great Western Railway, and by the turn of the century only a few boats were still using the canal. Bit by bit the original Monmouthshire Canal was closed, but the Brecon line was kept open as a water channel. In 1962 the network was formally 'abandoned', and parts were filled in.

However, with the development of the Brecon Beacons National Park, the amenity potential of the Brecon line was realised. In 1964 the slow task of restoration was begun by BWB, with the help of Brecon and Monmouth County Councils. The locks were restored, and soon boats were once more able to cruise from Pontymoile to Talybont. In 1970 the low fixed bridge at Talybont was replaced with a new lifting bridge, and once again navigation was open all along the old Brecknock & Abergavenny Canal. The Monmouthshire line from Pontymoile to the Usk at Newport may never be reopened in its entirety, for stretches have vanished completely; but parts have been restored as far south as Cwmbran, where it is proving a valuable asset to the developing new town.

Natural history

A diversity of interesting and colourful wild plants and animals can be seen along the Monmouthshire & Brecon Canal. For much of its length the canal is tree-lined, mostly by alders, which can be recognised by their smooth, roundish leaves with jagged edges and their clusters of little cones. Interspersed with the alders, or in small copses nearby, is a variety of other trees such as oak, ash, elm and sycamore. Between Llanfoist and Govilon fine beech trees clothe the hillside and reach down to the canal, and in spring wild cherries are conspicuously beautiful in blossom between Llangynidr and Crickhowell.

The smaller aquatic plants grow best in less shady places. Rooted in the mud at the bottom of the canal, and completely submerged in water, are the true aquatics like the featheryleaved water milfoil and Canadian pondweed. The latter, a North American plant, spread rapidly after its introduction into this country halfway through the last century. Other water plants to be seen include bur-reeds, with long ribbon-shaped leaves floating on the surface, and water plantains with oval leaves thrust above the water and tiny pink or white threepetalled flowers.

Bordering the canal grow many gaily coloured marsh plants, in bloom from July until autumn. Especially conspicuous are the tall 'codlins and cream', with rose flowers, and hemp agrimony with fluffy heads of pink flowers. The sweetly scented, feathery clusters of cream meadowsweet contrast effectively with the lovely blue of water forget-me-not. Marsh woundwort with its lilac flowers is frequent and here and there along the banks the blue trumpets of skullcap can be seen.

The animal life is also rich and varied. The kingfisher with its scintillating blue-green plumage is always an exciting sight. Fortunately it is now fairly frequent again along the canal. Another bird which comes to fish is the tall grey heron, which flaps away on slow wingbeats when disturbed. The largest bird likely to be encountered is the mute swan; a family party including four or five cygnets may often be seen near Brecon. Moorhens can be observed at several spots, either swimming along in their inimitable jerky style or walking about on the banks in search of food. Where the canal overlooks the River Usk as at Llanhamlach or crosses it via Brynich Aqueduct, the dipper—a dark, tubby, thrush-sized bird with a white front—may be seen bobbing up and down on stones in the river. Although its main habitat is the fast-flowing river, it may forsake this for the canal on occasions and be seen on the towpath.

In summer, from bramble thickets and hedgerows along the towpath issue the songs of whitethroats and garden warblers. Many small birds such as tree creepers, nuthatches and tits feed in the overhanging trees, and in winter the alders are sometimes thronged with twittering parties of siskins, searching the cones for seeds.

Of the wealth of smaller animal life along the canal, the dragonflies are perhaps the most noticeable, as they patrol to and fro over their particular stretch of water. Occasionally the female dragonflies may be seen dipping their long abdomens into the water at intervals to lay eggs on the submerged water plants. Pond skaters are the numerous small dark insects with long legs that dart away over the surface of the water at your approach. On marsh plants like the fragrant water mint, beautiful beetles with a greenish metallic lustre may be found. During May and June, orange-tip butterflies are on the wing along the banks, where the females (with grey, not orange-tipped wings) lay eggs on milkmaid plants, on which their caterpillars feed. Later in summer, speckled wood butterflies may also be seen flying or basking in sunny glades.

Brecon Beacons National Park

The Park covers 519 square miles of mountain and hill country, embracing parts of the old counties of Herefordshire, Monmouthshire, Breconshire and Carmarthenshire. Apart from a great variety of fine scenery, the Park also includes 3 nature reserves, a forest reserve, opportunities for fishing, caving, pony trekking, sailing and boating, and several towns of interest to tourists, notably Brecon, Crickhowell, Talgarth and Hay-on-Wye; in addition Abergavenny, Llandovery and Llandeilo are just outside the Park boundary.

Virtually all the canal is within the Park, —a factor that greatly strengthened the case for its restoration and reopening. The canal is an excellent introduction to the Park, crossing it roughly from south-east to north-west; in several places there are foot and bridle paths leading away into the mountains from the towpath. Various main roads cross the Park, and so access by car is easy, but the whole area is best explored on foot. A good place to start any exploration is the Mountain Centre, 1000ft up on Mynydd Illtud, above the village of Libanus, 4 miles south west of Brecon. There are rest and refreshment rooms, car parks and picnic sites overlooking the Brecon Beacons, and the wardens at the Centre give lectures to visitors and youth groups on the Park and the use of the countryside.

Pontypool

Before the closure of the Newport section, the
old Monmouthshire & Brecon Canal used to
run from Brecon to the estuary of the River Usk
at Newport, and thus to the sea. After a quarter
of a century of decay, the upper section, from
Pontypool to Brecon, was restored and
reopened to craft in 1970. Passing the turn-over
bridge, toll house and the site of the stop lock
that marked the junction with the southern
section, the canal turns north east, on to an
embankment that carries it past the Pilkington
Glass works, over the River Lwyd on an
aqueduct, and under the A4042 road bridge.
This is the most convenient access point for
Pontypool, Pontymoile and the railway station
(Pontypool Road). After a few canalside
gardens, all traces of the town are left behind,
and the canal starts its meandering contour
course towards Brecon. The character of this
canal is quickly apparent; it twists and turns,
clinging to the hillside on the west, while to the
east wide views open up across the rolling
pastures and woods of the Usk valley. The
winding course, and the frequent stone bridges
(all clearly numbered) make the canal
interesting, for every bend offers a different
view of the steep hills to the west and the valley
to the east, while the canal itself remains
entirely quiet, rural and isolated. Navigators
should look out for the cast-iron mile posts,
which survive irregularly along the length of
the canal. There are no villages by the canal in
this section, but services and pubs are never
more than a short walk away, at Pontymoile, at
Mamhilad and at Penperlleni. Main roads also
keep their distance, although they are generally
clearly visible in the valley below the canal.
After passing the long tunnel-like Saron bridge
(no. 74), the seclusion is interrupted by long
lines of moored boats, which are the prelude to
Goytre Wharf. Old lime kilns can be seen by
the wharf, indicating the agricultural nature of
the canal in its heyday. The wooded hills sweep
down to the wharf, giving it a most attractive
setting.

Penperlleni
Gwent. P.O. Tel. Stores, garage. Main road
village useful for supplies.
Mamhilad
Gwent. Tel. A little hillside hamlet scattered
round the church. Overshadowed by massive
yew trees, the pleasantly over-grown
churchyard has fine views across the valley.
Pontypool
Gwent. EC Thur. MD Wed, Fri, Sat. Pontypool
has been an industrial town since Roman times,
concentrating on the production of iron. This
reached a peak in the 18th and 19thC, but has
declined in recent times. In 1720 tinplate was
produced here for the first time in Britain, and
in the 19thC the town was a centre for
japanning—the coating of objects with an
extract of oils from coal, so producing a black
varnish similar to Japanese lacquer. Coal
mining has also been important. Despite this
industrial heritage, Pontypool has always
remained a farming centre, and so the hard
industrial elements are softened by the
traditions of a rural market town. The steep
walls of the Lwyd valley have also limited the
growth of the town, and made the centre very
self-contained.
Pontypool Park Originally the seat of the
Hanburys, the famous iron and steel family,
this Georgian mansion is now a school. The
park is open to the public. The magnificent
wrought iron entrance gates at Pontymoile (by
bridge 53) were given to John Hanbury by
Sarah Churchill, Duchess of Marlborough.
Torfaen Museum Trust Canal museum in the
old toll cottage. Details from Park Buildings,
Pontypool. (Ebbw Vale 790437). *Open
afternoons.*

BOATYARDS

Ⓑ **Red Line Boats** Goytre Wharf, Pontypool,
Gwent. (Nantyderry 880516). R S W P D Boat
hire, slipway, gas, boat building and repairs,
mooring, chandlery, toilets, showers, winter
storage, 12-seater trip boat.

PUBS

🍺 **Goytre Arms** Penperlleni. ¼ mile east of bridge 72. Food, garden, real ale, children welcome.

🍺 **Horseshoe Inn** Goetre Fawr. ¼ mile north of bridge 65.

🍺 **Star** Mamhilad. 200yds east of bridge 62. Food, real ale, children welcome.

🍺 **Horse & Jockey** Pontymoile, on A472. 100yds east of bridge 55.

🍺 **Bell Inn** High St, Pontypool.

🍺 **Forge Hammer** High St, Pontypool.

🍺 **The Open Hearth** Sebastopol. Canalside, between bridges 48 and 49, south of Pontymoile Basin. Moor at bridge 55. Food, garden, children welcome.

Gentle exercise along the 'Mon & Brec'. *Derek Pratt*

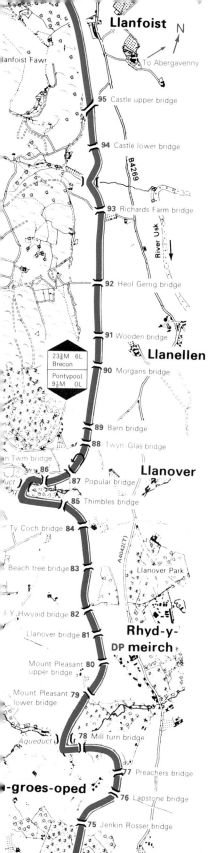

Abergavenny

Beyond Goytre Wharf, the canal continues its meandering course northwards, passing through a thick wooded cutting before returning to the pattern set in the previous section: steep wooded hills to the west, the wide valley rolling away to the east. The canal clings to its contour line high on the side of the hills, at times making horseshoe bends to avoid any change in level. At the apex of each such bend, there is generally a small stone aqueduct taking the canal over a stream that tumbles noisily down towards the valley. In several places these streams serve as feeders for the canal, half their water joining the canal, half passing beneath an aqueduct. After the first horseshoe bend, set among thick woods, the canal passes Llanover Park to the east; the house is out of sight, shielded by trees, but the village can be seen nestling in the hillside. The next bend is much wider; looking back, the course of the canal along the side of the hill can be clearly seen. After the bend there is a long straight for over a mile, which carries the canal through the trees above Llanellen. The River Usk is coming nearer all the time, and its course into Abergavenny is visible below. To the west the hills are now very steep, rising sharply to over 1800ft, at times almost vertically away from the canal. From its elevated position there is an excellent view of Abergavenny, laid out like a model in the valley below, nearly a mile from the canal. In the 19thC the hills to the west were heavily mined and quarried, and many tramways constructed to carry the coal, iron ore and limestone down to the canal to be loaded into boats. There are still traces of at least 10 of these tramways; often their course into the hills can be followed from the canal bridges. A good example leaves the canal at Llanfoist by the boathouse. The loading wharves, cut into the steep hillside, can also be seen in many places along the canal.

Abergavenny
Gwent. EC Thur. MD Tue. All services.
Abergavenny lies beside the fast flowing River Usk, surrounded on all sides by mountains and hills; the Sugar Loaf, Blorenge and the Skirrids overlook the town, a dramatic natural wall ranging up to 2000ft. Abergavenny enjoys this magnificent setting, living up to its reputation as the gateway to Wales. Primarily a market town, it contains the traditional mixture of buildings of all periods and styles, from the Tudor houses in the main street to the red stone of the 19thC Gothic town hall.
Abergavenny Castle The mound of the castle dominates the town. Built in the 11thC, the castle was the scene in 1177 of a treacherous massacre of several notable Welsh leaders; invited to the castle to dine by William de Braose, they were put to death with no warning. In this violent way William made sure of his control over the surrounding lands. Parts of walls, towers and a gateway survive. Ruins and grounds *open daily*.
St Mary's Church Originally the chapel of the Benedictine priory, the church was extensively rebuilt in the 14thC, after the destruction of the priory. It contains fine wooden 14thC choir stalls, a wooden figure of Jesse, and rich monuments in the Herbert chapel.
Abergavenny and District Museum Situated in the castle precincts, the museum contains items of local interest, Roman coins, tools and examples of local crafts. *Open daily.*
Sugar Loaf A conspicuous landmark 2 miles north west of Abergavenny, so named because of its flat shape. 2130 acres, including the 1955ft summit, are owned by the National Trust.
Rural Crafts Museum Llanvapley. 4 miles east of Abergavenny, on B4233. 500 tools, rural and farm equipment and implements, domestic bygones. *Open Sun afternoons.*
Llanellen
Gwent. P.O. Tel. Stores. Although modern housing has greatly extended Llanellen into a suburb of Abergavenny, it is still an attractive village, especially by the 3-arch stone bridge over the Usk. The 19thC church is pleasantly set among woods.

Llanover

Gwent. P.O. Tel. Garage. The famous bell Big Ben in Westminster was named after the politician Benjamin Hall (Lord Llanover), who was responsible for the construction of the tower whilst Chief Commissioner of Works. He also initiated the tramway from Buckland House Wharf to Rhymney Ironworks, east of Talybont reservoir. The estate village is particularly elegant; stone cottages and terraces all built in the same style, pleasingly laid out with generous grass verges and trees.

BOAT TRIPS

Owain Glyndwr 46-seater water bus operated by B & M Charters and based at bridge 76 near Goytre. (Raglan 690201).

PUBS

Many pubs and restaurants in Abergavenny.

Llanfoist Wharf.

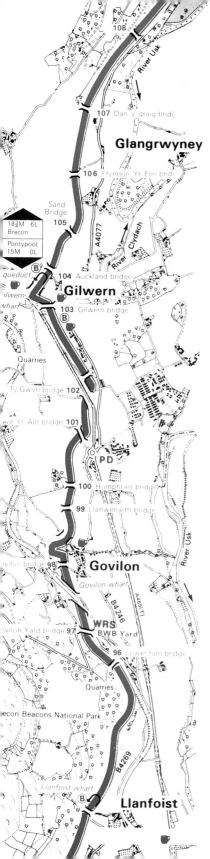

Govilon

The canal continues to follow its contour course
northwards, cut into the steep, rocky sides of
the hill. With Abergavenny spread out in the
valley below, and the wooded slopes climbing
up from the water, it is a very dramatic stretch.
Llanfoist comes into view, partly hidden by the
trees. The old wharf buildings, originally built
for the tramway that ran up into the hills from
the canal, are now a boatyard and hire cruiser
base. The boatyard bridge is the best place to
leave the canal on foot for Abergavenny.
Leaving Llanfoist, the canal continues through
the wooded side-cutting. As the course of the
long-abandoned railway swings in to join the
canal, the towpath changes sides to the west,
where it remains until Govilon. The village is
huddled beneath the canal; the wharf buildings
are now used by Govilon Boat Club, who
restored them. The BWB section office is also
here. After the big skewed rail bridge (now
disused) the canal makes another horseshoe
bend, crossing a stream on an aqueduct. As it
approaches Gilwern, the presence of the Heads
of the Valley road becomes more obvious, close
to the eastern bank. The canal passes above
Gilwern, which spreads down the hill to the
east, and then turns sharply before Gilwern
Wharf. The road and the hills swing away to
the west, leaving the canal to pass through a
thickly wooded stretch in comparative quiet;
however, the tumbling waters of the River Usk
are never far away.

Gilwern
Gwent. P.O. Tel. Stores. The village is built
along one main street, which falls steeply away
from the canal; there are fine views of the
country running down to the River Usk, ½
mile to the east.
Govilon
Gwent. P.O. Tel. Stores, garage. The canal
passes above the village, and little can be seen
from the water. Beside the aqueduct are steps
leading down to Govilon. The village is spread
out along the road, now quiet after the opening
of the new road to the east. It was at one time a
small industrial centre, with iron works and
lime-kilns, but these have long since vanished.
Llanfoist
Gwent. P.O. Tel. Stores, golf course. The
boatyard, housed in the old stone wharf
buildings, has given the little village a new lease
of life. There is a good walk from the boathouse
into the mountains, following the course of the
old tramway.

BOATYARDS

ⓑ **Castle Narrowboats** Church Rd Wharf,
Gilwern (830001). Ⓦ Pump-out. Narrowboat
hire, day boat hire.
ⓑ **Road House Holiday Hire Narrowboats**
Main Rd, Gilwern (830240). Pump-out. Gas,
narrowboat hire.
BWB Govilon Yard (Gilwern 830328) Ⓡ Ⓢ Ⓦ.
ⓑ **Beacon Park Boats** The Boatyard,
Llanfoist. (Abergavenny 78277, bookings
Cardiff 484677). Narrowboat hire.

PUBS

🍺 **Beaufort Arms** Gilwern. Food. B&B.
🍺 **Bridgend** Gilwern. Canalside at bridge 103.
Garden, children welcome.
🍺 **Corn Exchange** Gilwern. Food, garden, real
ale, children welcome.
🍺 **Navigation** Gilwern. Canalside at bridge
103. Fine picture of a navvy and his tools on
the sign. Food, garden, children welcome.
🍺 **Lion** Govilon, below the aqueduct. Food,
garden, children welcome.
🍺 **Bridge Inn** Llanfoist.
🍺 **Llanfoist Inn** Llanfoist. Food, garden,
children welcome.
🍺 **Bridgend** Govilon. Food, garden, real ale,
children welcome.

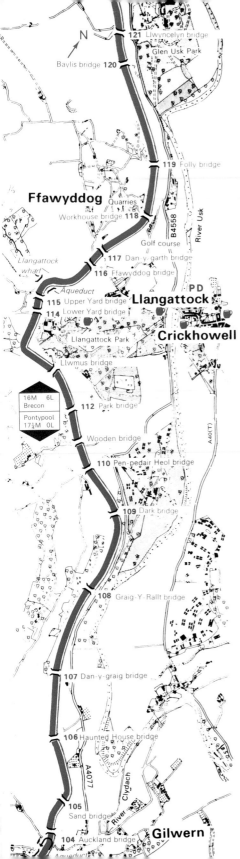

Crickhowell

Continuing north west, the canal clings to its contour on the side of the hill, which separates it from the River Usk for a while. As the canal passes the old army camp laid out in parkland to the east, the hills become less dramatic. The approach to Llangattock is through flatter country, but trees still surround the canal, hiding the extensive parkland that falls away to the east. Llangattock is set below the canal, best approached from bridges 114 and 115; beyond it lies Crickhowell, the fine houses rising out of the valley over the river. Llangattock Wharf is just beyond bridge 115: now a busy mooring site overlooked by the old stone wharf buildings, which include a range of lime kilns. This is a good base for exploring the Brecon Beacons; there are opportunities for caving in the surrounding hills, and horses can be hired in Crickhowell for trekking. Leaving Llangattock, the canal crosses a small aqueduct, and is then quickly back among the hills, whose steep wooded slopes fall sharply to the water's edge. As the River Usk and the canal close together again, there are fine views to the east across the valley. One of the best is across the golf course, which comes right up to the towpath. A short straight then takes the canal to Glen Usk Park, through woods that get progressively thicker.

Llangattock
Powys. P.O. Tel. Stores. This little village was once famous for its weaving and its lime-kilns. The hills behind the village are riddled with limestone caves and quarries. One cave, Agen Allwedd, has 11 miles of underground passages, the entrance is in the Craig-y-Cilau nature reserve. For access, follow the course of the old tramway west from bridge 114. Permits to enter must be obtained in advance from: Cave Management Committee, 10 Elms Road, Govilon, Gwent. Permits for rock climbing, and for specimen collecting, must also be obtained from: Nature Conservancy, Plas Gogerddan, Aberystwyth, Dyfed.

Crickhowell
Powys. EC Wed. MD Thur. P.O. Tel. Stores, garage, bank. The road down through Llangattock leads to the 13-arch medieval stone bridge over the Usk, the imposing entry to Crickhowell. This fine market town, once a centre for the production of Welsh flannel, is spread over the northern slopes of the Usk valley. The town is compact and elegant, with terraces of 18th and 19thC houses, and some handsome inns. In the centre are the scant remains of the Norman castle. Once controlling a large area, the castle was destroyed during the 15thC, and only the motte and bailey, parts of the curtain wall and a small tower survive. The 14thC parish church contains interesting stained glass. Crickhowell has long been a famous holiday centre, a role it still enjoys today. Apart from hill walking, there are opportunities for fishing and pony trekking.

PUBS
● **Horse Shoe** Llangattock. 200 yds from bridge 114 or 115. Food, garden, real ale, children welcome.
● **Bridgend Hotel** Crickhowell. At the end of the medieval bridge. Food. B&B.
●✕ **Bear Hotel** Crickhowell. Food. B&B.

Llangynidr

Leaving the wooded Glen Usk Park behind, the
canal continues its north westerly course along
the Usk valley. Among the trees to the east can
be seen the Italianate towers of Gliffaes. As the
canal approaches Llangynidr, it begins to
meander more, leaving the hills and woods
behind; river-like, it wanders through open
rolling pastureland beside the Usk, passing to
the south of the village. Bridge 129 is the best
access point for Llangynidr. The small
settlement by bridge 131 includes a shop,
telephone, tennis courts, and a garage. As this
is left behind, the canal reaches the first lock of
the Llangynidr flight of five; this, the first lock
on the navigable section of the canal, ends the
23-mile-long pound; the short climb to the
summit at Brecon starts here. Leaving Cwm
Crawnon, where there is a pub and restaurant,
the canal turns sharply over an aqueduct and
reaches the second lock. On the old wharf
beyond the lock is a toll house, now used by
BWB; there is a water point, and rubbish bins.
Thick woods now flank the canal as the steep
hills return on both sides. The Usk valley has
narrowed, and so canal and river flow close
together beside the hills; the canal is still high
above the river. In the middle of the woods are
the final 3 locks of the flight, following closely
upon each other. The surrounding woods and
hills make this one of the most beautiful
settings on the canal system. After a disastrous
breach in March 1975, the canal between
Llangynidr and Llanfoist was de-watered for
years while repairs were made.

Navigational note
Llangynidr locks should be left empty with
bottom gates open.

Cwm Crawnon
Powys. Clustered round the canal as it climbs
the Llangynidr locks, this hamlet is famous for
the Coach and Horses pub, with its French
cuisine.
Tretower Court and Castle
Powys. 2½ miles north west of Crickhowell on
A479. Ruins of a late 14thC fortified manor
house, which was built to replace a Norman
castle whose remains still exist nearby. The
ruined cylindrical keep is unusual.
Llangynidr
Powys. P.O. Tel. Stores. Spread out over a
plateau, this farming village is scattered round
the pretty 19thC church. The grandest house in
the village is the old rectory, whose grounds
run almost to the canal bank.

BOATYARDS
ⓑ **Country Crafts** Ty Newydd, Pencelli,
Brecon. (Llanfrynach 217). Hire craft.
BWB Llangynidr Maintenance Yard by bridge
134. R S W

PUBS
🍺 **Coach & Horses** Cwm Crawnon.
Llangynidr. Canalside at bridge 133. Food,
garden, real ale, children welcome.
🍺✕ **Red Lion** Llangynidr. (Bwlch 730223).
Food. B&B. Local trout and salmon served in
16thC surroundings. *Closed weekday lunchtimes
and Sun.*

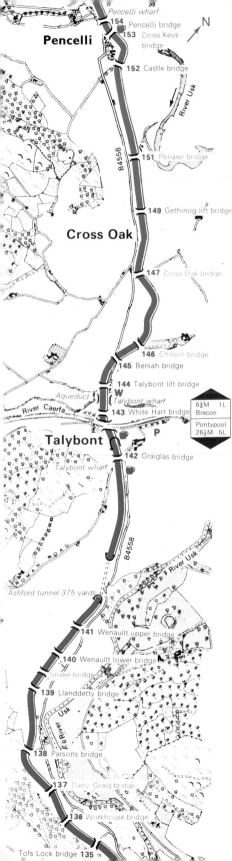

Talybont

Leaving the Llangynidr locks behind, the canal
continues through thick woods passing the 3
cottages by bridge 135 once a workhouse. The
narrow Usk valley pushes the two waterways
close together, although the canal stays high
above the river. The thick wooded walls of the
valley fall steeply on both sides. The minor
road that has accompanied the canal all along
the valley is still much in evidence, although
traffic is luckily very light. The valley starts to
open out, and as the hills recede, rolling
pastureland flanks the canal as it enters the
slight cutting that precedes the short Ashford
Tunnel. The tunnel, 375yds long, seems
particularly small as it has no portals to speak
of; a round hole disappears into the side of a
low hill, looking more like a large culvert than a
tunnel. The towpath goes over the top,
following the line of the tunnel and the B4558.
Leaving the tunnel behind, the canal goes
straight to Talybont through a low cutting.
Passing an old wharf where there is a pub on
the road beside the canal, bridge 142, and the
disused rail bridge, the canal goes through the
village on an embankment, crossing the fast
flowing Caerfanell river on an aqueduct. From
bridge 142 the remains of a Roman road run to
the hill fort above the village. The wharf was
used by the Bryn-Oer tramway, which brought
limestone down from the quarry above. Its
course can still be followed. Talybont stretches
along the road below the canal, seemingly a
typical canal village. At the end of the village is
the new lift bridge, the symbol of the
restoration of the canal. The bridge is
electrically operated and instructions are clearly
posted. Leaving the village, the canal enters a
different landscape. Pasturelands still roll
steeply away to the west, but to the east there
are wide flat lands; the canal is carried on a low
embankment which continues irregularly for
the next 3 miles. Three newly built
conventional lift bridges cross the canal. These
are sometimes fixed in the open position to stop
livestock crossing the canal; navigators should
always leave them as they find them. A very
wide towpath accompanies the canal along this
stretch, while on the west side the steep wooded
slopes conceal the minor road. A sharp bend
takes the canal into the village of Pencelli; the
mound of the old castle dominates the village
and the canal.

Pencelli
Powys. This little village was at one time the
head of a medieval lordship: but the only
indication of this today is the castle mound.
Talybont
Powys. P.O. Tel. Stores, garage. When the
railway and canal were both operating
commercially, Talybont must have been a busy
village. Today it is a quiet holiday centre with
facilities for fishing, pony trekking and hill
walking, although there is still a busy livestock
market. The large wharf overlooks the village,
which is clustered round the Caerfanell
aqueduct. The river falls rapidly from Talybont
reservoir in the hills to the south, to join the
Usk.
Llangorse Lake 3½ miles north of Talybont is
the largest natural lake in South Wales, 502
acres given over to pleasure and recreation.
Boating, yachting, water sports, fishing, pony
trekking, caravan parks and camping sites are
all available among spectacular scenery.
Wildlife is abundant, and the goosander is a
frequent visitor. The legendary town of Mara is
supposed to lie submerged in the lake, and in
fact a crannog, or lake dwelling set on stilts, has
been found near the lake's outlet.

PUBS
■ **Royal Oak** Pencelli. Canalside at bridge 154.
Food, garden, real ale, children welcome.
■ **Star Inn** Talybont. Canalside at bridge 143.
Food, garden, real ale, children welcome.
■ **White Hart** Talybont. Canalside at bridge
143. Food, real ale, children welcome.
■ **Travellers' Rest** Talybont. Canalside at
bridge 142. Food, garden, real ale, children
welcome.

Brecon

Leaving Pencelli, the canal starts on a long
horseshoe bend that carries it through flat
wooded country towards the crossing of the
Usk. After the last lift bridge, a low
embankment carries the canal across marshy
ground towards Llanfrynach, but it never goes
near the village. The best access point is the
B4558 bridge. Before this bridge, a small
aqueduct takes the canal over the Nant
Menascin; this aqueduct was rebuilt while the
canal was closed and so is narrower than the
rest. Beyond the aqueduct there is an old mill,
now converted to a private house, with a
covered loading bay over a small disused arm.
The canal completes the long curve back,
well above the fast flowing Usk. Llanhamlach
lies across the river. In addition to its
13thC church, the area is rich in prehistoric
remains. The Usk now stays in sight all the way
to Brecon, apart from one small interruption.
Bridge 162 takes the towpath to the west bank,
where it remains to the terminus, and then the
canal turns sharply on to the Brynich aqueduct.
This 4-arched stone structure takes the canal
across the Usk to the east side of the valley. To
the west can be seen the old bridge that takes
the B4558 across the river. Immediately beyond
the aqueduct is the last lock. Restored in 1970,
the lock has a particularly pretty cottage and
garden beside it. There is a shop and telephone
on the A40. The canal now goes straight to
Brecon, high on the hillside, overlooking the
Usk all the way. Although all of the canal is
very clean, the stretch into Brecon is
remarkably clear and free of weed. The canal
follows the road to the outskirts of the town,
passing the barracks, and then swings slightly
to the west, along the backs of the houses. The
entry into Brecon is attractive, with many
pretty houses and gardens flanking the canal.
Originally the canal went almost to the town
centre, turning sharply into a right-angled
basin, but now it stops short, just beyond
bridge 166. The course of the canal to the old
terminus can still be traced, although it has
vanished beneath a car park and a builder's
yard. A big brick warehouse, dated 1892,
marks the old head of the navigation.

Brecon
*Powys. EC Wed. MD Fri, P.O. Tel. Stores,
garage, bank, cinema, swimming pool.* Built at
the confluence of the Usk and Honddu rivers,
Brecon has long been the administrative centre
and market town for the Breconshire uplands.
It dates back to the Roman period, and
although little remains, the narrow streets that
surround the castle give an idea of medieval
Brecon. Today the town is famous as a touring
centre, its cathedral and generous 18thC
architecture making it seem more English than
Welsh. The Usk waterfront is especially
attractive, dominated by the old stone bridge.
Sarah Siddons and her brother Charles Kemble
lived in the High Street.
Brecon Cathedral Originally the Priory
Church of St John, founded by Bernard
Newmarch, it was given cathedral status in
1923. Most of the building is 13thC, although
the nave is a century later. There is some fine
glass, and side chapels dedicated to various
medieval trade guilds.
Brecon Castle Most of the remains of the
11thC castle now stand in the grounds of the
Brecon Hotel, and permission to view must be
obtained from the hotel. A large motte and
bailey, parts of the walls and two towers
survive. The destruction of the castle during
the Civil War was hastened by the inhabitants
of Brecon, who did not want either side to
occupy it.
Brecknock Museum Glamorgan Street.
(Brecon 2218). The collections include local
history, natural history and a large archaeology
section, from pre-Roman to medieval times.
The prize exhibit is a dug-out canoe found in
Llangorse Lake. *Closed Sun and Mon afternoon.*

Museum of the South Wales Borderers and the Monmouthshire Regiment The Barracks, Brecon (3111). History of two famous regiments over 280 years. *Open daily.*
Tourist Information 6 Glamorgan St, Brecon. (Brecon 4437) *Closed winter.*
Llanfrynach
Powys. An attractive village built in a square round the pretty church. Nearby is the site of a Roman bath house. The white painted pub dates from the 13thC.

PUBS
Many pubs and restaurants in Brecon, including:
🍺 **Wellington** Bulwark, Brecon.
🍺 **Boars Head** Watergate, Brecon.
🍺 **Gremlin** The Watton, Brecon.
🍺 **Old Ford** Llanhamlach. On A40. ½ mile east of bridge 160. Food.
🍺 **White Swan** Lanfrynach, ¾ mile from bridges 158 or 157. Food, garden, real ale, children welcome.

The beautifully sited Llangynidr locks. *Derek Pratt*

OXFORD

Maximum dimensions

Length: 70'
Beam: 7'
Headroom: 7'

Mileage

OXFORD (River Thames) to
Duke's Cut: 3
Thrupp: 6½
Lower Heyford: 14¾
Aynho Wharf: 20¼
Banbury: 27¼
Cropredy: 31½
Fenny Compton Wharf: 37¾
Napton Bottom Lock: 47
NAPTON JUNCTION (Grand Union Canal): 49¼
BRAUNSTON TURN (Grand Union Canal): 54¼
Hillmorton Bottom Lock: 61¾
Rugby Wharf Arm: 64½
Stretton Stop: 70
HAWKESBURY JUNCTION (Coventry Canal): 77

Locks: 42

This was one of the earliest and for many years one of the most important canals in southern England. It was authorised in 1769, when the Coventry Canal was in the offing, and was intended to fetch coal southwards from the Warwickshire coalfield to Banbury and Oxford, at the same time giving access to the River Thames. James Brindley was appointed engineer; he built a winding contour canal 91 miles long that soon began to look thoroughly out-dated and inefficient for the carriage of goods. Brindley died in 1772, and was replaced by Samuel Simcock; he completed the line from Longford, where a junction was made with the Coventry Canal, to Banbury in 1778. After a long pause, the canal was finally brought into Oxford in 1790, and thereafter through-traffic flowed constantly along this important new trade route.

In 1800, however, the Grand Junction Canal opened (excepting the tunnel at Blisworth) from London to Braunston, and the Warwick & Napton and Warwick & Birmingham canals completed the new short route from London to Birmingham. This had the natural—and intended—effect of drawing traffic off the Oxford Canal, especially south of Napton Junction; but the Oxford company protected itself very effectively against this powerful opposition by charging outrageously high rates for their 5½-mile stretch between Braunston and Napton, which had become part of the new London–Birmingham through route. Thus the Ox-

ford maintained its revenue and very high dividends for many years to come.

By the late 1820s, however, the Oxford Canal had become conspicuously out of date with its extravagant winding course; and under the threat of various schemes for big new canals which, if built, would render the Oxford Canal almost redundant, the company decided to modernise the northern part of their navigation. Tremendous engineering works were therefore carried out that completely changed the face of the canal north of Braunston. Aqueducts, massive embankments and deep cuttings were built, carrying the canal in great sweeps through the countryside and cutting almost 14 miles off the original 36 miles between Braunston Junction and the Coventry Canal. Much of the old main line suddenly became a series of loops and branches leading nowhere and crossed by elegant new towpath bridges inscribed 'Horseley Ironworks 1828'. Now most of these old loops are abandoned and weeded up, although their twisting course can still be easily traced.

This very expensive programme was well worth while. Although toll rates, and thus revenue, began to fall because of keen competition from the railways, dividends were kept at a high level for years; indeed a respectable profit was still shown right through to the 20th century. Now, there is no trade on the canal—but this beautiful waterway has become one of the most popular canals in Britain for pleasure cruising, fishing and walking.

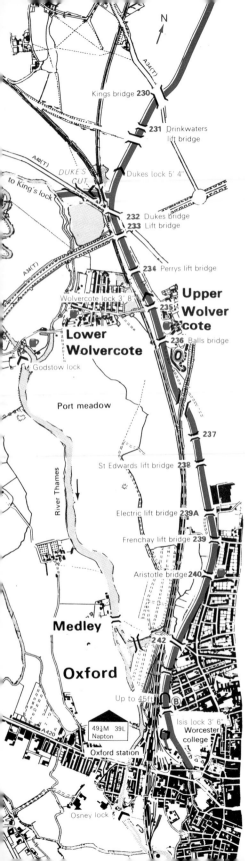

Oxford

The Oxford Canal can be reached from the
Thames in 2 places; one, via Duke's Cut, is
convenient but by-passes Oxford altogether;
the other, via a backwater under the north end
of Oxford station to the canal at Isis Lock, is
more enjoyable. A railway swing bridge here
was once a notorious obstruction, but this is
now left open. Past this bridge, boats continue
for 50yds along the backwater and should then
join the canal by turning sharp left up into Isis
Lock. The canal continues southwards for ¼
mile past Worcester College to its terminus near
Nuffield College. Isis Lock, with its pretty iron
turnover bridge, is wooded and secluded,
despite its nearness to the centre of Oxford.
The canal goes northwards, flanked by houses
to the east whose gardens run down to the
water. This is an attractive stretch of urban
canal. After passing several wharves the houses
give way to industry, while Port Meadow lies to
the west. At bridge 240 there is a P.O., stores
and off-licence, also swings for children. The
first of the typical Oxford Canal lift bridges
appears followed by an electric lift bridge,
opened by factory staff during work time, and
left open at other times. Beyond the railway
bridge is Wolvercote, where the canal starts the
long climb up to the Midlands. After a series of
main road bridges, carrying the A40 and the
A34, Duke's Cut branches off to the west to
join a back-water of the Thames, and the canal
moves into open country, leaving Oxford
behind. Those joining the River Thames from
the canal should obtain a copy of Nicholson's
'The Ordnance Survey Guide to the River
Thames'.

Wolvercote
Oxon. P.O. Tel. Stores, garage. Oxford spreads
north along the Woodstock and Banbury roads,
making Wolvercote inseparable from the city.
There is little of interest, although it is useful as
a supply centre, and there are swings for
children. The concrete footbridge that crosses
the canal and railway in one span is impressive.
Oxford
*Oxon. EC Thur, MD Wed. P.O. Tel. Stores,
garage, station, cinemas, theatres, university.*
Oxford was founded in the 10thC and has been
a university town since the 13thC. Its 39
colleges can be visited, but those noted here
have been selected as particularly
representative of their periods.
Merton College dates from 1264 and is one of
the earliest collegiate foundations that are
almost unrestored. Typical of the
Perpendicular and Decorative periods. The
Grove buildings are by Butterfield.
New College Founded by William of
Wykeham, Bishop of Winchester, in 1379. The
Perpendicular chapel was greatly restored by
Sir George Gilbert Scott in the 19thC.
Keble College Built by Butterfield in 1870
entirely in the Victorian Gothic style.
Sheldonian Theatre Broad St. Built by Sir
Christopher Wren in the 17thC under the
auspices of Gilbert Sheldon, Archbishop of
Canterbury, who disapproved of the annual
performances of plays in St Mary's Church.
University degrees are awarded here. It has an
attractive ceiling by Robert Streeter.
Ashmolean Museum Beaumont St.
Outstanding collection of Near Eastern and
European archaeology, the Farrer collection of
17th and 18thC silver, a display of early coins
and some drawings of Michelangelo and
Raphael. *Open weekdays and Sun afternoons.*
Christ Church Gallery Christ Church. Built by
Powell and Moya in 1967, it contains drawings
by Michelangelo, Veronese and Tintoretto, and
14th–18thC paintings, mainly Italian. *Open
afternoons.*
Museum of Modern Art Pembroke St. Gives
unusual art exhibitions—anything from
environment to architecture graphics and
photography. *Open Tue–Sat and Sun
afternoons.*

University Museum Parks Rd. A high Victorian Gothic building by Deane and Woodward. Natural history, including the head and claw of a dodo. *Open weekdays.*

Christ Church Meadows Approach from St Aldate's. A path leads down to the Thames, where the rowing eights are to be seen.

University Botanic Garden High St. Oldest botanic garden in Britain, founded by Henry Danvers, Earl of Danby. In the 17thC the garden was intended for the culture of medicinal plants, but today it fosters extensive collections of rare plants for research and teaching. The gateway is by Inigo Jones.

Information Bureau St Aldate's. (Oxford 48707).

BOATYARDS

Ⓑ **Black Prince Narrow Boats** Castle Mill Boatyard, Cardigan St, Oxford. (54043). Ⓡ Ⓢ Ⓔ Pump-out, gas, narrow boat hire, overnight mooring, maps. *Closed Wed and all winter.*

Ⓑ **College Cruisers** Combe Rd Wharf, Oxford. (Oxford 54343). Ⓡ Ⓦ Ⓓ Pump-out, narrow boat hire, repairs.

PUBS

🍺 **Red Lion** Wolvercote.

🍺 **White Hart** Wolvercote.

🍺 **Plough** Upper Wolvercote. Snacks, garden.

🍺✗ **Trout Inn** on the Thames, near Godstow Lock (10 mins walk from canal bridge 235). Dates from 12thC. *Meals served daily* (Oxford 54485).

🍺 **Gardeners Arms** Plantation Rd, Oxford. Children's room. ¼ mile east of bridge 242.

🍺 **The Fountain** Cardigan St, Oxford. 200yds east of bridge 242. Has antique juke-box and 'Aunt Sally' skittle game. It is worth the 1 mile walk from the terminus to visit.

🍺 **Turf Tavern** St Helen's Passage, New College Lane, Oxford. Hidden away. Excellent Stilton.

There are many other fine pubs, restaurants, wine bars and snack places in Oxford.

Oxford from the air. *Aerofilms*

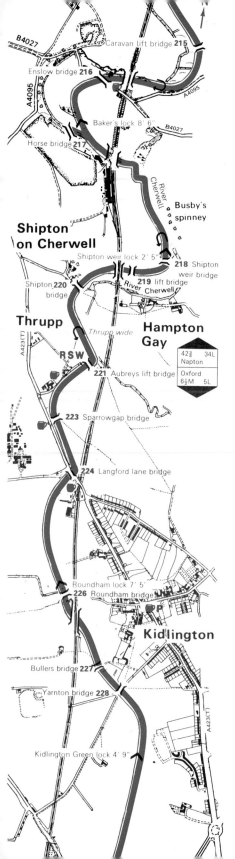

Kidlington

Continuing northwards the canal runs through
lightly wooded fields and meadows to
Kidlington, which is hidden from the canal by a
low cutting. Keeping Kidlington in the
distance, it then swings north east to join the
Cherwell valley at Thrupp. From Thrupp the
canal closely follows the Cherwell and adopts
the meandering characteristics of a contour
canal. Much of the canal is tree-lined, while its
shallow banks and close relationship with the
villages make it seem very river-like. At
Shipton Weir Lock, whose 1ft rise is made up
by its great width, the Cherwell and the canal
merge and share a common course for the next
mile (this stretch can be hazardous in times of
flood). The tall chimney at the quarry and
cement works on Bunker Hill dominate the
valley for several miles. The Cherwell swings
away west under an elegant iron bridge before
Baker's Lock, but soon returns to run parallel
to the canal. Wooded hills now determine the
course of the canal, which passes plenty of
villages and places of interest. Only Thrupp
yard and the moored maintenance boats, the
bridges and the occasional locks give away the
fact that this is a canal. The railway follows the
canal: the A423 crosses by Thrupp and the
A4095 by Bunker Hill. A delightful stretch of
rural canal.

Hampton Gay
Oxon. A deserted village. The church stands by
itself, overlooking the River Cherwell, it can
only be approached on foot, its seclusion and
peace rather disturbed by the railway that
almost runs through the churchyard. To the
east, half-hidden by trees, are the romantic
ruins of the manor: gaunt broken stone walls,
windows open to the sky. The whole is well
worth exploration, but is difficult to approach
owing to the presence of the River Cherwell.
Leave the canal at bridge 220 and walk east.
Shipton on Cherwell
Oxon. P.O. box. A magnificent situation: the
wooded church overlooks the bridge and the
canal, which curls round the foot of the church
yard. Behind, the grey stone manor and farm
look out over rolling fields to the west. The
well-concealed A423 does not intrude. Shipton
Bridge, ¼ mile to the east of the village, was
the scene of a railway disaster on Christmas Eve
1874. 9 carriages fell from the Bridge on to the
frozen canal below and 34 people were killed.
Blenheim Palace *Oxon.* 3 miles west of
Shipton, at Woodstock. The English Versailles,
built by Sir John Vanbrugh in 1722. Seat of the
Dukes of Marlborough and birthplace of Sir
Winston Churchill, who is buried in the nearby
village of Bladon. Grounds restyled by
Capability Brown include a large lake:
altogether a superb setting. Fine furniture,
paintings, tapestries. *Open daily. Mar–Oct.*
Thrupp
Oxon. P.O. box. Tel. A fine canal village,
terrace houses running along beside the
towpath, with a pub at one end and a BWB
yard at the other. The quality of the village
makes it an unusual survival of early canal
prosperity.
Kidlington
Oxon. P.O. Tel. Stores, garage, cinema. The
canal skirts round Kidlington, an extended
suburb of Oxford. Parts of an older village
survive to the north around the tall-spired
church, including Sir William Morton's 17thC
gabled almshouses. Nearby is the Oxford Air
Training School, one of only 20 such places in
the world training airline pilots. The town is
most easily reached from Bridge 228.

BOATYARDS
ⓑ **BWB Thrupp Yard** Kidlington. (Kidlington 2222). ⓇⓈⓌ Moorings.

BOAT TRIPS
Oxford Canal Trips 2½-hr trips at weekends from the Rock of Gibraltar, bridge 216. Details Freeland 881339.

PUBS
🍺 **Rock of Gibraltar** Canalside, at bridge 216. Food, garden with children's amusements. P.O. box.
🍺 **Boat** Thrupp. Canalside. Food.
🍺 **Jolly Boatman** Thrupp, by bridge 223. Canalside. Food.
🍺 **Wise Alderman** Kidlington. Canalside, by bridge 224. Lunchtime food.

Isis Lock, with it's pretty iron turnover bridge. *David Perrott*

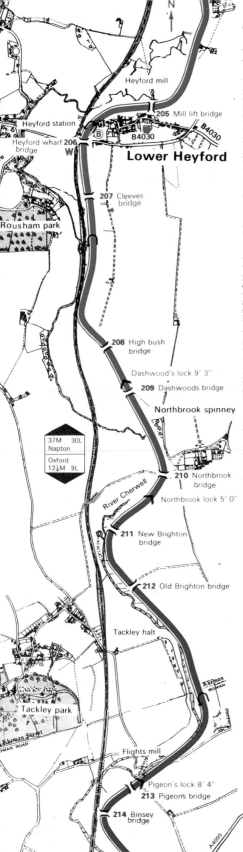

Lower Heyford

The canal continues to follow the Cherwell, winding its way through wooded undulating scenery. The canal does not intrude at all, in fact it is so well landscaped as to be often invisible from the hills on either side. At first the woods are thick, the over-hanging trees forming a tunnel through which the canal passes, bounded by old stone walls. Pigeon's Lock marks the centre of the woods, which gradually diminish to reveal rolling farmland to the east and the water-meadows of the Cherwell to the west. The canal passes over the route of Akeman Street, and then the trees and the isolation return to conceal the canal from the grounds of Rousham House. As it reaches Lower Heyford the landscape opens out. The locks continue the rise towards Claydon. Kirtlington and Tackley are set up on ridges away from the canal, but Lower Heyford actually reaches its banks. Here the wharf with its clapboarded warehouses and old crane is now a hire boat base. The railway follows the canal very closely: Heyford station is very convenient. The B4030 crosses here.

Lower Heyford
Oxon. P.O. Tel. Stores, station. Built among woods along the south bank of the Cherwell, and hence the canal. The church, with fine stained glass, overlooks the canal from a slight hill that conceals many of the cottages in a village where motor cars still seem intruders. To the north is a fine and very ancient water mill, screened by a line of willow trees that lead up to an unusual iron lift bridge, believed to be the only iron drawbridge in England.

Rousham House Steeple Aston. A lively picture of fighting during the Civil War is conjured up by the shooting holes made in the doors, which are preserved from the time when a Royalist garrison used the house. It dates from 1635, and was enlarged and its gardens landscaped in 1730 by William Kent. *Open Wed, Sun & B. Hol afternoons, Apr–Sep,. Gardens open daily.*

Northbrook Bridge The stone canal bridge adjoins a much earlier packhorse bridge that crosses the Cherwell to the east. Although stylistically different, the marriage is very striking, as both are the same rich golden colour; and the setting in Northbrook Spinney is delightful.

Tackley
Oxon. 1 mile north west of Pigeon's Lock across the Cherwell. (Access from the canal is by the footpath and a bridge leading from Pigeon's Lock. It is a pleasant walk). A residential stone village, spreading down towards the canal to include Nethercott where there is a small station, Tackley Halt. The church, set on a hill to the south, contains fine monuments.

Kirtlington
Oxon. 1 mile east of Pigeons Lock. *P.O. Tel. Stores, garage.* Stone village laid out around a green. To the east is Akeman Street, a Roman road that flanks the wooded grounds of Kirtlington park.

BOATYARDS

Ⓑ **Black Prince Narrow Boats** Canal Wharf, Lower Heyford. (Steeple Aston 40348). R S W D E Pump-out, narrow boat hire, gas, dry dock, boat building and repairs, chandlery, toilets, provisions.

PUBS

Red Lion Steeple Aston. Follow the path north from bridge 205. Food.
Bell 21 Market Square, Lower Heyford. Food, bar billiards. Picturesque 16thC inn.
Dashwood Arms Kirtlington. Food.
Gardiners Arms Tackley. Food.
Kings Arms Tackley. Food.
Oxford Arms Kirtlington. Food (hot dinners).

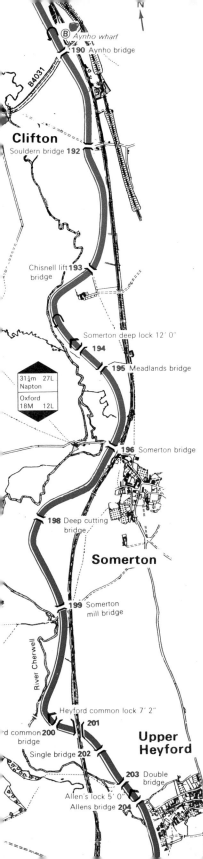

Somerton

Continuing north along the Cherwell valley, the canal wanders through water-meadows, the high towpath hedge often obscuring the fine views across the valley. As it curves towards Somerton the canal enters a short cutting and then moves out into open pastureland. Somerton climbs up the hillside to the east, altogether a very attractive situation. Throughout this stretch the canal is isolated in the middle of the landscape, the locks are generally remote, and set among trees, a pattern only broken at Heyford Common Lock. However, the open country continues after Somerton Deep Lock, and the canal pursues a straighter course towards Banbury. After Somerton two railways run side by side to the east of the canal, before joining at Aynho.

Aynho
Northants. EC Tue. P.O. Tel. Stores. The village is 1 mile east of Aynho Wharf, but must be seen. A self-contained village square sheltered from the road, very unchanged, very complete in rich stone. New houses have been carefully blended with the old. Note the peach trees that have been trained along the walls of many of the cottages. On the other side of the road is the formal classical façade of Aynho Park, a 17thC mansion rebuilt by Sir John Soane in the late 18thC. The house is large but restrained, and does not look out of the place in a village street. Fine paintings, furniture and Venetian glass. *Open Wed & Thur, afternoons May–Sep.* The church, beside the house was classicised at the same time: the strange façade added to the nave wall makes it a charming folly.

Clifton
Oxon. P.O. Tel. Stores. Small village overlooking the canal, more convenient for supplies than Aynho as it is nearer, but not as interesting in itself.

Somerton
Oxon. Tel. A straggling grey stone village winding up the hill to the east of the canal. On the highest point is the church with its decorated tower: there are good 16thC tombs inside. In all the villages along the Cherwell valley the churches are placed on mounds or higher ground, overlooking the valley.

Upper Heyford
Oxon. P.O. Tel. Store. A main street of thatched stone cottages falls steeply to the canal, with views across the valley to Steeple Aston. The general store is charmingly placed in the old nonconformist chapel. The huge USAF Heyford airfield, to the east, makes its presence felt. F-111's fly from here.

BOATYARDS
Ⓑ **Anglo Welsh Narrow Boats** Aynho Wharf, Banbury. (Deddington 38483). R S W D E Pump-out, narrow boat hire, gas, boat and engine repairs, mooring, toilets, provisions, canal shop. *Facilities available Mon–Fri.*

PUBS
🍺 **Great Western Arms** Aynho Wharf. Canalside. Food.
🍺✕ **Cartwright Arms Hotel** Aynho. Food.
🍺 **Duke of Cumberland's Head** Clifton. Food.
🍺 **Barley Mow** Upper Heyford. Food.

170 Haynes lift bridge

N

171 Foxes lift bridge

172 Nadkey bridge

Grant's lock 9' 6"
174 Grants bridge

Stevens lift bridge 175

Stevens lift 176 bridge

Twyford bridge 177

Twyford mill

River Cherwell

P

Tarvers bridge 179

King's Sutton lock 10' 8"

Scroobys lift bridge 181

Coles lift bridge 182

Kings Sutton station

King's Sutton

183 Coles lift bridge

A41(T)

A422

Haddons lift 186 bridge

Nell bridge lock 8' 8"

Nell bridge 187

27¾M 25L
Napton

Oxford
21½M 14L

Weir bridge 188

Aynho weir lock 1' 0"

Belchers 189 lift bridge

Aynho

King's Sutton

The canal continues through wooded open country with a background of hills to the east. The Cherwell crosses the canal at Aynho Weir Lock before continuing parallel to it and forming a large loop lined by trees as it approaches King's Sutton. Then the tall spire of the church comes into view. Locks continue the rise to Banbury: the very narrow Nell Bridge, where the A41 crosses the canal, is one of the oldest, having survived the various road-widening schemes. The railway follows the canal to the east. This pleasant rural stretch of the canal along the Cherwell valley is well punctuated by the characteristic wooden lift bridges: luckily most of these are nowadays left open (raised).

King's Sutton
Northants. P.O. Tel. Stores, garage, station. An attractive village of narrow streets that wander in every direction. The centre is round a green, at the top of a hill, where rows of thatched cottages, 2 pubs and the church stand in quiet harmony. The church is superb: beautifully proportioned with a tall, slender spire. The River Cherwell makes access to this village difficult from the canal; the only practicable access is by walking south east for 1½ miles from bridge 177.
Adderbury
Oxon. On the A41, west of bridge 177. Thatched cottages, an old yew tree and a graceful lychgate provide a fitting background to the Decorated and Perpendicular-style church, which is one of the finest in the country. Its 600-year-old spire is one of the well-known 3 that stand in line across the landscape in full view of the Oxford road.
Nell Bridge Farm By bridge 186. Eggs and milk.

PUBS
- **Bell** The Square, Kings Sutton. Food.
- **Butcher's Arms** Kings Sutton. Food.
- **Three Tuns** King's Sutton. Food.
- **White Horse** King's Sutton. Food.

Banbury

Continuing north west along the Cherwell valley the canal enters Banbury through housing estates and industrial area. North of Banbury the factories continue but gradually give way on the east to open fields. Your nose may tell you there is a General Foods Company factory west of bridge 162. To the west a main road follows the canal, accompanied by power lines and disused railways. Hardwick Lock marks the end of Banbury and the resumption of the more typical Oxford countryside. The canal swings north east and hills rise on the west. Locks continue the steady rise throughout this stretch; north of here all the locks feature double bottom gates, which make for lighter work. The railway follows the canal but crosses to the west after Banbury. The A422 crosses at Banbury.

Little Bourton
Oxon. ½ mile west of bridge 158. *P.O. box, Tel. Garage.* Quiet residential village to the west of the beautifully kept Little Bourton Lock and cottage. Stores in Great Bourton. 1 mile north.

Banbury
Oxon. EC Tue. MD Thur/Sat. P.O. Tel. Stores, garage, cinema, station. The view of Banbury from the canal is not really fair to the town; it is far more attractive than the dismal industry and housing estates imply. Originally a wool town, the castle was pulled down by Cromwell's forces in 1646 and no trace remains. The ancient cross of nursery rhyme fame in the town centre was pulled down in 1602, and the present cross is a 19thC replica. The church was built in 1793 by S. P. Cockrell. The original bake house, which produced the spiced Banbury cakes, was demolished in 1968. Unfortunately the undesirable section of the community tend to congregate by the canal, so navigators are advised to pass through with caution and not to linger.

Museum & Globe Room Marlborough Rd. Items of local interest.

Chacombe Priory Chacombe, Oxon. 2½ miles north east of Banbury, off B4036. The house dates mainly from 1600, although there is a 13thC chapel with fine early stained glass. Picture gallery, furniture and silver. *Open Sun and B. Hols Apr, May, Sep. Sat and Sun afternoons Jun, Aug.*

Broughton Castle Broughton, Oxon. 3 miles south west of Banbury, on B4035. Mainly moated Tudor castle with fine period fireplaces, ceilings and panelling. Collection of Civil War relics. *Open Wed, Sun, B. Hols afternoons Apr–Sep.*

Sulgrave Manor Sulgrave. 8 miles north east of Banbury. Small Elizabethan manor house completed in 1560 by Lawrence, direct ancestor of George Washington. The design of the American flag is reputed to come from the arms, consisting of 3 stars and 2 stripes, which are found in the main doorway. Contemporary furniture, portraits and personal possessions of George Washington. The Great Kitchen contains a range of impressive antique equipment. *Open daily (except Wed).*

BOATYARDS
Ⓑ **H. Tooley** Canalside by bridge 164. Builder and repairer of traditional wooden narrow boats. Drydock. Ⓓ.

Banbury Boatyard Services Old Corporation Wharf, Mill Lane, Banbury. (68539). Narrow boat builders and fitters, steel and wood. Engines supplied or serviced. Repairs and chandlery.

PUBS
🍺 **Bell Inn** Great Bourton. 1¼ miles west of bridge 153.
🍺 **Swan Inn** Great Bourton.
🍺 **Ye Olde Reindeer Inn** Parson St, Banbury. Dates from 1570.
🍺 **Wine Vaults** Parson St, Banbury. 300 years old.
🍺 **Wheatsheaf** George St, Banbury.
🍺 **Coach & Horses** Butchers' Row, Banbury.
🍺 **Plough** Little Bourton. Food.
🍺 **Bear** Market Place, Banbury. Food.

39 Reservoir bridge

Wormleighton reservoir

141 Boundary lift bridge

142 Feeder bridge

N

143 Hay bridge

N

Glebe farm

Claydon top **144** bridge
Claydon top lock

Claydon

Claydon locks 30' 6"

145 Claydon middle bridge
R

Claydon bottom lock
Claydon**146** bottom bridge

147

Forge farm

Elkington's lock 6' 5"

148 Elkingtons bridge

Varneys bridge **149**

Varney's lock 5' 10"

Broadmoor lock 7' 3"
Broadmoor bridge **150**

16¾M   17L
Napton

Oxford
32½M   22L

Prescote manor

Cropredy **152** Cropredy lock bridge
wharf**153** Cropredy lock 5' 6"
bridge

Cropredy

RSW

Cropredy bridge
battlefield 1644

Cropredy

Continuing north along the Cherwell valley the canal enters Cropredy, whose stone cottages and wharf have been visible for some time. The village flanks the canal on the west bank, and all services are beside Cropredy Bridge. After the village the high towpath hedge conceals the open fields beyond, although there are views across the valley to the west. Milk, eggs and sometimes, vegetables can be bought at Forge Farm. Around here the old ridge and furrow field patterns are very pronounced. Claydon comes into sight—here 5 locks take the canal to the summit level. Light woods border the canal, which is both shallow and very narrow in places. Near the second lock the remains of old stabling for boat horses can be seen; after the locks the canal twists and turns, swinging north west towards Fenny Compton. Hills and trees close in, preparing for the cutting that marks the course of the old tunnel. The feeder from Boddington reservoir, 2½ miles to the east, enters the canal through the tow path bridge 142. The railway, which moved to the west after Cropredy, reappears beside the canal. Bridge 141 is the last that the north-bound traveller sees of the very attractive wooden lift bridges that are such a well known feature of this canal. Much of the towpath is impassable on this section.

Claydon
Oxon. P.O. Tel. Stores. Set in a rolling open landscape to the west of the canal. Claydon is an old-fashioned brown stone village; in spite of some new development it preserves a quiet unpretentious charm. The curiously irregular church of St James the Great provides a focal point—parts of it date from before the 12thC and the tower, which has a saddle back roof, contains a clock. There is no face, but the hour is chimed. Opposite is the pub. Clattercote Priory, just to the south, still remains.
The Granary Museum Claydon. Andrew Fox's fascinating museum of local relics continues to grow and never fails to entrance visitors. Children love to handle the objects, and his recreation of a 19thC cottage kitchen is remarkably atmospheric. Admission is free, but there is a well stocked gift shop which invites spending.
Cropredy
Oxon. P.O. Tel. Stores, garage. Quiet village of wandering streets of old brick houses. There is no real centre, but the whole village is very close to the canal, especially the garage and stores. The stately sandstone church contains fine woodwork; the slow swing of the clock pendulum in the belfry seems to echo the sleepy nature of the village. Prescote Manor is now a craft centre *open Wed–Sun from Easter to Christmas.* Buttery.
Battle of Cropredy 29 June 1644. Cromwell's forces under Waller attacked Cropredy Bridge in an attempt to open a way to Oxford. Despite greatly inferior numbers the Royalist cavalry managed to scatter Waller's army and capture his artillery, thus protecting Oxford. A plaque on the river bridge recalls the battle.

BOATYARDS
Ⓑ **Cropredy Wharf** Cropredy. (215). Tea and coffee in the Barn Tea Rooms, gifts and crafts in the Stable. Children's play area. Also Ⓦ Ⓓ Ⓔ Pump-out, gas, long term mooring, winter storage, overnight mooring, books and maps, boat and engine repairs. Provisions at The Bridge Stores, an excellent general store and off-licence close by. Ⓔ at Cropredy Lock.
Bob Thacker Coal Wharf, Cropredy (661). Ⓔ

PUBS
🍺 **Brasenose Inn** Cropredy. Flagstone floors and low ceilings in the bar. Bass and M & B Springfield real ales, and Westons draught cider. Garden, food (*not Sun*).
🍺 **Red Lion** Cropredy (near bridge 152). 15thC pub serving Manns real ale. Dining room and bar food (*not winter Sun*).
🍺 **Sunrising** Claydon. Handsome village pub with cosy bar and fine fireplace. Hook Norton real ale, food, garden.

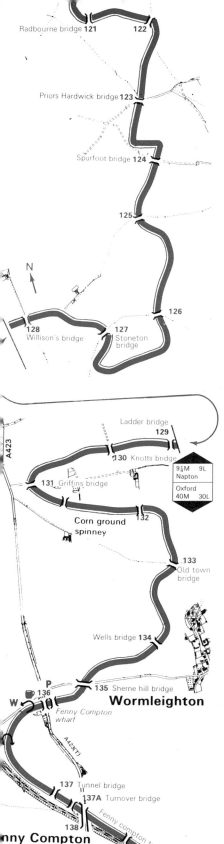

Fenny Compton

The canal continues along the Fenny Compton
'tunnel', a steep, thickly-wooded cutting which
ends as it swings in a wide loop eastwards
towards Fenny Compton Wharf. The hills
retreat for a while, although their influence is
still present in the extravagantly indirect course
taken by the canal: Brindley seems to have had
a horror of straight lines. The long winding
route involves a large number of brick arch
accommodation bridges and many are now
un-numbered—it is easy to become
disorientated here. The canal first runs west
before doubling back on itself and running east
to Stoneton Manor, where a steep ridge causes
it to resume a north-westerly direction towards
Napton. Fenny Compton and Wormleighton
are both about a mile from the canal; Priors
Hardwick is nearer, across the fields, but has no
supplies. The railway disappears to the west
after Fenny Compton Wharf; the A423 crosses
twice by Fenny Compton. Much of the tow
path is non-existent—where it has not eroded
away it is completely overgrown with brambles,
hawthorn, great willow-herb and
meadow-sweet.

Priors Hardwick
Warwicks. East of bridge 124. P.O. Tel.
Approachable from the canal by a footpath (all
gates along the way must be left closed). A
small, partly deserted village much of which
was pulled down by Cistercian monks in the
14thC. The squat stone church is partly 13thC
while the little cottage opposite the former
school looks as if it were straight out of a
picture book.

Wormleighton
Warwicks. P.O. Tel. A manorial village that
still retains a feeling of privacy. Its 13thC
brown stone church contains a Perpendicular
screen and Jacobean woodwork. Further up the
road from the canal (leave at bridge 135) is the
early 16thC brick manor house that must once
have been very impressive. South of the house
is a grand stone gatehouse dated 1613. A row of
Victorian mock-Tudor cottages completes the
village, which is well worth a visit for its feeling
of unity and self-reliance.

Fenny Compton
Warwicks. P.O. Tel. Stores, garage. 1 mile west
of the wharf. A scattered brown stone village,
whose attractiveness is rather marred by a large
housing estate near the canal. The church is
partly 14thC and partly Victorian, with a
curious offset tower; alongside is a fine brick
rectory of 1707. Most of the village follows the
road, which forms a central square containing
the most interesting buildings and shops. All
the houses are graced by well-laid out gardens.
Fenny Compton tunnel is no more, having been
converted into a cutting in 1868.

BOATYARDS

Ⓑ **Fenny Marine** Station Fields, Fenny
Compton, Warwicks. (Fenny Compton 461/2).
Large marina. Ⓡ Ⓢ Ⓦ Ⓟ Ⓓ Ⓔ Moorings, gas,
chandlery, provisions, pump-out, lavatories,
slipway, winter storage (hard standing).
Manufacturers of steel narrow boats and 20ft
fibreglass boats. *Closed winter weekends.*
Ⓑ **The Boat Breakdowns Co** Fenny Compton
Marina (Fenny Compton 588). 24-hr
breakdown service, workshop, dry dock.

PUBS

Ⓟ✕ **Butchers Arms** Priors Hardwick. Food.
Ⓟ✕ **George & Dragon** Fenny Compton
Wharf. Canalside. Food. Ⓦ Exotic birds in
garden.
Ⓟ **Merrie Lion** Fenny Compton.

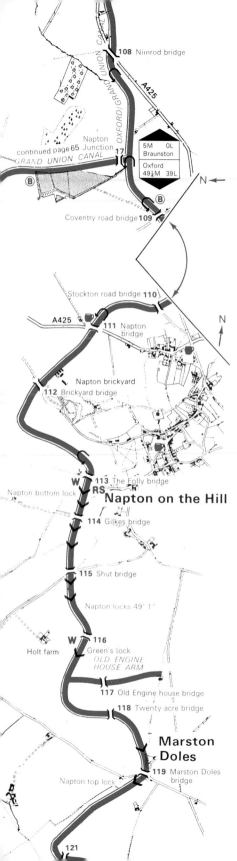

Napton

The canal continues northwards through
rolling open farmland, the view to the west
concealed by the towpath hedge. At Marston
Doles the country opens out and the windmill
on top of Napton Hill comes into view. Here
the summit level ends and the canal starts the
fall towards the junction that continues through
this heavily-locked section. The arm to the east,
now used for private moorings, leads to the site
of the former pump house. The canal swings to
the west of Napton Hill, passing Brickyard
Bridge and then turns east to meet the Grand
Union at the junction. Marston Doles is a
typical canal settlement, but Napton is set to
the east on the side of the hill. This is a very
quiet section, although the A425 crosses below
Napton. There are moorings available at
Napton Bottom Lock, and a canal shop for
provisions in the lock house.

Napton-on-the-Hill
Warwicks. P.O. Tel. Stores, garage. Rising to
over 400ft, Napton Hill dominates the
immediate landscape. The village is scattered
all over the hill, climbing steeply up the sides.
The shops and pubs are at the bottom,
however, and so only those wishing to enjoy the
view or visit the 13thC church need climb to the
top. Near the church is the restored windmill
alone on the hilltop. The canal wanders round
the base of the hill, by-passing the village
except for the wharf alongside Brickyard
Bridge.
Holt Farm Between Marston Doles and
Napton by Green's Lock. (Southam 2225).
Farm shop, souvenirs, off-licence and moorings
open daily until 19.30..
Marston Doles
Warwicks. Tel. Tiny settlement that owes its
existence to the canal. Towing horses used to be
stabled here. To the north, at the end of an
arm, are the remains of the pumping house that
used to pump water up to the summit from the
bottom of the Napton flight.

BOATYARDS

Ⓑ **Calcutt Boats** Calcutt Top Lock (on the
Grand Union). (Southam 3757). Ⓢ Ⓦ Ⓓ
Pump-out, gas, slipway, narrow boat hire and
building, repairs, mooring, chandlery, toilets
and provisions. Charter and hotel boats.
Ⓑ **Gordons Pleasure Cruisers** Napton
Marina, Stockton. (Southam 3644). Ⓡ Ⓢ Ⓦ Ⓓ
Pump-out, gas, showers, slipway, wet dock,
provisions, chandlery. Narrow boat hire,
building and repair.

PUBS

🍺✕ **Kings Head Inn** 200 yds south of bridge
109. (Southam 2202). Ind Coope real ale, food,
games room, garden.
🍺✕ **Napton Bridge Inn** Napton. Canalside at
bridge 111. (Southam 2466). A justly famous
pub serving Davenports real ale and food at the
bar or in the restaurant. Large garden with
swings.
🍺 **Crown** Napton. ½ mile east of bridge 113,
with PO and stores nearby. An excellent village
local with an airy lounge and a lively public bar.
Manns real ale, food lunchtime and evenings,
cheese skittles, garden and games room. A large
horse chestnut tree provides a shady drinking
area on the green.
🍺 **Hollybush** Priors Marston. 1½ miles east of
bridge 119. Fine 15thC inn serving Marstons
real ale along with guest beers. Garden, food.
Priors Marston stores (Byfield 60900) will
deliver to your boat.

Napton Locks. *Derek Pratt*

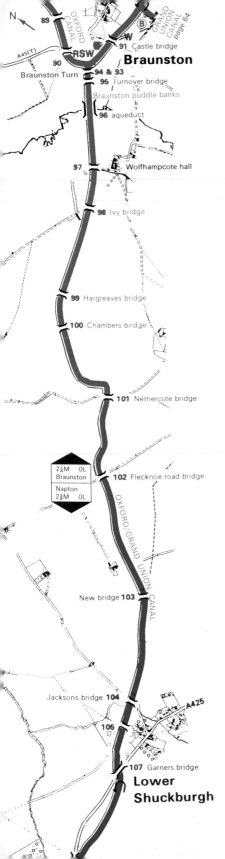

Braunston

Leaving Napton, the canal runs north east
towards Braunston Turn. This stretch of the
Oxford Canal was used jointly by the Grand
Junction Company, and as a result the Oxford
charged excessive toll rates in an attempt to get
even with their rival, whose more direct route
to London had attracted most of the traffic.
Flowing through open country with a
background of hills to the south, the canal is
quiet and empty after the activity around
Napton. The land is agricultural, with few
houses in sight: the surviving medieval ridge
and furrow field system on the south bank
reveals the age of the landscape. Note how the
canal cuts across the system at right angles.
There are no locks, no villages and few bridges:
a very pleasant rural stretch of canal. The A425
crosses through Lower Shuckburgh and the
A45 in Braunston. The Oxford Canal bears off
to the north at Braunston Turn: the Grand
Union goes off to the south east at this point,
passing through the canal centre of Braunston.
Boaters will find everything they are likely to
need here. There are good temporary moorings
either side of bridge 91.

Lower Shuckburgh
Warwick. P.O. box. A tiny village along the
main road. The church, built 1864, is attractive
in a Victorian way, with great use of contrasting
brickwork inside. The farm, west of bridge
104, sells eggs.

BOATYARDS
ⓑ **Ladyline Braunston Marina** On Grand
Union beyond bridge 91. (Rugby 890325).
Ⓡ Ⓢ Ⓦ Ⓟ Ⓓ Moorings, chandlery, boat sales
and repairs, gas, toilets, showers.
ⓑ **Braunston Boats** Just beyond Ladyline on
the Grand Union. (Rugby 891079). Ⓦ Ⓓ
Pump-out, gas, slipway, chandlery, boat
building and repair, narrow boat hire.

The Boat Shop Crafts and gifts on board a boat
moored at Braunston Turn. (Rugby 891037).

PUBS
🍺✗ **The Boatman** Braunston. Once the Rose
and Castle, now a comfortable and friendly
modern hotel/restaurant/pub. Watney and
Manns real ale, bar meals (vast helpings) and
candlelit dinners. Children's room, canalside
garden with swings, good overnight mooring
for patrons.
🍺 **The Old Plough** Braunston. Imposing
17thC pub serving Ansells real ale. Children's
room, bar food and garden.

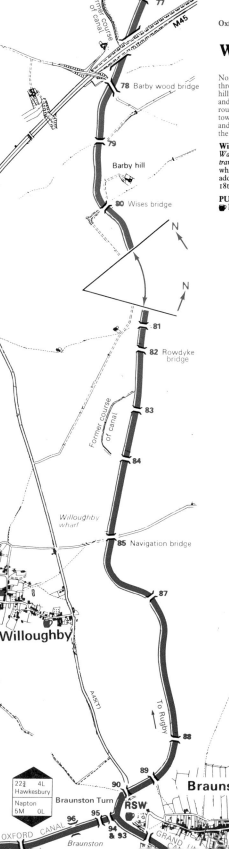

Willoughby

North west from Braunston the canal runs
through wide open country, backed by bare
hills to the east. At bridge 87 the medieval ridge
and furrow patterns are in evidence. Skirting
round Barby Hill, the canal swings north east
towards Hillmorton and Rugby. The railway
and the A45 run to the west of the canal, and
the M45 crosses after Barby Hill.

Willoughby
*Warwicks. P.O. Tel. Stores, garage (and
transport café).* Mellow red brick village to
which new buildings have been unobtrusively
added. The small church is dominated by a fine
18thC rectory. Excellent home bakery.

PUBS
🍺 **Rose Inn** Willoughby.

Map labels:

Rugby station

Rugby

CLIFTON ARM (disused)

66 Clifton bridge

B5414

Golf course

68

69 Clifton double bridge

Hillmorton

15½M 1L
Hawkesbury

Braunston
7½M 3L

BWB Hillmorton workshops

70
W
71 Granthams bridge

Hillmorton locks 18' 7"

72 Moors bridge

N

A428

73 Crick road bridge

Wharf farm

74 Tarrys bridge

B4038

75

76 Normans bridge to Barby

77 M45 motorway

Oxford   **146**

Hillmorton

After turning north east for 2 miles, the canal swings in a wide arc round Rugby. To the east the radio masts dominate the landscape. The canal descends Hillmorton locks, 3 paired narrow locks, (not often found), which fill and empty very quickly, are well maintained and a pleasure to use, and passes the attractively sited BWB maintenance yard and hire craft base. There is an excellent all purpose grocers shop at bridge 71. The railway accompanies the canal through Hillmorton and the A428 crosses south of the town. The little brick footbridge at the bottom locks is a delight to the eye.

Hillmorton
Warwicks. P.O. Tel. Stores, garage. Its church dates from c1300, but there have been additions as late as the 18thC. There is an interesting medieval cross in the centre of the village, but the independence this implies has long since been swallowed up by Rugby.

BOATYARDS
Ⓑ **Clifton Cruisers** Clifton Wharf, Vicarage Hill, Rugby. (Rugby 3570). Ⓡ Ⓢ Ⓦ Ⓓ Pump-out, gas, boat hire, repairs, toilets. *Phone first in winter.*
Ⓑ **BWB Hillmorton Locks** Hillmorton. (Rugby 73149). Ⓡ Ⓢ Ⓦ Ⓓ emergency only). Pump-out, gas, mooring, toilets, dry dock, hire craft. *Facilities Mon–Fri.*
Ⓑ **Rugby Boatbuilders** (Inland Marine Leisure) Hillmorton Wharf, Crick Road, Rugby. (Rugby 4438). Ⓢ Ⓦ Ⓓ Steel narrow boats built, repaired or fitted out. Engines overhauled. Pump-out, narrow boat hire, gas, dry dock, mooring, chandlery, toilets, gift shop. *Closed winter weekends.*

PUBS
🍺 **Stag & Pheasant** Hillmorton. Food.
🍺 **Old Royal Oak** Canalside at bridge 73. Handsome tall brick pub with a very tidy garden.
🍺 **Arnold Arms** Barby (1¼ miles south of bridge 76). Food.

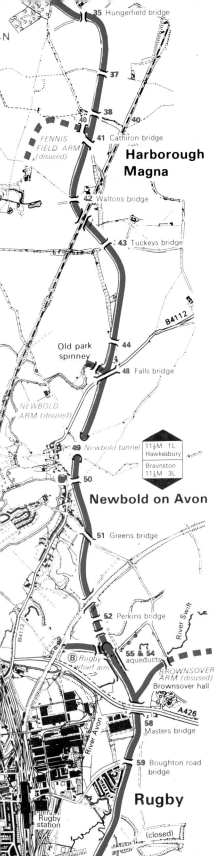

Rugby

Continuing the swing round Rugby, the canal
enters a side cut embankment whose tall
towpath hedge hides the town from view.
There are shops to the south of bridge 59 and a
picnic area below bridge 58. The River Avon is
crossed by an aqueduct, and the Rugby Arm
branches to the west; there is a boatyard on the
arm. A short open stretch and then another
deep cutting take the canal to Newbold, where
the short tunnel and thickly-wooded cutting
lead the canal into open countryside. The iron
bridges over the various arms reveal the course
of the old canal. The B4112 accompanies it
through Newbold.

Harborough Magna
Warwicks. P.O. Tel. Stores. Quiet red brick
village 1 mile to the north of the canal from
bridges 43 or 48. The 14thC church has many
Victorian additions, including an interesting
stained glass window.
Newbold-on-Avon
*Warwicks. P.O. Tel. Stores, garage, fish and
chips, launderette.* A pleasant village with an
interesting 15thC church and attractive
cottages. At the wharf near the tunnel mouth
are 2 pubs right next door to each other: why
not try both?
Newbold Tunnel This 250yd-long tunnel was
built during the shortening of the Oxford Canal
in the 1820s. The old route was at right angles
to the new, and the old tunnel mouth can be
seen from the south by Newbold Church. The
new tunnel was cut wide enough to allow for a
towpath on both sides, a luxury at that date.
Rugby
*Warwicks. EC Wed. MD Mon/Sat. P.O. Tel.
Stores, garage, station, cinema, theatre.* Famous
for Rugby school where Rugby football was
first played. St Andrew's parish church dates
from the 13thC, but was almost completely
rebuilt by Butterfield in 1877–79. The town
was important for its agriculture for over 600
years and then grew as a railway town, but
today heavy electrical industries flourish and
determine the character of the area.
Library Exhibition Gallery & Museum St
Matthew St. Regular loan exhibitions by local
societies and occasional exhibitions of the
borough's collections of modern art, which
include Paul Nash and Graham Sutherland.
The museum contains agricultural by-gones.
Open daily.

BOATYARDS

T.F. Yates East End of Newbold Tunnel.
(Rugby 845948). E
(B) **Willow Wren Hire Cruisers** Rugby Wharf,
off Consul Rd, Leicester Rd, Rugby. (Rugby
62183). R S W P D Pump-out, boat hire, gas,
boat building and repairs. toilets. Hotel boats.
Closed Sun.

PUBS

Golden Lion Harborough Magna. Food.
Boat Newbold Wharf. Canalside. Food,
skittles.
Barley Mow Newbold Wharf. Canalside.
Food, skittles, children's room.
Three Horseshoes Hotel Sheep St.
Rugby. Food.

Brinklow

Continuing north west, the canal runs through fine farming land and passes All Oaks Wood, where good moorings have been provided. By Brinklow the canal passes over an embankment, which was originally an aqueduct, the arches have long been filled in. Brinklow Arm, to the west, is unnavigable. The long embankment continues through Stretton stop and past Stretton Arm, used for mooring. Open, rolling fields follow, and then the canal enters a deep cutting spanned by the new motorway. The M6 cuts through this stretch, and has greatly altered the landscape. The elegant iron bridges that occur periodically mark the course of the old Oxford Canal, prior to the 1829 shortening. The railway follows the canal to the east. The A4114 crosses through Brinklow.

Brinklow
Warwicks. P.O. Tel. Stores, garage. A spacious pre-industrial village built along a wide main street, the A4114. The church is alongside the earthworks that mark the site of the castle built to defend the Fosse Way, and is unusual in having a distinctly sloping floor.

BOATYARDS
Ⓑ **Rose Narrowboats** Brinklow Marina, Stretton Stop. (Rugby 832449) Ⓡ Ⓦ Ⓟ Ⓓ Pump-out, gas, moorings, repairs, narrow boat hire, chandlery, provisions. Pottery made adjacent to the boatyard.

PUBS
🍺 **Railway Inn** Stretton Stop. Canalside. Food.
🍺 **White Lion** Brinklow. Food.
🍺 **Bull's Head** Brinklow. Food.
🍺 **Raven** Brinklow. Food.

20 aqueduct

OLD OXFORD CANAL

24 Nettlehill bridge

M6

Colehurst farm

26 Grimes bridge

27 Johnsons bridge

Stretton under Fosse

Smeeton lane aqueduct 28

Stretton wharf

Ⓑ Stretton stop

Fosse way

7¼M 1L Hawkesbury

Braunston 15½M 3L

Stretton road bridge 30

A427

31 aqueduct

Brinklow arches

32

BRINKLOW ARM (disused)

Brinklow

34 Easenhall lane bridge

Hungerfield farm

35 Hungerfield bridge

All oaks wood

37

Hawkesbury Junction

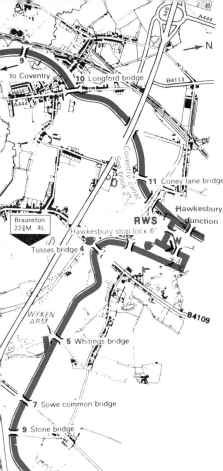

Continuing north west, the canal leaves the
cutting and crosses a long embankment, which
is shared by the railway. The open landscape
continues to Ansty, although the motorway is
never far away. After the village the first signs
of Coventry appear, with views of pylons and
housing estates. The new Wyken Colliery Arm
leaves to the west: it was built to replace the old
one eaten up by the motorway which comes
alongside the canal at this point. Sharp bends
then lead to the stop lock before Hawkesbury
Junction, the end of the Oxford Canal where it
joins the Coventry. The last stretch of the
Oxford is characterised by the 1820s
shortenings, the straight cuttings and
embankments obviously date from this period,
while the cast iron bridges mark the old route.
The railway turns away before Ansty.

Ansty
Warwicks. P.O. Tel. Stores, garage. Tiny village
that grew up along the canal, now disturbed by
the A46. To the north are the church and Hall
together, the Hall is mostly 18thC. This area
has been much altered by motorway
construction. Ansty Stores is extremely useful,
and runs a taxi service also.
Shilton
Warwicks. ½ mile north of bridge 17. *P.O. Tel.
Stores, garage.* Main road village left bewildered
by the railway and the A46.

PUBS

🍺 **Greyhound** Hawkesbury Junction.
Canalside. Food.
🍺 **Elephant and Castle** Canalside. By bridge 4.
M & B beers, food. Fishing tackle opposite.
🍺 **Crown** Ansty. Food.
🍺 **Crown** Shilton. Food.

The clock tower at Stourport. *David Perrott*

GLOUCESTER & SHARPNESS RIVER SEVERN

GLOUCESTER & SHARPNESS CANAL

Maximum dimensions

Length: 240'
Beam: 30'
Headroom: unlimited

Mileage

SHARPNESS Lock to
Purton: 2¼
Saul Junction: 8¾
GLOUCESTER Lock: 16¾

Locks: 2

RIVER SEVERN

Maximum dimensions

Gloucester to Worcester
Length: 135'
Beam: 21'
Headroom: 24' 6"
Worcester to Stourport
Length: 90'
Beam: 19'
Headroom: 20'

Mileage

GLOUCESTER Lock to
Ashleworth: 5
Haw Bridge: 8¼
TEWKESBURY Junction with River Avon:
13
Upton-upon-Severn: 19
DIGLIS Junction with Worcester &
Birmingham Canal: 29
Holt Fleet: 36
STOURPORT Junction with Staffs & Worcs
Canal: 42

Locks: 5

The River Severn has always been one of the principal navigations in England. Its great length has made it an important trade artery since the medieval period. With its tributary, the Avon, it cuts deep into the heart of England, linking the iron and coal fields with the Bristol Channel and the British coastal trade. By using the Severn, boats of a considerable size could sail into the Midlands, and into Wales as far as Welshpool. However the navigation, especially above Worcester, was always difficult, owing to currents, shoals, the demands of water supply for milling etc.

As boats increased in size, and the cargoes became heavier, the navigational problems increased. The larger boats in common use in the 18thC could rarely sail higher than Bewdley, and so by the end of the century this inland port was beginning to lose its significance. At the same time the sandbanks and shifting shoals in the Gloucester area were seriously affecting the trade on the river as a whole. In order for the river to survive as a viable trade route, it became necessary for drastic improvements to be made. Various Acts were passed to ensure the maintenance of the towing path, although the Severn maintained its tradition of using gangs of men to bow-haul boats until well into the 19thC. In 1803 over 150 men were still employed in what Telford called 'this barbarous and expensive slave-like office' on the section between Bewdley and Coalbrookdale.

The demands of increasing navigation, and the spread of canals in the West Midlands (the Staffordshire & Worcestershire Canal linking the Severn with Birmingham and the rest of the network was opened in 1772) led to the passing of an Act in 1793 that authorised a canal to be built from Berkeley Pill to Gloucester. Work began on Gloucester Docks in 1794, and over the next few years 5½ miles of canal were cut. Shortage of money then caused work to be stopped, and so the canal remained useless and incomplete. In 1817 Telford was commissioned by the government to report on the feasibility of the canal, with particular reference to the maintenance of navigation on the Severn. He reported in favour of continuing and completing the canal, but recommended that it should run to Sharpness instead of to Berkeley. The government then put up the money for the canal, mainly to relieve acute problems of unemployment, and after considerable delays the Gloucester & Sharpness Canal was opened throughout in 1827.

Some of the structural problems were caused by the decision to build the canal to ship standard. (At the time of opening, this was the broadest, deepest canal in the world.) But although it greatly increased the cost, this far-sighted decision has ensured that the canal remains in use, and even today Gloucester and Sharpness docks are commercial ports.

Once the canal was in use, considerable dredging works and improvements became necessary to maintain the navigation of the upper Severn to Worcester and Stourport. This work, carried out extensively since the formation of the Severn Commission in 1842, included the building of locks and weirs, and the canalisation of parts of the river. The links with the Midlands canal network helped the Severn to flourish, and railway competition increased rather than decreased the traffic both in the docks and on the ship canal. In 1874 Sharpness docks were enlarged and modernised, to handle ships of up to 1000 tons. The same year the Gloucester & Berkeley Canal Company leased the Worcester & Birmingham Canal, to maintain their hold on the trade routes to the Midlands. By 1888 the Severn had a minimum depth of over 6ft, and in most places the depth was 8 to 9ft. Trade continued to thrive, and the recession in the 1920s was soon overcome by the rapidly growing oil traffic, which became the mainstay of the river. Although commercial traffic has declined there are strong signs of a revival. The BWB depot at Worcester is expanding, and there are plans to upgrade the G & S Canal to take vessels of 2500 tonnes, and the River Severn to take vessels of 1500 tonnes, thus creating a 'Severn Corridor'.

Natural history

Spring is a good time to visit the River Severn, when the river banks are speckled white with cow parsley and the riverside alders and willows are bearing their catkin flowers, providing valuable nectar and pollen for early moths and bees. In March and April millions of young eels come up-river with the high spring tides after a 3-year, 3000-mile journey from their breeding grounds in the western Atlantic. The elvers are followed by twaite shad, a sea fish which migrates into fresh water to spawn, and these provide sport for anglers as the fish try to ascend the weirs at Tewkesbury and Gloucester. Other migrants from the sea include 3ft-long sea lam-preys and 9-in river lampreys (which are both parasitic, sucking the blood from other fish), sea trout and salmon. Spring is also the time to listen for nightingales, which sometimes sing in the riverside woodlands, and to watch the caddis flies, may flies and stone flies which have newly emerged from their aquatic larvae and now dance across the surface of the water until they have mated, laid their eggs or fallen prey to some surface-feeding fish such as bleak or dace. Other fish found in the Severn include bottom-feeders such as bream, carp, roach, gudgeon, loach and occasionally barbel (which was introduced about 15 years ago), as well as carnivores such as pike, perch and eel.

It is perhaps in August that the river banks look best, with colourful clumps of yellow tansy, purple loosestrife and great willowherb with drooping heads of pink flowers. The recently introduced Himalayan balsam with its handsome pink and white flowers now grows in large clumps at Mythe Bridge near Tewkesbury, Sandhurst near Gloucester and near Gloucester Docks. In marshy areas, riverside pools and withy beds the reedmace grows with brown club-like heads, the common reed with 6ft-high stems and plumed flowerheads, and the greater and lesser pond sedges, which bear separate spikes of male (upper) and female (lower) flowers. These areas are the home of the sedge, reed and marsh warbler, although the last-named is rare nowadays.

Very few other birds nest along the Severn, although sand martins and kingfishers sometimes excavate nesting holes where the banks are steep, moorhen and mallard are found in the riverside bushes and two heron colonies are known to inhabit tall trees a little way inland from the tidal part of the river below Gloucester. The best place to look for water birds is undoubtedly the area between Frampton and Slimbridge where the extensive mud flats and sand banks exposed at low tide provide an attractive resting place for spring and autumn passage migrants. This area is especially good for winter visitors such as shoveller, pintail, wigeon, teal, lapwing, golden plover, ringed plover, dunlin, curlew, redshank and turnstone, and holds a roosting colony of about 20,000 common gulls. Two species of geese also come to feed on the riverside pastures in winter: up to 5000 whitefronted geese from Siberia and 100 pinkfooted geese from Greenland.

For the most part, the mammals of our rivers are secretive and nocturnal but water vole holes are a common sight in the river banks and the observant walker can sometimes recognise the tracks or other signs of our rare native otter or the accidentally introduced North American mink, a beautifully sleek black animal a little larger than a stoat, which originally escaped from fur farms but is now breeding in the wild along all parts of the Severn which run through Gloucestershire.

Sharpness

The Gloucester & Sharpness Ship Canal, which
was built to bypass the dangerous winding
stretch of the tidal River Severn between these
two places, has its southern terminus at
Sharpness, where there are docks and a large
lock up from the Severn. The Gloucester &
Sharpness Canal is nowadays the only
navigable route between the Severn Estuary
and the Severn Navigation above Gloucester, so
all boats heading upstream must pass through
Sharpness Lock and Docks. It should be noted
that the entrance to the lock dries out
completely at low water, so boats heading in
from the estuary should time their arrival
accurately. The best time to arrive at the lock is
about 2½ hours before high water when
locking down, and about 1 hour before high
water when locking up. (The lock is operated
only for 2 hours preceding high water).
It is important to give prior notice of one's
intentions to the BWB at Dursley 811644.
Boatmen wishing to proceed down the Severn
Estuary from Sharpness are advised not to do so
without a pilot. It is important to keep to the
marked channel, and the tide runs extremely
fast. Immediately above the lock are Sharpness
Docks, which handle ships from all over
Europe. The docks are a very busy area and an
important source of revenue to BWB's Freight
Services Divison. Pleasure boats are
encouraged to move on quickly through the 2
swing bridges out of the docks and onto the
ship canal itself. Just north of the 2 swing
bridges is an arm off to the west: this leads to a
tidal basin which is now, unfortunately,
disused. However the length of the arm leading
to it is used for permanent and temporary
pleasure craft moorings, and there is a small
boatyard at the end of it. It is a fascinating place
to walk round and see the tidal Severn flowing
strongly at the foot of the stone walls. Across
the river is the tree-lined west bank of the river,
only ½ a mile across at this point. A railway
line runs along the bottom of the hills. However
the old 22-arched railway bridge that used to
cross the river just north of here has been
completely demolished, and only the merest
traces of some of the stone piers can be seen at
low water. The bridge was badly damaged one
foggy night in November 1959, when a vessel
collided with it; the bridge then stood with a
hole in the middle until it was demolished and
the iron girders sold to—of all places—Chile,
where they now form a road-carrying viaduct.
Along the main line of the canal, the circular
stone structure is all that remains of the
railway's swing bridge over the canal. A mile
from Sharpness Docks, the canal is lined with
trees on each side—an uncharacteristically
river-like stretch that is belied by the occasional
glimpse of the Severn flowing alongside. Old
timber ponds open off the canal to the right.
Timber was stored afloat here 'in the round'.
Then a curve leads to the little village of Purton
and its 2 swing bridges. There is only one bridge
keeper and he spends most of his time at the
upper swing bridge. (Dursley 811384). The
navigation snakes through the village, passing
the big new waterworks before settling down to
a steady course of wide, straight reaches. It
traverses a quiet, green and predictably flat
landscape that is well studded with trees and
always bounded to the north by saltings and the
mud-flats of the Severn Estuary—which is here
much wider than at Sharpness. At Patch Bridge
(Cambridge 324) there are 2 pubs; this is the
best access point to the Slimbridge Wildfowl
Trust. (*See over*). There is a water point by the
bridge.

Navigational notes

1 As this is a commercial Waterway, moor only
    at recognised sites: Old Arm, Sharpness;
    Patch Bridge; Fretherne Bridge; Sellars
    Bridge; Bakers Quay; Gloucester Docks.
2 The mechanical swing bridges are manned
    08.00–18.45 (16.30 winter), lunch break
    13.00–13.30, and are guarded by traffic
    lights. Proceed only on the green.
3 Information on river levels and tide times can
    be obtained by ringing Bewdley 296929.

Shepherd's Patch

This little settlement existed long before the canal: it used to be where the shepherds watched over their flocks grazing the Severn Estuary. There are 2 pubs here, a gift shop, café and youth hostel.

Slimbridge Wildfowl Trust Conveniently situated just ½ mile north west of the canal at Patch bridge, the Trust is well worth visiting. It is close to the River Severn and apart from containing the largest collection of captive wildfowl (160 kinds) in the world, the Trust's grounds and adjacent water-meadows attract many thousands of migrant birds—white fronted geese, Bewick's Swans and all kinds of ducks and waders. Visitors are free to walk all round the Trust's grounds and study the inhabitants, which are fascinating for their variety, quantity and behaviour. The Trust also incorporates an important research establishment that studies all biological aspects of wildfowl, with special reference to ecological trends—it also plays an important role in the defence of the various species from extinction and can already be credited with the rescue of several important species. *Open throughout the year except on Christmas Day.*

Purton

Glos. P.O. Tel. Stores. A tiny village of lean, modest houses. It derives an unusual charm from being bisected by the ship canal. The canal is not particularly wide here, and to have a large German coaster quietly throbbing past the cowering post office seems an incredible distortion of scale. The village has, surprisingly, 2 pubs—one is on the canal bank, the other is 100yds away on an enviable site beside the Severn Estuary. There used to be a ford for cattle across the river nearby—the herdsman had to judge the time to cross the treacherous river to within a few minutes. Just outside Purton, a huge waterworks has been built for the city of Bristol, where up to 24 million gallons of water can be drawn daily from the ship canal, purified and pumped through a new 4ft pipe-line down to Bristol for drinking purposes. Small reservoirs have been constructed on the other side of the canal: these will provide a temporary feed if and when a recording device beside the canal nearer Gloucester indicates that the water is too heavily polluted to draw on.

Sharpness

Glos. Tel. Bank (Mon, Thu & Fri only). Stores & garage distant. Sharpness exists only for its docks with their tall cranes, old and new warehouses and ever-changing display of foreign ships. It has a strange atmosphere and an interesting situation beside the River Severn. The Severn is wide here, and wild: the tidal range at Sharpness is believed to be the second biggest in the world and the current is very swift, especially when accompanied by the very high winds that often race up the estuary from the sea. Across the water is the hilly Forest of Dean, with a main railway line running almost along the shore. It is only half a mile away, but it could as well be another country, so remote does it seem. In terms of population, Sharpness is very strung out; here and there is a row of terraced cottages, inhabited mainly by dock workers. Along the lockside—the focus of the docks—are the buildings housing the offices of various shipping firms, HM Customs & Excise and the BWB. The annual tonnage handled here is now approaching the million mark, with cargoes consisting mainly of animal feedstuffs, grain, fertilisers, timber and scrap metal, coming from Ireland, Europe, Russia and Scandinavia. Finnish wooden telegraph poles are also imported at Sharpness. Ships handled here displace up to 5000 tons (the limiting dimensions of the entrance lock are 55ft beam by 21ft 6in draught). An interesting development at Sharpness is the recent conversion of the old Merchant Navy training camp (on the hill by Sharpness Marine) into an outdoor leisure activity centre for the youth of land-locked Birmingham.

BOATYARDS

Ⓑ **Sharpness Marine** Floating Yacht Services Store. The Old Dock, Sharpness, Glos. (Dursley 811476). Ⓦ Ⓟ Ⓓ Gas, chandlery, mooring, repairs, slipway, food.

BWB Sharpness Office beside Sharpness Lock. (Dursley 811644.)

PUBS

Ⓟ **Patch Hotel**, opposite the Tudor Arms.

Ⓟ✕ **Tudor Arms** Shepherd's Patch, a few yards from Patch bridge. Restaurant and bar snacks, children's room.

Ⓟ **Berkeley Hunt**, Purton, by the lower bridge.

Ⓟ **Berkeley Arms**, Purton. 150yds from the lower bridge. Situated beside the river with an excellent view along it.

Ⓟ **Severn Bridge & Railway** Sharpness, on a hill to the north east of the docks. The pub sign shows a picture of the former railway bridge.

Ⓟ **Sharpness Hotel** Sharpness, on a hill to the north west of the docks. A large building on the hill near the Sharpness Marine boatyard.

Ⓟ **Lammastide Inn** 1 mile east of Sharpness at Brookend. Comfortable pub with 'own brew' beer among others.

An unusual visitor at Sharpness: a Thames Sailing Barge on it's way up to Gloucester.

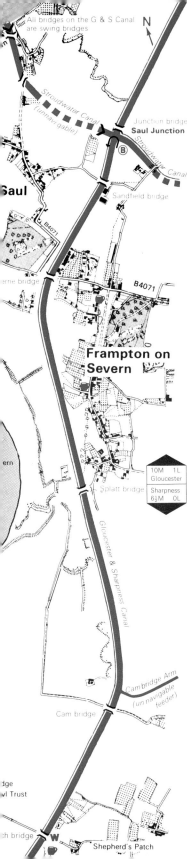

All bridges on the G & S Canal
are swing bridges

N

Stroudwater Canal
(unnavigable)

Junction bridge
Saul Junction

Stroudwater
Canal

Saul

Sandfield bridge

B4071

erne bridge

B4071

**Frampton on
Severn**

ern

10M   1L
Gloucester
Sharpness
6½M   0L

Splatt bridge

Gloucester & Sharpness Canal

Cambridge Arm
(unnavigable
feeder)

Cam bridge

dge
vl Trust

ch bridge   W

Shepherd's Patch

Saul Junction

The Ship Canal continues towards Gloucester, with the spacious Severn Estuary over to the west. Swing bridges punctuate the canal and at almost every bridge is a bridge keeper's cottage (Junction bridge–Gloucester 740444, Cambridge–Cambridge 272). These cottages are peculiar to the Gloucester & Sharpness Canal and have great charm—they are only small single-storey buildings, but each one has a substantial classical façade with fluted Doric columns and a pediment. At Cam Bridge is an unnavigable arm that feeds the canal with water from the Cotswolds. At Frampton on Severn the church is passed on the east side, then after a long straight the navigation bends to the north east. Trees encroach here on one side, and several bridges lead past scattered houses to Saul Junction. Over to the east the great Cotswold ridge marches parallel to the canal.

Saul Junction This unusual waterway 'crossroad' is where the Stroudwater Canal intersects the Gloucester & Sharpness Canal. The former canal was an extension of the Thames & Severn Canal, which used to run from the Thames at Lechlade, through the Cotswolds via the great Sapperton Tunnel and thus to Stroud. 12 locks brought the Stroudwater Canal down from this point to Saul, where it crossed the Ship Canal and continued to Framilode. Here it locked down into the tidal River Severn. Like the Thames & Severn, the Stroudwater Canal has been disused for many years, and the old lock by Saul Junction is derelict. However a 300yd stretch to the south east from the junction to the first bridge (now lowered) is navigable and in use as a mooring site. At the junction itself is a swing bridge and a cottage (previously the Junction Inn) as well as plenty of boats at the yard. The village of Saul is half a mile to the west. It is worth walking the mile from Saul Junction to the River Severn. The towpath is in good shape and this isolated section of the Stroudwater Canal is still in water. There is a pub (the Ship) along the way and from the riverside church in Framilode a footpath runs beside the Severn to the Darell Arms, whose gardens overlook the river. Restoration of both the Stroudwater and the Thames & Severn canals is underway.

Frampton on Severn
Glos. P.O. Tel. Stores, garage. A beautiful linear village notable mainly for its green, which is about 100yds wide and fully half a mile long. All manner of attractive houses attach themselves to the edge of this magnificent expanse of common land, and the occasional cars that drive down the middle of it are kept in their proper scale. Trees and ponds are scattered along it; the gateway that guards the Court is on the east side. The Church of St Mary is at the south end of the village, near the canal, it is mainly of the 14thC. The stained glass and monuments are worth a look, and the Romanesque lead font is one of only 6 in Gloucestershire.

Frampton Court Facing the village green is this Georgian mansion (1731–33) whose gardens contain a Gothic Orangery (1745) and an octagonal dovecote. *Visits by written application to the owners in residence only.*

BOATYARDS
ⓑ **R. W. Davis & Son** Junction Dry Dock, Saul, Gloucester. (Gloucester 740233). Boat building, repairs and surveys.

PUBS
🍺 **Bell Hotel** Frampton on Severn, ¼ mile south east of Fretherne Bridge.
🍺 **Three Horseshoes** Frampton, halfway along the green.

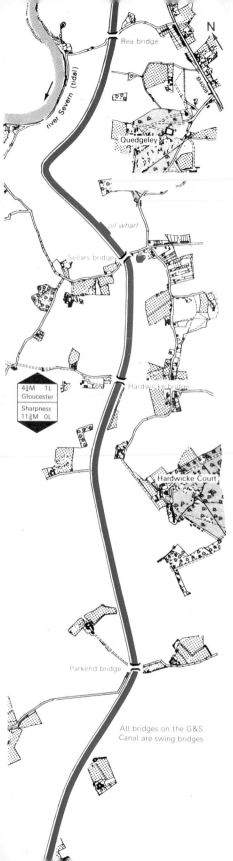

Hardwicke

On from Saul, the canal continues through
undramatic country, which is slightly wooded.
There are no villages on this section, but several
farms are situated near the canal. Towards
Sellars Bridge (Gloucester 720251), the
navigation enters a cutting for the first time
since Sharpness. There is a pub by this bridge,
and just to the north is an oil wharf for small
ships. This is the furthest (northernmost) point
which the oil traffic reaches on the Severn
Navigation—oil used to be carried further on
past Gloucester and right up to Stourport in
barges, but this is all finished now. North of
Quedgeley Wharf the canal approaches the
River Severn (hidden behind a flood bank and
far narrower up here than downstream);
turning sharply eastward, the canal reaches Rea
Bridge.

Navigational note
The 3 bridges, Sellars, Rea and Sims (*see next
page*) have a greater headroom (over 7ft) than
the others on the Gloucester & Sharpness
Canal. Boats normally used on the narrow
canals will find no difficulty in getting under
these 3 bridges without them being opened,
although they do so at their own risk. Boats
should not pass under these bridges without
receiving a green light from the keeper.

The Severn Bore This famous natural
phenomenon occurs on the section of the river
that is bypassed by the Gloucester & Sharpness
Canal. The Bore is a wave that travels
upstream: it is created by the strong tidal flow
encountering the 'land water' and chasing it
back up the shallow, winding river. One of the
best places from which to see the Severn Bore is
Stonebench, Elmore—only 500yds west of
Lower Rea bridge on the G & S Canal.
(Another good place is Maisemore Weir, above
Gloucester.) A Bore occurs on the spring tides
but a substantial wave of over 7 to 9ft is a rarer
occurrence. SAE to Area Amenity Assistant,
BWB Dock Office, Gloucester for annual
predictions.

PUBS

 Pilot Canalside, at Sellars Bridge.
 Anchor Epney (on the river 1½ miles west
of Park End Bridge).

Gloucester

At Rea Bridge the canal enters a cutting and describes a sharp double bend, from which one emerges into a completely different landscape: the quiet countryside has disappeared, its place taken by outlying industrial works on either side of the main road that runs noisily parallel to the navigation. The Ship Canal, strangely enough, plays little part in the generation of wealth that this industry represents, but north of Hempstead Bridge (Gloucester 21880) is a large timber wharf for discharging ships bringing imported wood. Further on is the oil dock, a grain silo and a general cargo quay. Ahead is Gloucester, and the extensive docks that are laid out virtually in the town centre. These are superb docks, for all around are the great warehouses ranged along the quays. Boatmen wishing to moor here—the best place for visiting Gloucester—should go to the office by the lock and seek advice from the BWB official. Gloucester Lock (Gloucester 25525) marks the northern end of the Gloucester & Sharpness Canal, and lowers boats back into the River Severn, reminding one that the ship canal is well above the river level. It has to be kept filled with water by pumping up from the river. No boats at the tail of Gloucester Lock should follow the river to the south west, for Llanthony Lock is closed and only a weir awaits them. North of Gloucester Lock, the river is bounded on the town side by a high quay, with moorings more suitable for large vessels than for motor cruisers. Gloucester gaol is nearby. Proceeding upstream, boatmen will find themselves on a dull length of river, narrow and hemmed in by high banks. A sharp bend requires a careful look-out; beyond it are road and rail bridges. The river winds along in its own isolated way, flanked mainly by trees. At one point it approaches a minor road; the former pub here is now a private house. Further upstream is the junction with the big western channel of the Severn, whose separate course between here and Gloucester explains the narrowness of the navigation channel. There is in fact a lock (Maisemore Lock, now closed) just 300yds along the western channel of the Severn. This is a relic of the days before the ship canal was built: it used to give access from the upper Severn to the Herefordshire & Gloucestershire Canal (now derelict), which joined the Severn near Gloucester.

Navigational notes
1 Information on river levels and tide times can be obtained by ringing Bewdley 296929. As with all river navigations, the Severn must be treated with respect, especially after periods of prolonged rain, when the current increases. If you are in any doubt regarding your safety on the river, moor up out of the main stream and seek *expert* advice.
2 All locks on the River Severn are manned. The are open:
08.00–19.15 summer
08.00–16.30 winter
Meal breaks 13.00–13.30, 17.00–17.30. Do not enter a lock unless the green light is showing.

Gloucester
MD: Street Market Sat, Cattle Market Mon and Thur. All services. Now a busy manufacturing town, commercial centre and port, Gloucester was once the Roman colony of Glevum. The town was laid out in a cross plan, with north, south, east and west gates. This geography still survives, if only in name. Traces of Roman habitation are much more difficult to find than in other Roman towns in Britain, but when the Bell Hotel was being demolished in recent years, excavations revealed 1000 square feet of paved courtyard, believed to be the site of the Roman forum. There are a few interesting old buildings in the town centre, notably the 12thC Fleece Hotel and numbers 11–15 Southgate, but otherwise the town centre is of less interest than one might expect. However the glorious cathedral provides an oasis of peace and beauty in the town. The other area of real interest is the docks.

Gloucester Cathedral Founded as an abbey in 1089 by Abbot Serlo, this splendid building is essentially Norman, but extensive remodelling of the choir and transepts between 1330 and 1370 shows fine examples of early Perpendicular architecture. These alterations were authorised by King Edward III, whose father Edward II was murdered at Berkeley (2 miles south of Sharpness). Gloucester Cathedral was the only place that would offer him burial in consecrated ground, and his tomb here became the object of pilgrimage. The new king showed his gratitude to the then Abbot of Gloucester with financial assistance. The great east window is particularly fine—the glass dates almost entirely from 1350, when the window was built, and is one of the first examples of a church window depicting rows of people. But perhaps the most interesting part of the present building is the adjacent cloisters: they feature the earliest known fan-vaulting (mid-14thC). It is still in good condition and is delightfully ornate.

City Museum & Art Gallery Brunswick Rd. Exhibits of furniture, glass, silver, costumes and coins; also local archaeology, geology and natural history. *Open weekdays.*

Folklife and Regimental Museum 99–103 Westgate St. Housed in 3 Tudor timber-framed buildings known as Bishop Hooper's Lodging and scheduled as an ancient monument. Fine collection of local history and bygones: there is a whole section on the River Severn, its vessels and the salmon and eel fishing industries that it once supported. Relics of the siege of Gloucester (1643) are here, also the collection of the Gloucester Regiment. *Open weekdays.*

Gloucester Docks These extensive docks close to the centre of Gloucester are, to many people, really much more interesting than the town itself. They are at the north end of the Gloucester & Sharpness Ship Canal, where it

locks down into the Severn and were built around 1827. Imported timber and grain are two of the main cargoes brought up here—they arrive mostly in big barges from ports down the Bristol Channel, for nowadays only a few coasters a week navigate the length of the canal. One may be sure that if the canal had not the generous dimensions that it has, Gloucester Docks would be disused by now, like the wharves up-river at Worcester and Stourport. The 7-storey dock warehouses are magnificent. Fully 9 of the original buildings still stand, lining the waterside like block houses and concealing it from the town. The docks have now gained an interesting new feature, for the old Llanthony swing bridge carrying a road across the docks has been recently replaced by an elegant steel bascule bridge, which carries heavier traffic and is faster to operate than the old one. Gloucester Docks add up to a fascinating scene and are now the subject of extensive restoration scheme, which includes the establishment of a waterways museum. 20 of the buildings are 'listed' as of historical importance.

Tourist Information 6 College St, Gloucester. (421188).

BOATYARDS

BWB Gloucester Area Engineer's Office Dock Office, Gloucester (25524).

BOAT TRIPS

Cotswold Narrowboats 18 Meysey Close, Meysey Hampton, Cirencester, Glos. (Poulton 529). Trips from Bakers Quay, Gloucester. **Gloucester Packet** A narrow boat based at Bakers Quay, Gloucester. For charter details ring Starline Travel, Gloucester 416881.

Gloucester Docks. The fine buildings here are now to be restored.

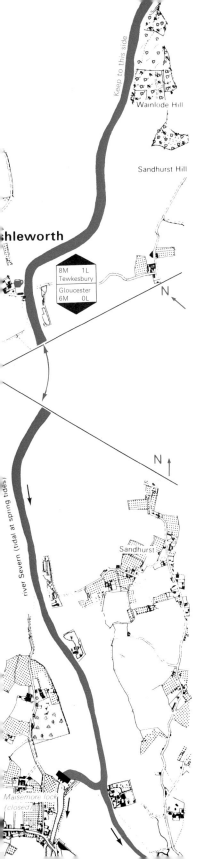

Ashleworth

Leaving the junction (known as the 'Upper
Parting') of the east and west channels of the
River Severn, the river from this point
northwards is predictably wider. Its character
changes very little in all its journey to
Stourport—most of the way it is lined by trees
and high banks. The surrounding countryside
that accompanies the river is quite pretty but
because of the banks, the boater will see little
beyond except for the occasional hills. The
walker along the banks is luckier, in having
good views of the river and the surrounding
countryside; but the towpath has mostly been
eroded away. Away from the centre the river is
often extremely shallow; there are anyway few
mooring places, so access to the villages on
either side is severely limited. After a series of
long reaches, the spire of Ashleworth Church
appears on the left side as the river bends to the
east towards the hills that rise steeply from the
river-bank. Unfortunately access to Ashleworth
from the river is poor. The main hill here is
Wainlode Hill, which reaches a height of almost
300ft.

Navigational note
1 Because of Wainlode Hill's susceptibility to
erosion by the river, old barges have been
sunk in the river near the east bank of the
section on this page, in order to protect the
river bank. All boats should keep to the
north side of the river to avoid the hulks. The
area is marked by posts.

Ashleworth Quay
Glos. Behind the tiny isolated pub is a
fascinating group of 15thC buildings, all
virtually intact. Ashleworth Court, a long, low,
stone building, was completed in 1460 and
stands next to the church. (*Open only to parties
on written application to the owner in residence.*)
The church, with its pretty spire, is nearby; but
of greater interest is the big stone tithe barn
(125ft by 25ft). This is owned by the National
Trust but is still used as a working barn by the
farmer—*open daily during daylight hours.*
Ashleworth Manor and the rest of the village
are set well back from the river. The Manor is
contemporary with the Court, and is of
timber-framed construction. *It is open only by
written appointment to the owner in residence.*
There used of course to be a jetty at Ashleworth
Quay; but this has varnished now, and boat
crews wishing to get ashore must either ground
their craft and wade ashore through the mud to
the bank or tie up to an overhanging tree where
there is enough water (a few yards downstream
of the pub).

PUBS
🍺 **Boat** Ashleworth. A delightful isolated pub
on the river. Access is difficult (shallow water).
🍺 **Queen's Arms** Village Green, Ashleworth.

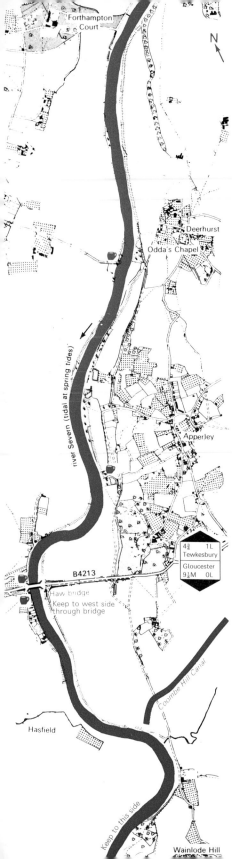

Haw Bridge

The towering mass of Wainlode Hill slowly
recedes as the tree-lined river curves round to
the north west. The silted-up lock on the east
bank is the entrance to the former Coombe Hill
Canal, now partly restored, but land-locked.
The modern bridge to the north is Haw Bridge.
There are pubs and good moorings. Navigators
should keep away from the east bank near this
bridge—there is a submerged obstruction. The
river winds through an S-bend, passing a
riverside pub and a line of hills to the east; then
it straightens out somewhat as it heads for
Tewkesbury. Yet another riverside pub, the
Yew Tree Inn, is passed—a half-sunken barge
serves as a mooring. A sailing club is based
here. Opposite is Odda's chapel, but access is
bad because of the rocky banks.

Deerhurst
Glos. Tel. Stores. The most important feature of
this small village is the beautiful Church of St
Mary, parts of which dates back to the year
804. The font with its trumpet-spiral motif
dates from the late 9thC and for some time the
bowl was used as a wash tub in a farm. It was
discovered and reunited with the stem in the
late 19thC, and is now thought to be one of the
best preserved Saxon fonts in England. The
church contains some interesting brasses and
15thC stained glass. Access is bad from the
river, as the banks are rocky.
Odda's chapel About 200yds south west of the
church. This Anglo-Saxon chapel dates from
1056; for years part of a farmhouse, it was
rediscovered for what it is during repairs in
1885. *Open at any reasonable time.*
Hawbridge The old cast iron bridge, built in
1824, was knocked down accidentally by a
barge in December 1958, when the river was in
spate. The replacement bridge was opened in
1961, a few yards downstream of the old one.
There are two pubs at the bridge, but little else.
The villages of Tirley and Hasfield are a mile to
the north west.
Coombe Hill Canal This short canal, running
eastwards from the Severn for 2¾ miles was
built in 1796 to facilitate the carriage of coal to
Cheltenham. There were 2 locks. Despite high
tolls, the canal never made any money, and
changed hands several times during the 19thC.
In 1875 the lock gates were swept away by
floods, and the canal was formally abandoned
the following year. Having lain derelict for
many years, it was purchased by the Severn &
Canal Carrying Company for £35,000 (7 times
the original company's capital). The canal and
wharf manager's house, near the basin, has now
been restored, and a museum and trips along
the canal were planned before the company
went into liquidation. The future is unceratin.

PUBS

🍺✕ **Yew Tree Inn** on west bank of river,
opposite Deerhurst. Large pub at the end of a
lane. Sailing club based here; food always
available. Reasonable temporary moorings.
The quiet village of Chaceley (*P.O. Tel.*) is a
mile up the lane.
🍺✕ **Coal House** on east bank of river near
Apperley. Moorings not brilliant, but food is
available, also a skittle alley.
🍺 **New Bridge** Haw Bridge.
🍺 **Haw Bridge Inn** at Haw Bridge. Moorings.
Skittle room.

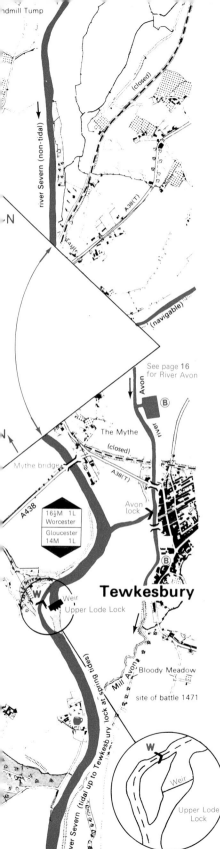

Mythe Bridge

The river now passes another pub, facing a
sailing club. There is a private ferry between
them; access to the pub is difficult because of
shallow water. 1 of the 2 channels of the
Warwickshire Avon enters here from
Tewkesbury: the Battle of Tewkesbury was
fought just to the east of here in 1471. Marked
by the abbey, Tewkesbury can be seen to the
north east, but the Severn sweeps round to the
west of the town, leaving an enormous expanse
of flat, empty meadow between them. The big
lock (Tewkesbury 293138) is well concealed on
a corner between the weir and a backwater.
(The weir is, incidentally, the highest point to
which normal spring tides flow). Upstream of
the lock is a junction with the main (navigable)
course of the River Avon—boats heading for
the Lower and Upper Avon navigations should
turn east here, as should boats intending to visit
Tewkesbury. Beware of the shallow spit
projecting south west from the tip of the
junction. Continuing up the Severn, one
reaches the single 170ft-span of the cast iron
Mythe Bridge over the river, built by Thomas
Telford in 1828. Steep wooded hills rise on the
east bank by this bridge, but the river bears off
to the north west and soon leaves them behind.
Its character remains virtually unchanged—it is
lined by high banks and trees, untouched by
villages or towns, and seemingly isolated from
the countryside that its wide course divides so
effectively.

The River Avon in Tewkesbury It is certainly
worth turning off the Severn into the River
Avon—this is the way to Tewkesbury.
Evesham and Stratford-upon-Avon. Boaters
not wishing to buy the short-term pass on to the
Lower Avon Navigation may tie up just below
the big Healing's Mill to visit Tewkesbury, but
those who decide to go through the pretty Avon
Lock (operated by a lock keeper) will find it a
worthwhile diversion. *See page 16.* See the
River Avon section for all details and boatyard
services in the town.

PUBS

🍺 **Lower Lode** ¾ mile below Tewkesbury
lock, but mooring is difficult.

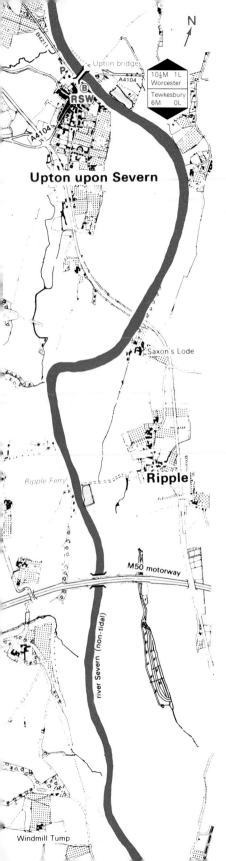

Upton upon Severn

The River Severn continues on its predictable, undramatic course northwards, flanked by wooded banks that prevent any views of the countryside. There are few signs of habitation or human activity apart from boats and anglers. The big steel viaduct carrying the M50 motorway provides a rare feature of interest. The significant-looking pipes sticking out of the ground on the east bank at this point betray the existence of an old underground oil depot, but it is now disused. A mile further on, things improve as the old church tower at Upton upon Severn comes into view, followed by the graceful modern bridge and interesting waterfront of this very attractive small town. Plenty of boats are moored here—there are temporary public moorings on the west bank, just downstream of the bridge.

Upton upon Severn
Hereford & Worcs. EC Thur. P.O. Tel. Stores, garage, banks. This delightful town is well provided with fascinating old timbered and early Georgian buildings, and it is doubly welcome for being situated on the river bank. The best area is nearest the river, where various pubs and venerable hotels beckon; nearby is the prominent 13thC tower with its 18thC copper-covered cupola, all that remains of the church that was demolished in 1937. The tower and the former churchyard have recently been restored as a public garden. The 'new' church of SS Peter and Paul was built in 1878, on the edge of the town—a good place for it. There are good shops in Upton, including a delicatessen, and it is the best place along the Severn (apart from Worcester) to forsake a boat for a trip to the famous Malvern Hills, which rise to the west. Great Malvern is under 6 miles to the north west, and the hills are visible from the Severn.

Ripple
Hereford & Worcs. P.O. Tel. Stores. Although set back from the river, Ripple is well worth a visit. It is a pretty village, the houses scattered irregularly along the road. The large church is very fine and dates almost entirely from the late 12thC. Only the chancel is late 13thC. The central tower at one time had a spire. Inside are 15thC choir stalls, carved with astrological symbols.

BOATYARDS

Ⓑ **Upton Marina** Upton upon Severn, Worcs. (Upton 3111). Ⓡ Ⓢ Ⓦ Ⓟ Ⓓ Ⓔ Pump-out, slipway, gas, dry dock, repairs, mooring, chandlery, toilets. Corsair Cruisers and Walker Boats are based here.

PUBS

The only riverside pubs on this section are in Upton.
● **Plough Inn** Upton, near the bridge.
●✕ **Star Hotel** Upton. Near the river. Lunches and dinners *daily*. Residential.
● **Swan** Upton, beside the river.
● **Ye Olde Anchor Inn** Upton, near the church. This pub is dated 1601.
●✕ **White Lion Hotel** High Street, Upton.
● **Railway Inn** Ripple.

Hanley Castle

Leaving Upton, the river resumes its
high-banked course through the countryside.
On the west bank, but hardly visible from a
boat, is the village of Hanley Castle. Further
up, on the east bank, is a wooded ridge with a
curious turreted house projecting from the
trees. The village of Severn Stoke is to the east;
it is reached by a lane from a jetty on the river.
West of here is an enjoyably romantic stretch of
river, where tall, steep red cliffs rise sharply
from the water to over 100ft. Trees and shrubs
struggle to grow from this treacherous slope,
and somewhere hidden at the top is Rhydd
Court. The steep hill recedes, allowing a large
caravan site to nestle by the river. A scattering
of bungalows appears; then the river leaves
houses and hills and wanders off north east.
Distantly, to the west, can be seen the grey
lumps of the Malvern Hills.

Severn Stoke
Hereford & Worcs. P.O. Tel. Stores. The village
is scattered along the main road, and has no real
centre. The best part is near the pretty
half-timbered pub with its rose garden. Nearby
is the church with its curious 14thC side tower.

Hanley Castle
Hereford & Worcs. P.O. Tel. Stores. The early
13thC castle, built by King John, has now
vanished, leaving only its moat as a memorial.
But the village that grew up around it still
thrives. It is extremely pretty, with a good
collection of half-timbered and brick cottages
around the little green. Overlooking the green
is the church, set in an attractive churchyard. It
is a curious building, half 14thC stone, half
17thC brick, with a squat brick tower. Nearby
are the 17thC almshouses and grammar school,
the whole group a remarkable indication of
village life long ago. A lane leads to the village
from the river, but mooring is difficult. It is not
too far to walk from Upton.

PUBS

🍺 **Rose & Crown** Severn Stoke. Off the main
road near the church.
🍺 **Three Kings** Hanley Castle. In the village
centre. Food, garden.

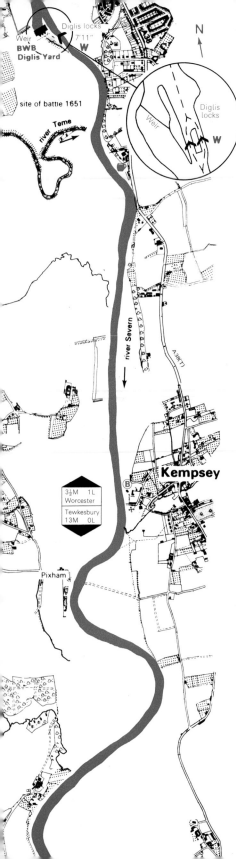

Kempsey

The river winds past the hamlet of Pixham, then the bold tower of Kempsey Church appears on the east bank, and a line of moored boats betrays the presence of a boatyard. There are temporary moorings along here for visitors to the village. Upstream, the river straightens out as it makes for Worcester. The Malvern Hills may be glimpsed occasionally, forming the western horizon. Soon the Severn narrows somewhat as a wooded ridge encroaches from the east. The Severn Motor Yacht Club is based here—it is well-named, for the cruisers moored along here are lavish and grand. There is a pub up among the trees near the club. The Battle of Worcester was fought in 1651 near where the little River Teme joins the Severn. Above here is the pair of Diglis Locks (Worcester 354280), on the outskirts of Worcester. There is a BWB maintenance yard and a large freight depot above the locks, so dredgers and tugs are often seen.

Battle of Worcester, 3rd September 1651 On 22nd August 1651 the young Charles Stuart (later Charles II), having been proclaimed king by the rebels at Scone, reached Worcester with his Scottish army of 17,000. The Roundhead General Lambert was sent off in pursuit with his northern cavalry, and captured the Severn Bridge at Upton upon Severn, cutting off Charles' retreat. Meanwhile another army of 28,000 under Cromwell advanced on Worcester from Nottingham. Charles, realising that he would have to fight at Worcester, organised his defences around the rivers Severn and Teme. After receiving further reinforcements from Banbury, the Roundhead armies advanced across the Severn, using a pontoon made of boats: meanwhile their cavalry crossed by a ford south of Powick Bridge, on the Teme. Heavy fighting broke out, and Charles' Scottish infantry, taken by surprise, were soon driven back. Charles tried to redeem the battle by leading a brave charge out of the east gate of Worcester: supported by cavalry this would have succeeded, but by this time the Scottish cavalry had fled. Cromwell held his ground and forced the Royalists back into the town, killing many in the narrow streets. This Roundhead victory ended the Royalist hopes; Charles fled with a few followers, and after the famous Boscobel Oak episode he made his way back to France.

Kempsey
Hereford & Worcs. P.O. Tel. Stores. A dull village in which acres of new housing have swamped the old. One or two beautiful thatched cottages have survived to defy the invasion of modernity; but it is the church that should be visited, for the enormous scale of this building is matched by interior grandeur. It was constructed to cater for the Bishop of Worcester and his huge retinue—the Bishop's Palace used to stand just a few yards west of the church. Hence the generous proportions of, especially, the chancel and sanctuary. Note the medieval glass in the chancel.

BOATYARDS

BWB Diglis Maintenance Yard Diglis Lock. (Worcester 356264).
Ⓑ **Seaborn Yacht Company** Court Meadow, Kempsey, Worcs. (Worcester 820295) Ⓡ Ⓢ Ⓦ Pump-out (*not Sat*). Boat hire, slipway, gas, boat building and repairs, mooring, toilets, showers, winter storage. *Closed winter Suns.*

PUBS

🍺 **Ketch Inn** On A38 overlooking the river.
🍺 **Anchor** Kempsey.
🍺 **Farmers Arms** Kempsey Common. Food, skittles.

Hallow

A443

A449

A44

A449

B4206

Race Course

Worcester

Foregate Station

12½M 3L
Stourport
16½M 1L

Worcester & Birmingham Canal
See page 183

3
2
1
W
B
B
Weir
Diglis Basin
See next page

BWB Diglis Yard

Diglis locks 7
W See enlargement
on page 164

site of battle 1651

river Teme

river Severn

Worcester

Just above Diglis Locks is the terminal basin
where the oil tankers used to come to unload
before the traffic finished some years ago. A few
hundred yards on are the disused wharves and
the two locks that lead into Diglis Basin, the
Worcester & Birmingham Canal. (*See page
181*). Worcester Cathedral is well in view now;
the big square tower commands the town and
the riverside. Two other church towers
contribute to the scene, and the unspoilt nature
of the west bank makes Worcester's riverside a
pretty one. Anglers fish from a path along the
east bank, seemingly just below the great west
window of the cathedral, while 'fours' and
'eights' appear from rowing clubs. There are 2
bridges over the river in Worcester—a 5-arched
stone road bridge and, just north of it, a curious
iron railway bridge. The best temporary
moorings are between these bridges, on the east
bank. North of the railway, the west bank is
built up while the east bank is green and
tree-lined, with the race course right by the
river. At its northern end is a busy waterworks,
contrasting with the bijou houses that adjoin it.
North of here the river moves out into
pleasantly wooded country; the only trace of
civilisation is the glimpse of the occasional farm
and a pretty, secluded riverside pub with good
moorings. There is a field of hops nearby.

Worcester
EC Thur. MD Sat. 2 stations. All services. The
'Faithful City', Worcester has shown loyalty
and devotion to the Crown for the last 900
years. Hence the name of Royal Worcester
Porcelain, which is still one of the biggest firms
in the town. Other industries include glove
manufacturing and the making of a certain
brown sauce. Worcester has plenty to offer the
visitor, although one's enjoyment is lessened by
the constant flow of heavy traffic through the
town. Foregate Street has many irregular
Georgian buildings with attractive pediments.
A railway bridges the street, but does not
intrude, for the girders are suitably decorated
and trains are infrequent. However the best
area is around Friar Street, and of course the
cathedral.
The Cathedral An imposing building that
dates from 1074 (when Bishop Wulstan started
to rebuild the Saxon church), but has work
representative of the 5 subsequent centuries.
There is a wealth of stained glass and
monuments to see—including the tomb of King
John, which lies in the chancel. Carved out of
Purbeck marble in 1216, this is the oldest royal
effigy in England. When he was dying at
Newark, King John demanded to be buried at
Worcester Cathedral between 2 saints: but the
saints have gone now. The best way into the
cathedral is from the Close with its immaculate
lawns and houses, passing through the cloisters
where one may inspect 5 of the cathedral's old
bells. (2 of these were cast in 1374). The
gardens at the west end of the building look out
over the Severn and over to the Malvern
Hills—a particularly fine sight at sunset.
The Three Choirs Festival is held annually in
rotation at the cathedrals of Worcester,
Gloucester and Hereford, during the last week
in *Aug.* This famous festival has inspired some
fine music, one notable composer being
Vaughan Williams. For further information
about the festival, contact the Town Clerk in
any of the 3 cities.
The Commandery by Kings Head Lock, on
the Worcester & Birmingham Canal. This was
founded as a small hospital by Bishop Wulstan
in 1085, but the present timbered building
dates from the reign of Henry VII in the 15thC.
It served as Charles Stuart's headquarters
before the Battle of Worcester in 1651. The
glory of the building is the superb galleried hall
with its ancient windows and the Elizabethan
staircase. Teas. *Open Tue–Sat and Sun
afternoons.*
Tudor House Folk Museum Friar St. A new
museum of local antiquities, furniture and
porcelain housed in traditional Elizabethan
buildings. (The wattle and daub that make up
the walls can be clearly seen in places).
Amongst other exhibits are a modern copy of a
traditional coracle, a tiny fishing craft used for
thousands of years on the river Severn, and a

painting of the Waterman's Church in Worcester—a chapel on a floating barge, last used in the 1870s, when it was taken ashore and set up on dry land. *Closed Thur and Sun.*

The Dyson Perrins Museum of Worcester Porcelain The Royal Porcelain Works, Severn St. Here, where it should be, is the most comprehensive collection of Worcester porcelain in the world, from 1751 to the present day. *Open Mon–Sat Apr–Oct. Tours of the porcelain works can be arranged.*

The Guildhall High St. Built in 1721–23 by a local architect, Thomas White, this building has a splendidly elaborate façade with statues of Charles I and Charles II on either side of the doorway and of Queen Anne on the pediment. It contains a very fine assembly room.

City Museum and Art Gallery Foregate St. Collections of folk life material and natural history illustrating man and his environment in the Severn valley. In the Art Gallery are a permanent collection and loan exhibitions. Also museum of the Worcestershire Regiment. *Open Mon–Sat.*

The Greyfriars Friar St. (NT property). Dating from 1480, this was once part of a Franciscan priory and is one of the finest half-timbered houses in the country. Charles II escaped from this house after the Battle of

Worcester on 3rd September 1651. It is an antique shop now.
Tourist information Worcester 23471.

BOATYARDS

Ⓑ **Tolladine Boat Services** Diglis Basin. Worcester. (Worcester 352142). Boat builders, repairers and engineers. 10-ton gantry crane and moorings (some undercover).
Ⓑ **Diglis Boat Co** Wharf Cottage, Diglis Basin. (Worcester 354039). Ⓡ Ⓢ Ⓦ Dry dock, boat building & repairs, toilets. Boat brokerage a speciality.

PUBS

🍺✕ **Camp House Inn** Grimley. An isolated riverside pub below Bevere Lock. Snacks, garden and good moorings. The drinking water here is pumped up electrically from a well.
🍺✕ **Crown** Hallow. Restaurant (on the A443).
🍺 **Severn View Hotel** Worcester. Near the river by the railway bridge. A choice of real ales.
🍺 **Old Rectifying House** Worcester, by the road bridge. B&B.
🍺✕ **Diglis Hotel** Worcester, on the river by the cathedral. Restaurant.
🍺 **Anchor Inn** Near Diglis Basin. Snacks.

DIGLIS BASIN
Enlargement from map page 165

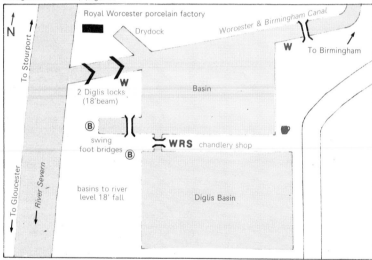

There is always lots to see at Diglis. *David Perrott*

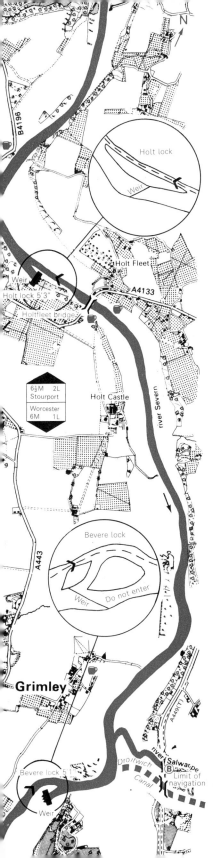

Holt Castle

Just upstream of the Camp House Inn is Bevere
Lock (Worcester 640275), which is certainly
one of the prettiest on the Severn. There is a
delightful rose garden, tended by the lock
keeper and his wife. The island adjoining the
lock is connected to the land on the far side by a
graceful iron footbridge. Continuing upstream
of the lock, the river is approached by wooded
hills on its east bank, while on the other side the
plain green fields continue, edged by high
banks and trees. At one point the little River
Salwarpe and the disused Droitwich Canal
enter together from the east. The Salwarpe is
navigable for craft up to 35ft as far as Judge's
Boatyard at Hawford, but there are no visitors
moorings. The canal has yet to be restored. The
village of Grimley is at the end of a lane leading
up from the river, but it is difficult to
distinguish this track, and there are no
moorings. The river continues north west now,
until Holt Castle is reached, a curious
composite building overlooking the river.
Beside it is the discreet tower of a small church.
Further on is the delicate iron span of Holt
Fleet Bridge, and beyond it a steep wooded
hillside, with pubs and caravans nearby. Above
Holt Lock (Worcester 620218), the steep
wooded hills continue, rising straight up from
the river bank. It is a pleasant scene, and there
is a riverside pub nearby. The next few miles
form an attractive reach, with steep wooded
hills rising from the river bank on one side,
then on the other. There is a riverside pub
along here, with a small settlement of
inoffensive-looking chalets.

Holt
Hereford & Worcs. P.O. Tel. Stores. Holt is a
scattering of assorted settlements, around the
river. The elegant narrow bridge here was built
by Telford in 1828. Holt Fleet exploits the river
in a most unattractive fashion, being composed
of a large sprawling caravan site, whose
television aerials and wires swamp the
riverside. There are two large pubs. Holt Castle
is up on the hill, overlooking the river. The
'castle' is a 14thC tower, for the rest of the
building is a 19thC battlemented mansion.
Nearby, set among the fruit fields, is the
church, a fine late Norman building with
interesting carving around the doorways, and
rich in interior ornamentation.

Grimley
Hereford & Worcs. P.O. Tel. Stores. A small
farming village close to, but hidden from, the
river. The well placed church has some
Norman work, but has been heavily restored; it
has a curious outside staircase by the door.
Access from the river is not easy, but there is a
pub.

The Droitwich Canal This attractive rural
waterway, which leaves the Severn ½ mile
north east of Bevere Lock, used to go to
Droitwich—5¾ miles and 8 locks away. It was
then joined by the Droitwich Junction Canal,
whose 7 locks led it a further 1½ miles to
terminate in a junction with the Worcester &
Birmingham Canal at Hanbury Wharf (*see page
185*). Both the Droitwich canals have been
derelict for most of this century, but they are
now reviving. The local council, Droitwich
Town Development, is gradually implementing
a scheme to open up the Droitwich Canal from
the town to the River Severn, and it is hoped
later to extend the restoration to the Junction
Canal. When and if this happens, it will restore
a 22-mile ring of cruising waterways.

BOATYARDS
Ⓑ **George Judge** Mill House, Hawford.
(Worcester 51283). Just east of the A449 bridge
on the River Salwarpe. Ⓦ Gas, boat sales and
repairs, chandlery, provisions, Café, camping
and caravan site, long-term mooring. Visitor
mooring is very restricted, and craft over 35ft
cannot turn.

PUBS
🍺 **Lenchford** Holt. Riverside, upstream of
Holt Lock.
🍺 **Holt Fleet Hotel** Holt Fleet, by the bridge.
🍺 **Wharf Hotel** Holt Fleet, north bank by
caravan site.
🍺✕ **Waggon Wheel** Grimley. Food.

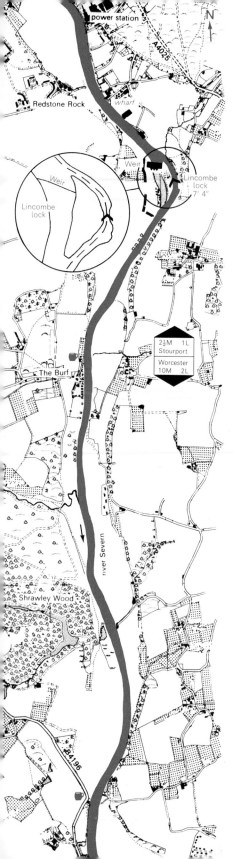

The Burf

The reach from Lenchford to Stourport is one
of the most pleasant on the Severn. Unlike
much of its journey further downstream, the
river runs here through a well-defined valley,
with steep wooded hills never far away from
either bank. The hills on the west bank are the
more impressive and the more thickly wooded,
although the old church at Shrawley can
sometimes be seen peering over the woods.
Roads keep their distance, but at the site of
Hampstall Ferry (The Burf) there is a small
village and a riverside pub, with good
moorings. From here very steep hills encroach
on the east bank of the river, almost hanging
over it at Lincomb Lock (Stourport 2887). This
pretty lock is now the northernmost on the
river, for signs of Stourport soon come into
view. First there are the abandoned oil
wharves, whose rusty pipes and terminals are a
sad reminder of the former traffic. On the
opposite side of the river, at the foot of a cliff, is
the Redstone Rock—an unexpected outcrop of
crumbling red sandstone. There was once a
hermitage in caves here. On towards Stourport,
there is a modest restaurant on the east bank
and, beyond it, Stourport Power Station. The
River Stour flows in here.

The Burf
An isolated riverside settlement, comprised
mainly of new housing for retired persons.

PUBS
✕❢ **Fountain Grill & Snack Bar**, on east bank
of river below Stourport Power Station.
Licensed restaurant. Moorings.
🍺 **Hamstall Inn** The Burf, overlooking the
river. Good moorings. Food.

Stourport-on-Severn

At Stourport Power Station the little River
Salwarpe flows in from the east, and just to
the north the Staffordshire & Worcestershire Canal
drops down into the Severn from the unseen
basins. There are 2 sets of locks—narrow canal
boats should use the upstream set. Just above
these locks is Stourport Bridge, a heavy iron
structure built in 1870.

The River Severn is not officially navigable for
more than a couple of hundred yards above
Stourport Bridge, at which point BWB's
jurisdiction as navigation authority ends.
However in suitable conditions small boats not
drawing more than 1ft 9in can penetrate
upstream to within a mile of Bewdley Bridge. A
shoal across the river impedes further progress,
and boatmen must tie up or wade ashore when
they reach the shoal. 'Bradshaw's Canals and
Navigable Rivers, 1904' states that a few craft,
in times of full water, proceed as far as Arley
Quarry, 5 miles above Bewdley, although the
trade is very small. There is a road into
Bewdley on either side of the river (the B4194
on the west bank being the most direct).
Alternatively, one can avoid all this by leaving
the boat in Stourport and taking a bus to
Bewdley, an excursion well worth the effort.

The River Severn above Bewdley
In the 19thC the Severn was fully navigable for
a long way past Stourport: it used to be a vital
trade artery right up into Wales, through
Bridgnorth, Shrewsbury and Newtown. It used
to connect with the Montgomery Canal at
Newtown, the Shrewsbury Canal at
Shrewsbury, and the Shropshire Canal at Hay.
It is unfortunate that this upper section is
unnavigable, for the river is much prettier than
further south: it runs along a narrow valley,
hemmed in by steep and wooded hills.
However, there is a public right of way along
one or both banks up to Bridgnorth and
beyond, and this can form an interesting walk.
Another attraction north of Bewdley is the
Severn Valley Railway, a private railway which
runs a summer service of steam trains between
Bridgnorth and Hampton Loade.

Bewdley
*Hereford & Worcs. EC Wed. P.O. Tel. Stores,
garage, bank.* Bewdley is a magnificent small
18thC riverside town, still remarkably intact. It
is blessed with a fine river frontage and elegant
bridge that make the most of the wide Severn,
and a handsome main street that leads away
from the river to terminate at the church. The
scale of the whole town is very pleasing, a
comfortable mixture of old timber-framed
buildings and plainer, more elegant 17th and
18thC structures. Most of the town is on the
west bank, and so Telford's 3-arch stone
bridge, built in 1798 to replace an earlier
medieval structure, forms a fitting entrance to
Bewdley. Old warehouses, hotels, and grand
houses flank the quays and small motorboats
can be hired from which to enjoy the view.

Stourport-on-Severn
*Hereford & Worcs. EC Wed. P.O. Tel. Stores,
garage, bank.* When the engineer James
Brindley surveyed the line for the Staffordshire
& Worcestershire Canal in the early 1760s, he
intended to meet the River Severn at Bewdley,
which was already an established river port.
But the residents there objected to his plans,
and so he chose instead the hamlet of Lower
Mitton, 4 miles downstream, where the little
River Stour flowed into the Severn. Basins and
locks were built for the boats, warehouses for
the cargoes and cottages for the workmen. The
canal company even built in 1788 the great
Tontine Hotel beside the locks. The hamlet
soon earned the name of Stourport, becoming a
busy and wealthy town. The 2 basins were
expanded to 5 (one has since been filled in) and
the locks were duplicated. Nowadays, plenty
remains of Stourport's former glory, for the
basins are always full of boats (there is a boat
club and boatyards). The delightful clock tower
still functions, a canal maintenance yard carries
on in the old workshops by the locks, and the
Tontine Hotel still has a licence. Mart Lane (on
the north east side of the basins) is worth a
look—the original 18thC terrace of workmen's
cottages still stands. Numbers 2, 3 and 4 are
listed as ancient monuments. In contrast with

the basin area, the town of Stourport is not
interesting, and although it was built on
account of the canal, the town has no
relationship at all with the basins now. It seems
to have grown up away from the canal.

BOATYARDS

ⓑ **BWB Stourport Yard** Stourport Basin.
(Stourport 77661) R̲ S̲ W̲ close by.
ⓑ **Dartline** Parkes passage, off York St.
Stourport on Severn (2970). R̲ S̲ W̲ D̲
Pump-out (*Mon–Fri*). Boat hire, mooring,
toilets, winter storage.
ⓑ **Plain Sailing** Stourport Basin. (Stourport
2044) R̲ S̲ W̲ Slipway, gas, dry dock, mooring,
chandlery, toilets, provisions.
ⓑ **Severn Valley Cruisers** York St Boatyard.
Stourport. (Stourport 71165). R̲ W̲ D̲
Pump-out (*not Sat*).Boat hire, slipway, gas,
boat building & repair, mooring, chandlery,
toilets, winter storage.

BOAT TRIPS

Severn Steamboat Co. Trips from Stourport
to Worcester and back on *Weds July & Aug.*
Also trips on the river *mid-summer* according to
demand and boat charter. Details Stourport
71177.

PUBS

Bewdley is a town with many fine pubs,
including:
🍺 **Angel** Lode St, town centre, Bewdley.
🍺 **Black Boy** Wyre Hill. Garden (*Not* Black
Boy *Hotel*).
🍺 **Cock and Magpies** Severnside North,
Bewdley.
🍺 **Mug House** Severnside North, Bewdley.
🍺 **Pack Horse** High St, Bewdley.
🍺 **Rising Sun** Kidderminster Rd,
Wribbenhall. Garden.
🍺 **Woodcolliers Arms** Welchgate, Bewdley.
Lunchtime snacks.
🍺 **Tontine Hotel** Stourport Basin. Food,
garden, children's room. Banks's real ale.
🍺 **Bridge Inn** Bridge St, near Severn bridge.
Garden, snacks, ghost.
🍺 **Black Star** Mitton St, Stourport. Canalside.
🍺 **Angel Hotel** Severnside, near the Tontine.
🍺 **Bird in Hand** Holly Bush, Stourport.
Canalside garden.
✕🍷 **Lock, Stock & Barrel** 2a High St,
Stourport. (Stourport 6014). Intimate
restaurant. *Closed Sun.* By bridge 5.

STOURPORT BASINS - Enlargment from map page 169

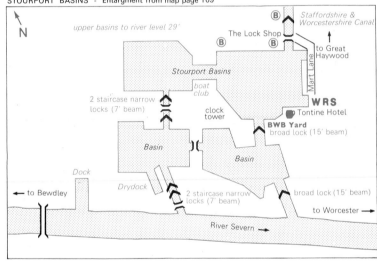

The old quayside, Bewdley. *David Perrott*

STRATFORD-ON-AVON

Maximum dimensions

Length: 70'
Beam: 7'
Headroom: 6'

Mileage

KING'S NORTON JUNCTION to
Hockley Heath: 9¾
LAPWORTH Junction with Grand Union
Canal: 12½
Preston Bagot: 16¼
Wootton Wawen Basin: 18½
Wilmcote: 22
STRATFORD-ON-AVON Junction with
River Avon: 25½

Locks: 55

The opening of the Oxford Canal in 1790 and of the Coventry Canal throughout shortly afterwards opened up a continuous waterway from London to the rapidly developing industrial area based on Birmingham. It also gave access, via the Trent & Mersey Canal, to the expanding pottery industry based on Stoke-on-Trent, to the Mersey, and to the East Midland coalfield. When the Warwick & Birmingham and Warwick & Napton Canals were projected to pass within 8 miles of Stratford-on-Avon, the business interests of that town realised that the prosperity being generated by these new trade arteries would pass them by unless Stratford acquired direct access to the network. And so, after the usual preliminaries, on the 28th of March 1793 an Act of Parliament was passed for the construction of the Stratford-on-Avon Canal, to start at King's Norton on the Worcester & Birmingham Canal (itself a long way from completion at that time). The junction was to be less than 3 miles from the junction of the Worcester & Birmingham with the Dudley Canal, and would thus provide a direct route to a major coal producing area without passing through Birmingham.

Progress was rapid at first; but almost the total estimated cost of the complete canal was spent in the first 3 years, on cutting the 9¾ lock-free miles to Hockley Heath. It took another 4 years, more negotiations, a revision of the route and another Act of Parliament to get things going again. By 1803 the canal was open from King's Norton Junction to its junction with the Warwick & Birmingham Canal (now part of the Grand Union main line) near Lapworth, with through traffic along the whole of this northern section. Even more delays now followed, with little enthusiasm on the part of private investors to put up more money. Cutting recommenced in 1812, the route being revised yet again in 1815 to include the present

junction with the River Avon at Stratford. (From here, the Avon was navigable down to the Severn at Tewkesbury.)

In its most prosperous period, the canal's annual traffic exceeded 180,000 tons, including 50,000 tons of coal through the complete canal, down to Stratford. By 1835 the canal was suffering from railway competition. This grew so rapidly that in 1845 the Canal Company decided to sell out to the Great Western Railway. There was opposition, however, and it was not until 1st January 1856 that the sale was considered complete. Thus the canal had been in full, independent operation for less than 40 years. Traffic was not immediately suppressed by the new owners, but long-distance haulage was the first to suffer as it was a more direct threat to the railway. In 1890 the tonnage carried was still ¼ of what it had been 50 years before, but the fall in ton-miles was much greater.

This pattern of decline continued in the 20thC, and by the 1950s only an occasional working boat was using the northern section; the southern section (Lapworth to Stratford) was badly silted, some locks were unusable and some of the short pounds below Wilmcote were dry. It is believed that the last boat to reach Stratford did so in the early 1930s but there is evidence that a pleasure cruiser reached Wilmcote during the Easter holiday of 1947.

After the 1939–45 war interest began to grow in boating as a recreation. In 1955 a Board of Survey had recommended sweeping canal closures, including the southern section of the Stratford Canal. Public protest was such that a Committee of Enquiry was set up in 1958, and this prompted the start of a massive campaign to save the canal. The campaign was successful: the decision not to abandon the canal was announced by the Ministry on the 22nd of May 1959. On October 16th of the same year the National Trust announced that it had agreed a lease from the British Transport Commission under which the Trust would assume responsibility for restoring and maintaining the southern section. The transfer took place on the 29th September 1960 and restoration work began in earnest in March of the following year. The terms of the arrangement included a contribution towards the cost of restoration but a very substantial sum was provided by the Trust, which maintained the southern section at its own expense. (The freehold was transferred by BWB to the Trust in 1965.)

The re-opening ceremony was performed by Queen Elizabeth the Queen Mother on the 11th of July 1964, after more than 4 years of hard work by prison labourers, canal enthusiasts, Army units and a handful of National Trust staff. Regrettably in recent years the NT has found itself unable to maintain the canal in a satisfactory condition, and by the end of 1981 a backlog of work amounting to £500,000 had accumulated. It was then suggested that the southern Stratford-on-Avon Canal could be administered by a newly formed Stratford Canal Trust, in an attempt to ensure a secure future for this waterway—however, as yet nothing has been finalised.

Natural history

Between the green tunnel of trees near King's Norton and the lily-covered basin at Stratford, there is great scope for seeing the wild life and plants that frequent this delightful Warwickshire canal. After passing through Shirley, the canal enters the old Forest of Arden and for miles the banks are bordered by sturdy oaks and hazel bushes, which are a great attraction to grey squirrels. Here, the harsh calls of jays and the rattle of magpies are familiar sounds. It is worth making a halt at Earlswood, for it is only a few minutes' walk to the feeder reservoirs which attract naturalists from all over the Midlands. Here, at any time of the year, several pairs of great crested grebes can be seen carrying out their curious courtship ritual; the birds face each other, shake their heads from side to side, then dive and present offerings of weed. In early summer the young grebes can sometimes be seen riding on the parents' backs.

East of the open fields of Hockley Heath, the canal descends through the Lapworth flight. The locks and bridges are interesting as the walls are often covered with profusion of plant life, including the small ferns of the spleenwort family. Further down, in the southern section past lock 29, there is a magnificent display of hartstongue ferns growing near a demolished railway bridge. Past lock 27, the western bank is lined with large alders and pollarded willows, the haunt of tits and warblers. During late summer these trees provide a roosting place for countless swallows.

At Yarningale, the canal crosses a tributary of the River Alne, which flows parallel for several miles. The dipper, which is rather lik a blackbird but with a white breast, is sometimes seen around here, skimming over the water or perched on a stone. It is unique in being able to 'fly' underwater, as well as walk on the stream bed in search of insects. From Preston Bagot to Bishopton, the canal passes through one of the richest parts of Warwickshire as far as wildlife is concerned. Badgers are very common in the area and can sometimes be observed from the canal several hours before sunset; with luck, weasels can be seen hunting on the banks. These animals can be observed only when the boat is moored and quiet. It is worth a pause at bridge 51 and a walk up the bridle path to Austy Wood. Apart from numerous warblers, this wood houses a large number of great spotted woodpeckers, whose drumming can be heard during spring. In this area, Canada geese and several species of ducks frequently fly over to Wootton Pool. The harsh 'kwark' of the heron is a familiar sound, for there is a small heronry at the Pool and the birds are busy at their nests from March until August. At least 4 pairs of kingfisher have their homes on the Stratford Canal, and they may occasionally be seen perched on lock gates as they watch for rising fish. Another interesting bird, which can be heard singing during late afternoon and evening, is the grasshopper warbler; it sounds just like a grasshopper or a fisherman's reel. The moorhen is the most common water-bird on the canal; 57 have been counted in the 5 mile stretch between Lowsonford and Wilmcote. The moorhen nests from early spring to late September, so great care should be taken to avoid clumps of reeds in which a nest may be concealed. Many nests are easy to spot from a boat and, as a rule, they are limited to one side of the canal—opposite the towpath. Moorhens feed on almost anything; they can be seen pecking at blackberries, pulling leaves off plants or foraging in the fields amongst cows. At night they frequently roost in the alder trees lining the bank.

Wild flowers of the canal are too numerous to list. Purple loosestrife is one of the most showy flowers but is not found above Wootton Wawen. It is one of the food plants of the elephant hawkmoth caterpillar, a creature some 3in long with a pair of conspicuous eye spots near the front of its body. The arrowhead is generally considered to be quite rare in the British Isles, but towards Stratford its peculiar arrow-shaped leaves and spikes of white flowers are abundant in summer. The flowering rush is fairly common throughout the canal. Anyone particularly interested in pond life should dip his net at the winding holes where all manner of aquatic insects are to be found among the pink spikes of bistort.

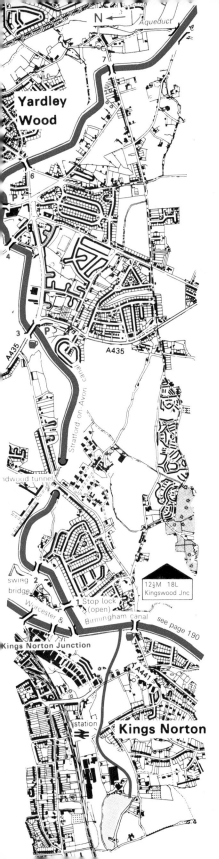

King's Norton

The west end of this delightful canal is at
King's Norton, just outside Birmingham. As
may be guessed from the map, the first 5 miles
of the navigation pass entirely through
residential outskirts of the Birmingham
conurbation. The canal veteran might expect
this to be a dull or scruffy stretch, but he would
be wrong: in fact the Stratford Canal is
bordered all the way with dense but varied
vegetation and, thus protected from the inroads
of the suburbs, forms a quiet, winding ribbon
of green all the way through to the real
countryside. In conjunction with the northern
section of the Worcester & Birmingham Canal,
this is a far more scenically interesting route
between Lapworth and Birmingham than via
the Grand Union Canal.

Leaving the Worcester & Birmingham (*see page
189*) at King's Norton Junction, the
Stratford-on-Avon Canal proceeds straight to
the well-known King's Norton stop lock. In the
days of the private canal companies, stop locks
were common at junctions, as one canal sought
to protect its water supply from any newcomer;
but King's Norton stop lock is unusual in
having 2 wooden guillotine gates mounted in
iron frames balanced by chains and
counterweights. The machinery is now seized
up, and boats pass under the 2 gates without
stopping. The next bridge is a small swing
bridge, then round the corner is Brandwood
Tunnel. Further east is a beautiful tree-lined
cutting, then a bridge with a pub beside it
(*petrol and telephone nearby*) and the remains of
an old arm just beyond it. A water point is
outside a cottage near bridge 5. The canal
continues through pleasant wooded
cuttings—access is bad at most of the bridges,
so the seclusion is virtually complete.

Brandwood Tunnel 352yds long, this tunnel
has no towpath. Horse-drawn boats had to be
hauled through by means of an iron hand-rail
on the side. Lengths of this rail can still be seen
in the tunnel.

PUBS

🍺 **Horse Shoe** Canalside, at bridge 3. Cold
food. *Telephone and petrol nearby*.

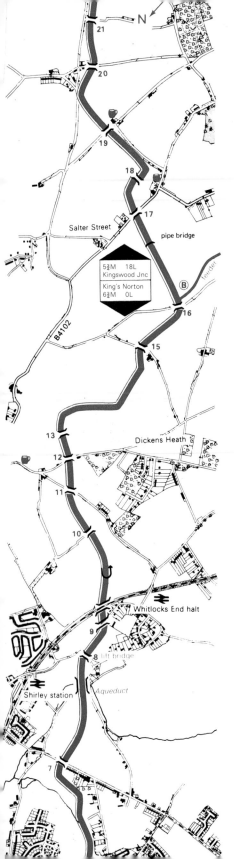

Earlswood

Passing over a small aqueduct, the canal reaches a steel lift bridge, which has to be raised and lowered with a windlass. (There are 2 more of these bridges nearer Lapworth). Passing under a railway bridge, the canal sheds all traces of the suburbs but maintains its twisting course in wooded cuttings through quiet countryside. The bridges over the navigation are mostly the generous brick arched bridges typical of the canal between King's Norton and Lapworth Locks (in contrast to the much smaller bridges further south), but few roads of any significance come near the canal. At bridge 16 the canal emerges from a long cutting and is joined by a feeder from the nearby Earlswood Reservoirs. Several boats are moored along it, for at the junction there is a boatyard and the mooring site of the Earlswood Motor Yacht Club. There are no villages along this rural stretch of canal, but at Salter Street there is a modern school and a strange Victorian church. At bridge 19 (which spans a cutting) is a cider house. One of the buildings here was once a brewhouse.

Earlswood Reservoir Half a mile south of bridge 16 is this canal-feeding reservoir, surrounded by trees and divided into 3 lakes: Windmill Pool, Engine Pool and Terry's Pool. There is a sailing club on Terry's Pool, and fishing available to the general public on the other 2. The BWB bailiff will supply information about the lakes. (Lapworth 2091).

BOATYARDS

ⓑ **Earlswood Marine Services** Lady La, Earlswood, Warwicks. (Earlswood 2552). R S W D E Gas, chandlery, slipway, moorings. Large trip boats for hire. Licensed club. Base of the Earlswood Yacht Club; visitors welcome. *Open all year.*

BOAT TRIPS

'Cepheus' Full-length motor narrow boat available for party bookings from Earlswood. Bar on board, and carries a maximum of 45 to 50 passengers. All enquiries to Earlswood Marine Services (*see above*). *Open all year.*

PUBS

● **Blue Bell** Cider house. Canalside, at bridge 19. Good mooring jetty.
● **Bull's Head** ¼ mile south of bridge 17. Old country pub.
● **Red Lion** 500yds south of bridge 16, near Earlswood Reservoir.
● **The Drawbridge** By bridge 8. Davenports real ale, lunchtime food, garden.

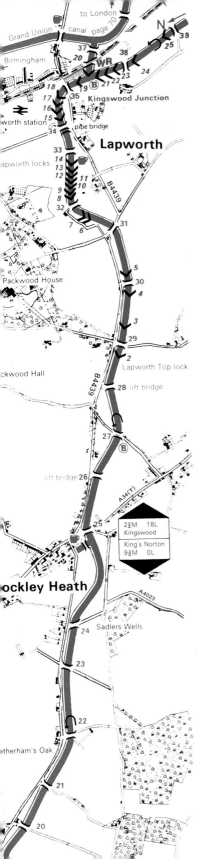

Lapworth Locks

The canal continues to wind gently south eastwards through the quiet countryside, sometimes in minor cuttings and often flanked by trees. To begin with, there are no locks, and the bridges—especially those in the cuttings—are still the big brick arches worthy of a broader canal. At Hockley Heath (bridge 25) there is a tiny arm that once served a coal wharf. Nearby the Wharf Inn overlooks the canal. East of here things change dramatically, for the first of the 55 narrow locks down to Stratford is reached. (The top lock is numbered 2, the old stop lock at King's Norton being number 1). The surroundings of the top lock are indeed pleasant: a white house surrounded by walls and hemmed in by trees stands beside the lock, while a cottage with a delightful garden faces the towpath just below. To the south west can be seen the spire of Lapworth Church. After the first 4 locks is a ½-mile breathing space, then the Lapworth flight begins in earnest, with each of the next 9 locks spaced only a few yards from its neighbour. The short intervening pounds have been enlarged to provide a bigger working reservoir of water, so that one side of each lock is virtually an isthmus. The locks have double bottom gates and are not heavy going. They are interspersed with the old cast-iron split bridges that are such a charming feature of the Stratford-on-Avon Canal. These bridges are built in 2 halves, separated by a 1in gap so that the towing line between a horse and a boat could be dropped through the gap without having to disconnect the horse. Below lock 19 is Kingswood Junction: boats heading for Stratford should keep right here. A short branch to the left through lock 20 leads under the railway line to the Grand Union Canal.

Lapworth
Warwicks. P.O. Tel. Stores, garage, station.
Indivisible from Kingswood, this is more a residential area than a village. Two canals pass through Lapworth: the heavily locked Stratford-on-Avon Canal and, to the east, the main line of the Grand Union Canal. These 2 waterways, and the short spur that connects them, are easily the most interesting aspect of Lapworth. There are usually plenty of boats about, especially on the southern section of the Stratford Canal (below lock 21), the canalside buildings are attractive and there are 2 small reservoirs at the junction. The mostly 15thC church is quite separate from the village and is 1½ miles west of the junction; it contains an interesting monument by Eric Gill, 1928.
Packwood House NT Property. Lapworth. (2024). ½-mile north of the B4439 road bridge. A 16thC timber-framed house, enlarged in the 17thC by John Fetherstone. It was he who created the clipped yew garden that is held to represent the Sermon on the Mount. The house contains collections of tapestry, needlework and furniture. *Open Apr–Sep, Wed to Sun and B. Hols afternoons only.*
Hockley Heath
Warwicks. P.O. Tel. Stores, garage. A featureless place, but the several shops are conveniently close to the canal bridge.

BOATYARDS

Ⓑ **Swallow Cruisers** Wharf Lane, Hockley Heath, Warwicks. (Lapworth 3442). Beside bridge 27. Slipway, gas, boat & engine repairs, mooring, chandlery, toilets.
Ⓑ **Canal Depot** Lapworth Junction. (Lapworth 3370). Ⓡ Ⓢ Ⓦ Licences issued for the southern section of the Stratford-on-Avon Canal. *Closed Nov–Mar.*

PUBS

🍺 **Navigation** Lapworth. Canalside, on Grand Union Canal at bridge 65.
🍺 **Boot Inn** Lapworth, near lock 14.
🍺 **Wharf Inn** Hockley Heath. Canalside, at bridge 25. Food and a garden down to the canal.

A barrel roofed cottage and split bridge, both typical of the Stratford-on-Avon Canal. *Derek Pratt*

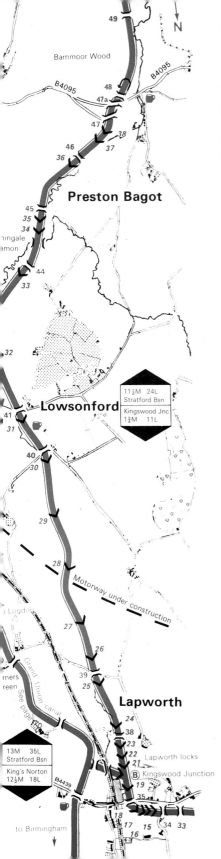

Preston Bagot

At Kingswood Junction the Stratford Canal
continues south, locking steadily downward.
The locks have single gates and very small
paddles, so they are slow to fill and empty. At
some of them are the little iron split bridges
over the lock-tail; and at intervals may be seen
the delightful barrel-roofed lock-cottages which
are just as much a hallmark of this canal as are
the bridges. Most of these cottages are
inhabited and well cared for—a great contrast
to many of the cottages on the canal system.
Indeed the whole of the southern Stratford has
the appearance of a canal that is cherished by
the people living along it—the towpath is in
places beautifully mown, the hedges trimmed
and the locks and bridges painted. The canal
goes through folds of very pretty, wooded
country, rarely encountering a main road or
more than a scattering of houses. This virtual
seclusion is maintained right through to
Stratford. At Lowsonford is a pub where boats
may moor in among the weeping willows of the
garden; at Yarningale the canal, having
followed a small stream for several miles,
crosses it on a tiny iron aqueduct adjoining lock
34.

Navigational note
The southern section of the Stratford-on-Avon
Canal—i.e. from Lapworth to Stratford—is not
administered by British Waterways Board. A
special licence to navigate the canal must be
obtained from the Canal Office by lock 21.
Facilities for boats are also available.

Preston Bagot
Warwicks. A small, scattered settlement with
attractive, ancient houses here and there,
including the 16thC manor. The Church of All
Saints has a Norman nave and other Norman
details, with Victorian additions.
Lowsonford
*Warwicks. P.O. Tel. Stores (all just west of lock
30).* Another small and scattered hamlet,
tucked away by the canal.

PUBS
● **Old Crab Mill** Preston Bagot, 350yds west
of the new road bridge. *Telephone outside.*
●✕ **Fleur de Lys** Lowsonford, by the canal
north of lock 31. Ancient building with large
garden. Food.
● **Tom o' the Wood** Finwood Rd, Rowington.
Canalside, on the Grand Union canal. ½ mile
south east of Stratford Canal bridge 39, beyond
the railway. Whitbread and Flowers real ale,
food, garden.

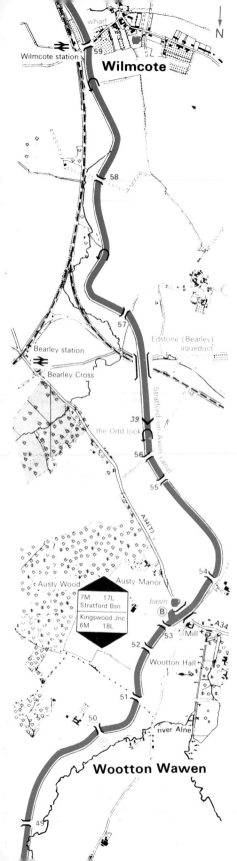

Wilmcote

Lock 38 at Preston Bagot introduces 2 long
pounds, which are welcome on such a heavily
locked canal. The canal continues through
delightfully quiet country, passing a farm as the
big Austy Wood looms up on the hill to the
east. (The low stone hall is Austy Manor.)
Beyond bridge 53 the canal widens into a
basin—a boatyard and a pub are here—and
then crosses the A34 road on a cast-iron
aqueduct. Soon it enters a slight cutting—rare
on the southern section of this canal—and then
straightens out at lock 39—known as the Odd
Lock. Further south the canal rises on an
embankment and is then carried across the
water-meadows, a road and a railway by the
splendid Edstone aqueduct. At the south end is
a very pretty cottage and garden. The
navigation now winds along a secluded course
to Wilmcote. Just north of the village are the
remains of a bridge—this used to carry a horse
tramway that served nearby quarries. The
winding hole and the cottages on the towpath at
this point were built for the quarry trade.
Wilmcote is close to the canal.

Wilmcote
Warwicks. P.O. Tel. Stores, garage. A small and
attractive village, typical of this part of the
world. A beautiful lime tree on the green is the
centre of the village: nearby are a fine old pub, a
residential hotel and the most well-known
building in the village—Mary Arden's Cottage.
The school and a vicarage by the church were
built by William Butterfield c1848. The little
railway station is to the east of the canal: with
its trim roses and well-painted structures it is
kept very much in the old tradition.
Mary Arden's Cottage Wilmcote. This was the
home of Shakespeare's mother, and is a
beautiful 15thC timbered farmhouse. The long,
low house crouches behind luxurious and
well-tended flower beds, and contains a
museum of agricultural implements and local
rural bygones. It is owned by the Shakespeare
Birthplace Trust. *Open weekdays, and Sun
afternoons in summer.*
Edstone (or Bearley) Aqueduct This major
aqueduct, approaching 200yds in length,
consists of a narrow cast-iron trough carried on
brick piers across a shallow valley. As with the
2 other—but much smaller—iron aqueducts on
this canal (at Yarningale and Wootton Wawen)
the towpath runs along the level of the bottom
of the tank, so that towing horses and
pedestrians get a duck's eye view of passing
boats. This feature makes the aqueducts on this
canal very unusual.
Wootton Wawen
Warwicks. P.O. Tel. Stores, garage, station.
This scattered but very pretty village is half a
mile west of the basin. The village has been
designated a Conservation Area. There are
plenty of timbered houses and the late 17thC
Hall looks superb across the parkland and
pond; but the chief glory is the Church of St
Peter on its rise overlooking the whole village.
This church should certainly be visited. Its
unusual building history has given it a
pleasantly disorderly external appearance, but
inside there are really rare and fascinating
things to see. The church is the only one in
Warwickshire that derives from Saxon times,
and the original sanctuary in the centre of the
11thC church survives intact, still the focus of
the church after over 900 years. The nave is
conspicuously Norman, the chancel is bare but
large, with a superb 14thC east window. The
Lady Chapel is probably the oddest part of the
whole building—it is like a barn in more ways
than one. It is enormous, with a primitive tiled
roof and a completely irregular brick floor.
Birds are often to be found, enjoying the shelter
it provides. All around the walls is a medley of
monuments. It all adds up to an intriguing
building.
Wootton Wawen Basin This wide, embanked
basin was built when construction of the canal
was halted here for a while. A hire cruiser
base—one of the few on this canal—has been
built here, and was in 1972 awarded a Civic
Trust commendation for its design. With a

nearby pub and petrol station, the wharf is a popular halt with both boaters and motorists. A cast-iron aqueduct carries the canal over the A34 by the basin. This aqueduct has often been damaged by lorries hitting the underside, so now a triangular road sign warning motorists of the headroom is mounted on the aqueduct. Unfortunately this sign has been positioned so that it almost completely obscures the original iron plaque that commemorates the opening of the aqueduct in 1813. Just down the hill from the aqueduct is a fine brick watermill, in good repair. This dates from the late 18thC.

BOATYARDS

Ⓑ **Anglo Welsh Narrow Boats**. The Wharf, Wootton Wawen, Solihull, Warwicks.

(Henley-in-Arden 3427). RSWDE
Pump-out (*Mon–Fri*). Boat hire, gas, boat & engine repairs, mooring, toilets. *Closed Sun*.

PUBS

Swan House Wilmcote. Choice of real ales in a friendly hotel. Food, garden.

Mason's Arms Wilmcote. Snacks and hot meals *daily*. Permanent exhibition of paintings by the landlord's wife.

Olde Bull's Head Wootton Wawen. ½ mile west of the aqueduct. 13thC building. Full restaurant meals daily.

Navigation Wootton Wawen, at the basin. Meals at or near the bar *daily (except Tue)* during licensed hours. Omelettes, steaks, snacks etc.

Mary Arden's cottage at Wilmcote.

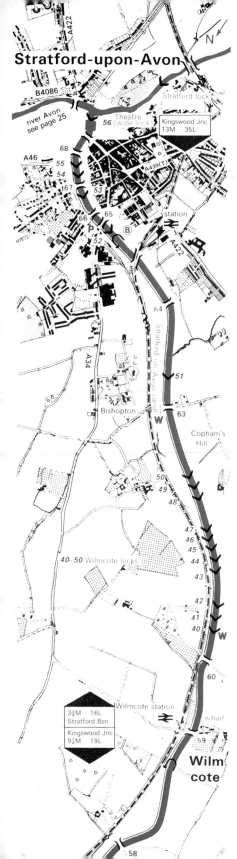

Stratford-upon-Avon

South of Wilmcote, the 2 long pounds from Preston Bagot are terminated by a dense flight of locks—there are 11 in the Wilmcote flight, in groups of 3, 5 and 3. They are set in pleasant open country, in which Stratford can occasionally be seen to the east. Meanwhile the countryside seems flatter, even though there are more locks to come. At bridge 64, a slight bend suddenly reveals the nether regions—gas holders and industrial works—of Stratford. Past 2 railway bridges, a grassy wharf on the right is a boatyard attached to an engineering works. At the next bridge is a winding hole, petrol station and telephone box; then the canal disappears down its own private and inaccessible corridor towards the River Avon. It drops steeply through several locks, accompanied by the little-used towpath; then the towpath disappears altogether, the canal passes through the lowest bridge since Lapworth and one suddenly emerges at the splendid great basin in the middle of the riverside parkland beside the Shakespeare Memorial Theatre. The contrast is astonishing—here is an unwalled, public and attractive basin, constantly surrounded by the famous Stratford tourists, while only a few yards away the canal is completely shut away in a world of its own, forgotten by all except boaters. This seems all the more odd in view of the attention the canal received when it was restored, and ceremonially re-opened by the Queen Mother. For some reason the fine basin has no mooring rings or bollards, so stakes have to be driven into the surrounds (take care your ropes do not trip the many passers-by).

Stratford-upon-Avon
See page 25 for details

BOATYARDS

Ⓑ **Western Cruisers** Western Rd, Stratford-on-Avon, Warwicks. (Stratford 69636). ℝⓈⓌⅅ Pump-out (*Mar–Oct*) Boat hire, gas, boat & engine repairs, mooring, chandlery, toilets, showers, bread & milk.
Ⓑ **Stratford-upon-Avon Marine** Clopton Bridge, Stratford-on-Avon, Warwicks. (Stratford 69669/69773). ℝⓈⓌⅅⒺ Pump-out, gas, chandlery, boat hire, boat building & repairs, mooring, toilets, showers. *Closed Sat afternoon and Sun in winter.*

PUBS

None on the canal. Plenty in Stratford—*see page 26.*

WORCESTER & BIRMINGHAM

Maximum dimensions
Length: 71′ 6″
Beam: 7′
Headroom: 6′

Mileage
WORCESTER, Diglis Basin to
Tibberton: 5¾
Dunhampstead: 7½
Hanbury Wharf: 9¼
Stoke Wharf: 12¾
Tardebigge Top Lock: 15½
Bittell Reservoirs: 20½
KING'S NORTON JUNCTION: 24½
BIRMINGHAM Worcester Bar Basin: 30

Locks: 58

The Bill for the Worcester & Birmingham Canal was passed in 1791 in spite of fierce opposition from the Staffordshire & Worcestershire Canal proprietors, who saw trade on their route to the Severn threatened. The supporters of the Bill claimed that the route from Birmingham and the Black Country towns would be much shorter, enabling traffic to avoid the then notorious shallows in the Severn below Stourport. The Birmingham Canal Company also opposed the Bill and succeeded in obtaining a clause preventing the new navigation from approaching within 7ft of their water. This resulted in the famous Worcester Bar separating the 2 canals in the centre of Birmingham.

Construction of the canal began at the Birmingham end following the line originally surveyed by John Snape and Josiah Clowes. Even at this early stage difficulties with water supply were encountered. The Company were obliged by the Act authorising the canal to safeguard water supplies to the mills on the streams south of Birmingham. To do this, and to supply water for the summit level, 10 reservoirs were planned or constructed. The high cost of these engineering works led to a change of policy: instead of building a broad canal, the company decided to build it with narrow locks, in order to save money in construction and water in operation.

Work on King's Norton Tunnel, described at the time as 'a stupendous undertaking', began in 1794; by 1807 boats could get from Birmingham to Tardebigge Wharf. Here work came to a standstill for several years while the company considered alternative cheaper ways of completing the line down to the Severn. Work eventually started again under a new engineer, John Woodhouse, a great exponent of boat lifts. He proposed reducing the number of locks down to Worcester from 76 to 12, using lifts to descend most of the fall. The company

were less enthusiastic and limited his enterprises to 1 experimental lift at Tardebigge. This seems to have worked reasonably well but the company were still sceptical. They called in the famous canal engineer John Rennie, who decided that the mechanism would not withstand the rough treatment that it would doubtless receive from the boatmen. Consequently locks were built but reduced in number to 58. The site of the lift became the top lock of the Tardebigge flight—which accounts for its unusual depth.

After this, work progressed steadily and the canal was completed in 1815. In the same year an agreement with the Birmingham Canal proprietors permitted the cutting of a stop-lock through the Worcester Bar. The canal had cost £610,000, exceeding its original estimate by many thousands of pounds. Industrial goods and coal were carried down to Worcester, often for onward shipping to Bristol, while grain, timber and agricultural produce were returned to the growing towns of the Midlands. The canal basins in Worcester became important warehousing and transhipment points: Diglis Basin had warehousing for general merchandise, grain and wine, and Lowesmoor Basin specialised in coal and timber. Prosperous businesses were conducted from these wharves and they were an important port of call for the main canal carriers. However the opening of railways in the area in the 1840s and 1850s reduced this traffic considerably and had a profound effect on the fortunes of the canal.

In an attempt to win back salt carrying, the canal company cut the Droitwich Junction Canal in 1852 to connect the Droitwich Barge Canal and the town of Droitwich with their main line at Hanbury Wharf. Toll income and profits continued their relentless decline, however, and after 1864 the company was unable to pay a dividend. In 1874 the canal was bought by the Sharpness New Docks Company. (The words 'Sharpness New Docks and Gloucester & Birmingham Navigation Company' can still be seen on old notices on some of the bridges.) The new management commenced a programme of works to improve the canal in the hope of attracting trade but, in effect, the canal was subsidised by the Gloucester & Berkeley Ship Canal for the rest of its working life.

The animals that used to draw the boats along the Worcester & Birmingham Canal were mainly donkeys worked in pairs instead of the more usual horse. Why this should have been so is not recorded but both horse and donkey were unsatisfactory on the summit level with its 4 tunnels, for only the short Edgbaston Tunnel has a towpath through it. To overcome the delays caused by the need to 'leg' boats through the other tunnels, steam tugs were introduced in the 1870s and successfully hauled trains of boats through the tunnels for many years.

By the early 1900s the commercial future of the canal was uncertain, although the works were in much better condition than on many other canals. Schemes to enlarge the navigation as part of a Bristol–Birmingham route came to nothing. Commercial carrying continued until about 1964, the traffic being mostly between the 2 Cadbury factories of Bournville and Blackpole, and to Frampton on the Gloucester & Sharpness Canal. After nationalisation, several proposals were made to abandon the canal but the 1960s brought a dramatic increase in the number of pleasure boats using the waterway thus securing its future use. Now it is part of the popular cruising circuits comprising the River Severn, the Staffordshire & Worcestershire Canal and part of the Birmingham Canal Navigations, and the Rivers Severn and Avon and Stratford-on-Avon route.

Natural history

The Worcester & Birmingham Canal has a rich variety of plant, bird and insect life throughout its length. Apart from its general interest it provides material for more serious study since it flows past extensive salt deposits left by an ancient sea of the Triassic period, consequently the water is quite brackish in some localities. After emerging from the gloom of the West Hill Tunnel it is worth pausing at the exit not only to admire the tree-covered avenue but to examine the variety of ferns and liverworts which grow on the dripping clay of the high banks. A mile or so downstream, a mooring at Bittell is a must, for the reservoirs are among the best-known bird haunts in this part of the country, particularly for wild duck. One large reservoir (Bittell Lower) lies immediately against the west bank

of the canal. There are always great crested grebe and mallard here, but the commonest water bird is the coot.

The Tardebigge flight of locks gives splendid views over open meadow land where the song of the skylark is usually heard in summer. Here clumps of great willowherb and orange balsam line the banks. The orange balsam was introduced from America, being first recorded in Surrey in 1822; it has now spread along the river and canal system to most of England. When touched, the pods shoot out their seeds to a distance of several feet.

Where the vegetation is dense the harsh scolding of the sedge warbler can be heard; it is particularly frequent in this reach of the canal where caddis flies and other insects are abundant. Two common dragonflies are the large yellow aeshna and the delicate damselfly *ischura elegans*, which has a vivid blue spot on the abdomen. When the locks are emptied the walls can be seen to be covered with thousands of aquatic snails (limnaea). With such an abundance of aquatic organisms it is not surprising that the Worcester & Birmingham Canal is a favourite among anglers.

The calls of redshank and common sandpiper are not unfamiliar at Tardebigge for these waders often fly over on their way to Tardebigge reservoir, which is beside the locks. In addition to waders and waterbirds, herons are usually to be seen feeding in the shallows. In late summer varieties such as the wood sandpiper and the black tern may be occasionally seen at both the Bittell and Tardebigge reservoirs.

At Stoke Prior a subtle change comes over the canal, for the water becomes rather brackish. One interesting waterweed is the enteromorpha—a kind of alga which looks like floating transparent tubes about ½in across. Although the canal is enclosed by brick walls for a short distance, a mass of rosebay willowherb clothes the industrial scars in summer and parts of the waterway are covered with yellow water lilies.

From the Astwood flight to past Hanbury there are many beds of phragmites (reeds) on the west bank. Reed warblers are common in this area as they can only weave their suspended nests in the stems of these plants. Moorhens are common throughout the canal and, in places where bushes and trees hang into the water, families of mallard can usually be seen. Where the bank is low, a grass snake may sometimes be observed swimming in the water hunting for frogs or small fish. The water vole is commom everywhere. Being rather short-sighted and slightly deaf it can sometimes be watched from a distance of 3ft for, like many creatures of the canal, it expects intruders only from the towpath.

indlip Park

22

10 Tolladine lock 7'

21

20

A449(T)

9 Blackpole lock 7'

A4536

19

18

17

N ←

16

7' 0" 8

15 7' 0"

A4536

14

Worcester & Birmingham Canal

6

5' 7' 0"

13

12

N

11

10

B Foregate Station

Shrub Hill Station

7

6

Worcester

5

4 Blockhouse lock 11' 0"

river Severn Navigation see page 165

3 Kings Head lock 11' 0"

A44

24½M 56L King's Norton

Diglis

Detail on page 187

glis locks & 2

Diglis Basin

B B

A38

Weir

Diglis locks

BWB Diglis Yard

Worcester

The Worcester & Birmingham Canal begins at Diglis, on the south side of Worcester. It leaves the River Severn a few hundred yards north of the Diglis Locks, climbs 2 wide (18ft) locks and opens out into one of the 2 Diglis Basins, where a large number of pleasure boats are moored, several of them boatyards: a couple of boatyards and other boating facilities are available here. Past the basin, the canal becomes hemmed in by the town as it enters the first of many deep, narrow locks up to Birmingham. By lock 13 is the Commandery (*see below*). The canal curves round the east side of Worcester, between the town and Shrub Hill station. Access to the town centre is possible at most of the bridges, although the canal is virtually ignored by the town—it is lined by old buildings and intermittent waste ground, and hardly anywhere is it consciously used as a positive part of the urban scene. However, during the summer wild flowers, brambles and buddleia bring a touch of colour. At one point, near the railway viaduct that leads to Foregate station and the west, the towpath rises over the entrance to the Lowesmoore Basin and wharves. Fish and chips are available in Southfield St, beyond the viaduct. A series of 4 locks lifts the canal up and away from the outskirts, then it is crossed by a railway line, with an isolated industrial estate beside it. The canal turns east for several miles, negotiating Blackpole Lock and then Tolladine Lock. Worcester is well behind, and the canal is in open country, but the A449 runs parallel. Hindlip Park is to the north.

Worcester

For notes on Worcester, *see page 165*.
Diglis Basin This is a fascinating terminus at the junction of the River Severn and the Worcester & Birmingham Canal. It consists of basins, boatyards, old warehouses and a dry dock. Commercial craft have been entirely replaced by a mixture of pleasure boats designed for narrow canals rivers and the sea. There are plenty of facilities, 2 boatyards, a chandlery, and the usual BWB facilities. Permission to use the dry-dock should be sought from the BWB basin attendant (Worcester 351174), whose house is at the top of the 2 locks down into the river. The locks will take boats up to 72ft by 18ft 6in, although obviously only narrow boats can proceed along the canal beyond the first lock. The locks (which can be operated only by the basin attendant, between *08.00 and 20.00*, with breaks, for lunch and dinner) incorporate a side pond to save water; and near the second lock is a small pump-house that raises water from the river to maintain the level in the basin.
The Commandery By Kings Head Lock. Founded as a small hospital by Bishop Wulstan in 1085, the present timbered building dates from the reign of Henry VII in the 15thC. It served as Charles Stuart's headquarters before the Battle of Worcester in 1651. The glory of the building is the superb galleried hall with its ancient windows and the Elizabethan staircase. Teas. *Open Tue–Sat and Sun afternoons.*

BOATYARDS

Ⓑ **Viking Afloat** Lowesmoore Basin, Lowesmore Terrace, Worcester. (Worcester 612707) Ⓡ Ⓢ Ⓦ Pump-out, gas, hire craft, souvenirs.
Ⓑ **Diglis Boat Co** Wharf Cottage, Diglis Basin (Worcester 354039). Ⓡ Ⓢ Ⓦ Dry-dock, boat building & repairs, toilets. Boat brokerage a speciality.

PUBS

🍺 **Cavalier Tavern** Worcester. Canalside, at bridge 11. Comfortable modern pub serving Flowers real ale and food. Garden.
🍺 **Bridge** Worcester. Canalside, at bridge 9.
🍺 **Bricklayers Arms** Worcester. 10yds from Blockhouse Lock. Back street local serving Banks's real ale.
🍺 **Anchor** Diglis, on the road just outside the basin grounds.

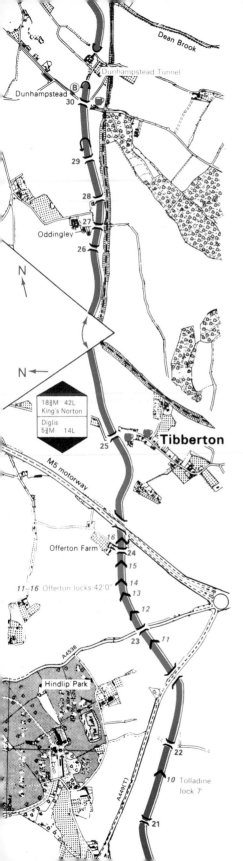

Dunhampstead

This is a very pleasant stretch of rural canal, entirely typical of the Worcester & Birmingham. Having left the outskirts of Worcester, and accompanied by a minor road, the canal now goes under the A449 and ascends the 6 Offerton locks, which are set in pleasant pastureland with a pretty cottage by lock 15. The M5 motorway crosses on its skewed steel bridge; it vanishes immediately as the canal enters a short, curving cutting that brings one to the village of Tibberton. There are 2 pubs nearby, and fruit trees remind one of Worcestershire's orchards. The canal moves towards a ridge of hills to the east, but a railway line intercedes to prevent the canal reaching the side of the valley. This is the main Bristol–Birmingham line, which carries many fast passenger trains, but the only station near the canal is at Bromsgrove. At Oddingley there is a little church and a timbered farm that look out together over the canal; further on are the crowded moorings at Dunhampstead Wharf (popular pub nearby). A wooded cutting leads to Dunhampstead Tunnel, the first of 5 between here and Birmingham. There is no towpath in the tunnel; horses used to walk over the hill while boatmen pulled the boats through by the handrail (still in place) along each side of the tunnel. It is 236yds long.

Dunhampstead
Hereford & Worcs. P.O. Tel. Stores (the shop is a few hundred yards north west of bridge 30). A hamlet consisting of no more than 5 buildings, including the railway signal box. The only life in the area, apart from the trains that roar past the woods, is provided by the canal and the nearby pub. To the north is the tunnel.
Tibberton
Hereford & Worcs. P.O. Tel. Stores (all to the south of the pubs). A small but expanding canalside village, of little interest. There is a fine old rectory by the Victorian church. Milk is sold by bridge 25.

BOATYARDS

Ⓑ **Brook Line** Dunhampstead Wharf. Oddingly. (Droitwich 773889). Ⓡ Ⓢ Ⓦ Ⓓ Pump-out, boat hire, gas, boat building & repair, chandlery, toilets, winter storage. Trip boat and day boats. Craft shop opposite.

PUBS

🍺 **The Firs Inn** Dunhampstead. Very smart and comfortable pub, with excellent food. Garden.
🍺 **Bridge Inn** Tibberton. Handsome village local serving Banks's real ale. Lots of toys in the garden for the children.
🍺 **Speed the Plough** Tibberton. Attractive cottagey pub with small beer garden. Banks's real ale, food *Mon–Sat.*

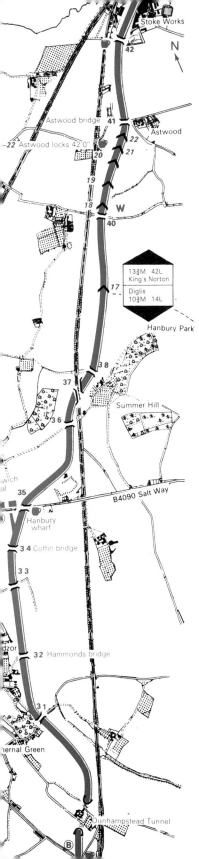

Hanbury Wharf

Leaving Dunhampstead Tunnel, the canal
enters flatter countryside as the hills recede to
the east. The pretty, residential settlement of
Shernal Green flanks the canal, while Hadzor
House (late 18thC in the classical tradition) is
visible in the trees on the west side of the canal.
This straight stretch is terminated by the very
busy area of Hanbury Wharf, where an old arm
and a new building comprise a boatyard for
small pleasure boats. There is a pub by the
main road bridge—the Droitwich Junction
Canal (unnavigable but undergoing restoration)
joins here. North of here the ridge of hills
approaches again from the east. Navigators
should relish this 5½-mile level—it is easily the
longest pound between Worcester and
Tardebigge Top Lock. But as the canal passes
under the railway to take up an uninterrupted
position on its east side, the ridge of hills nears
again, accompanied by attractive parkland.
Milk, eggs and tea and coffee in jugs are sold
from the cottage at Astwood bottom lock, by
the water point. Ahead are the 6 locks in the
Astwood flight, set in pleasant open
pastureland. Near the top is a pub, beside the
railway line; and beyond the cottages at
Astwood Bridge is a semi built-up area—a
minor road joins the canal, lined by workmen's
terraced cottages. A useful grocery store and
post office is here, as well as two more pubs,
one of these having a verandah fronting the
canal. To the north of this settlement is the
reason for its existence—a huge industrial
chemical works. The canal goes through the
middle of this works, much of which is now
changing use.

Stoke Works Now closed, this establishment
was built in 1828 to pump brine (salt) from
underground sources for industrial uses, and
provided much of the canal's trade (later gained
by the railways). Now an industrial estate,
where the housing fronts the tree lined canal,
and all is very tidy.
Hanbury Hall *NT property. (Access via the
public footpath leading south east from lock 17).*
Set in spacious and well-wooded park, this is a
Wren-style red brick house built in 1701 and
little altered since then. On show are the long
room and main staircase with painted ceilings
by Thornhill. *Open: Wed and Sat afternoons
Apr–Sep.*
Hanbury Wharf An interesting canal
settlement at the junction of the Droitwich
Junction and Worcester & Birmingham canals.
A short arm leads to the original wharf, but the
old canal cottages here are now overshadowed
by the big new shed that houses a busy modern
boatyard. Construction of the Droitwich
Junction Canal from here down to Droitwich (2
miles to the west), and of the Droitwich Canal
on to the River Severn, presumably lessened
the usefulness of Hanbury Wharf.

BOATYARDS

Ⓑ **Droitwich Marine** Hanbury Rd, Droitwich,
Worcs. (Droitwich 773002). Ⓡ Ⓢ Ⓦ Boat sales,
gas, chandlery, toilets, showers.

PUBS

🍺 **Boat and Railway** Canalside, just south of
bridge 42. Traditional pub with a terrace on to
the canal. Hansons real ale. There is a
temporary mooring nearby for fish and chips
and provisions.
🍺 **Bowling Green** Beside railway bridge,
200yds south west of bridge 41. Garden,
bowling green, snacks.
🍺 **Eagle & Sun** Hanbury Wharf. Canalside, at
bridge 35. Comfortable, with several cosy
rooms. Excellent food *Mon–Sat*, with
lunchtime cold buffet during the summer. Bass
and M & B real ale.

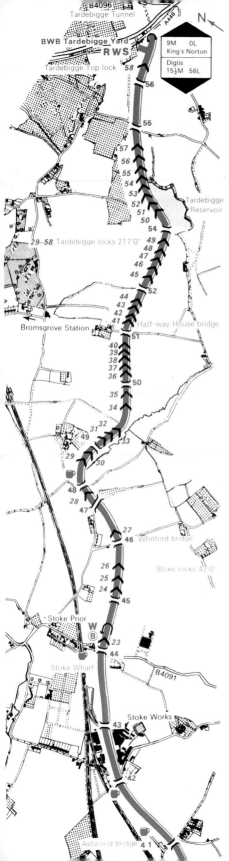

Tardebigge Locks

Approaching Stoke Wharf from the old works, boaters will note the hills to the north east with some misgiving. At Stoke Wharf is the first lock for over a mile; beyond is a crowded mooring site, and then more locks, flanked by trees and pasture land. These locks (numbers 23–28) form the Stoke flight, but in fact there is only a short breathing space of a few hundred yards, with a well-placed pub, before the first of the 30 Tardebigge locks is reached. Forward progress becomes a crawl as this great flight is climbed, but the pleasures of the surroundings make the effort worthwhile. The locks wind up through pretty, folding countryside, leaving the busy railway behind in the west. There are attractive, well-cared-for cottages scattered along the flight, generally near the bridges; their gardens overlook the canal. The locks themselves have great charm, being equipped throughout with traditional wooden gates and balance beams. Large paddles speed up locking, and so a reasonably well co-ordinated crew of 2 can work through a lock every 5 minutes. Regrettably, there is no pub at the top, the next being well beyond Shortwood Tunnel. The remote rural course of the canal takes it well wide of Bromsgrove, but Bromsgrove station is only a mile north west of bridge 51. Between locks 50 and 54 Tardebigge reservoir can be seen behind an embankment on the east bank. This feeder reservoir is particularly popular with fishermen. As the reservoir is about 50ft below the summit level, a steam engine was installed to pump water up the hill. The engine-house still stands near the canal, now converted into a restaurant/disco. Tardebigge Top Lock has a fall of 14ft, one of the deepest narrow locks in the country. When the canal was built, there was a vertical boat lift here. The usual technical problems caused the lift to be replaced by the deep lock, and there is little trace of it now. Above the lock is Tardebigge Wharf, overlooked by the elegant spire of Tardebigge Church, up on the hill to the east. At the wharf is an attractive BWB maintenance yard, and a large mooring site. Leaving the wharf and its cottages behind, the canal vanishes into a tunnel, passing under a main road (A448) at the tunnel mouth.

Tardebigge
Hereford & Worcs. Stores (on A448 10 mins walk from south end of Tardebigge Tunnel). A small farming village flanking the main road. Apart from the settlement near the canal, the best part of the village is up on the hill, around the fine 18thC church with its delicate spire. At the top of the locks a plaque commemorates the founding of the Inland Waterways Assocation in 1946 by L. T. C. Rolt and Robert Aickman, aboard the narrow boat 'Cressy', moored at this spot.

Stoke Wharf
A pretty canal settlement in the best tradition—a lock, a wharf and warehouse, and a pleasant line of houses facing the canal, now housing a boatyard. Stoke Wharf is the only compact element of Stoke Prior—perhaps the heart of the village was drawn to the canal when the latter was built, and has remained there ever since. Stoke Prior Church, which is mainly of the 12thC, stands by itself ½ a mile north of the wharf, the other side of the busy railway junction. Stoke Prior is not a good place for shopping: it is better to victual up at the settlement near bridge 42. However there is a pub near the wharf.

Avoncroft Museum of Buildings, Stoke Prior
1 mile north of Stoke Wharf, off B4091. Old buildings rescued from demolition are re-erected and displayed here. Exhibits include an 18thC post mill, a local nail and chain works, a 15thC timber-framed house from Bromsgrove, and the 14thC roof of Guesten Hall, Worcester. There is also a reconstruction of an Iron Age hut. *Open mid Mar–mid Oct, Tue–Sun.*

BOATYARDS

Ⓑ **BWB Tardebigge Yard** Tardebigge Top Lock. (Bromsgrove 72572). ⓇⓈⓌ Dry dock available, also permanent moorings.
Ⓑ **Black Prince Narrow Boats** Stoke Wharf, Nr Bromsgrove, Worcs. (Bromsgrove 78289). ⓇⓈⓌⒹⒺ Pump-out, boat hire, gas, mooring, chandlery, toilets.

PUBS

✕ **The Engine House** Tardebigge, by lock 57. Smart restaurant and disco *open Thur, Fri and Sat eve.* Suitable only for the well-dressed. Nearest pint to the canal is at bridge 61.
☕ **Queen's head** Canalside at bridge 48. Busy pub with good food and Hansons real ale. Terrace by the water.
☕ **Navigation** Behind Stoke Wharf. A fine spacious pub serving Davenports real ale. Food, garden.

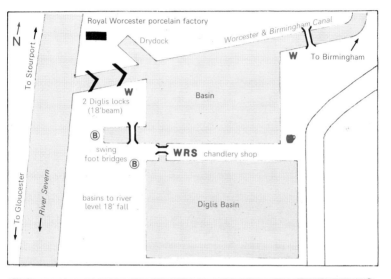

The long haul up Tardebigge Locks. *Derek Pratt*

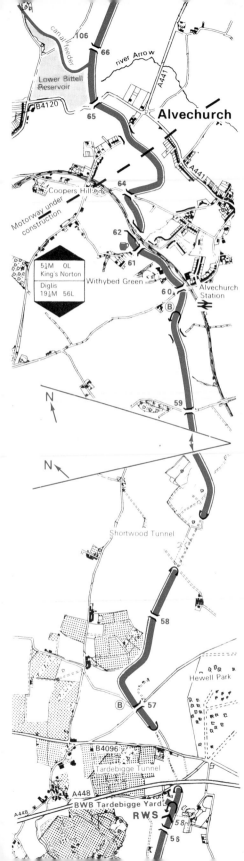

Alvechurch

This is a most delightful stretch of canal that winds through the hilly Worcestershire countryside. The flat Severn valley seems very distant as the canal plunges first into Tardebigge and then Shortwood Tunnel. There is a boatyard between the tunnels. East of Shortwood Tunnel and the surrounding fruit plantations, the canal emerges high up on the side of a low wooded hill, overlooking the modest valley of the River Arrow. In the distance is the hum of traffic on the A441. The canal continues northward, winding steadily through this tranquil landscape until the small town of Alvechurch is reached. The town is set below the canal in a hollow, its church up on a hill; the canal winds tortuously along the steep hills round the outskirts, passing a boatyard, a station and a charming canal pub. Then the canal turns abruptly north; ahead in the distance is the ridge of hills that is pierced by King's Norton Tunnel. Unexpectedly, an aqueduct carries the canal over a little lane that leads to Barnt Green and its station (a mile to the west). Past the aqueduct and through bridge 65, Lower Bittell reservoir comes into view, beside and below the navigation. The canal crosses the valley on an embankment; at the north end of this is a very pretty cottage, which stands at the point where the feeder from Upper Bittell reservoir enters the canal. With these on two sides and an overflow weir and the lower reservoir on the third, the house seems to be virtually surrounded by water.

Bittell reservoirs
These 2 reservoirs were built by the canal company, the upper to feed the canal, the lower being a compensation to local mill owners for the loss of water resulting from construction of the canal. The reservoirs are nowadays popular among anglers and bird watchers.

Alvechurch
Hereford & Worcs. P.O. Tel. Stores, garage, bank, station. A pleasant little town with some fine half-timbered houses, Alvechurch is situated at the bottom of a hollow and surrounded by folds of green hills. However through-traffic on the A441 does not improve the place and there are plans for a southern bypass. The church stands alone on a hill; it is of Norman origin but was largely rebuilt by Butterfield in 1861. There are some interesting monuments within.

Shortwood and Tardebigge Tunnels 608yds long and 568yds long respectively, these are 2 out of the 4 tunnels on the 14-mile summit level of the Worcester & Birmingham Canal. Neither contains a towpath, and until the turn of the century a company tug used to pull all boats through Tardebigge, Shortwood and the great King's Norton Tunnel. Navigators will find Shortwood Tunnel extremely wet and walkers will find the path obscured by wheat fields and difficult to follow.

BOATYARDS

ⓑ **Alvechurch Boat Centre** Scarfield Wharf, Alvechurch, Birmingham. (021 445 2909). At bridge 60. R S W P D E Pump-out, narrow boat hire. Marine engineering of all kinds; boat fitting out, repairs and sales. Engine installation and repairs, gas, chandlery, slipway, permanent moorings, winter storage, toilets. Groceries nearby, over canal bridge.

ⓑ **Dartline** Old Wharf, Tardebigge. (Bromsgrove 73898). R W D Pump-out, gas, narrow boat hire. Shop, trip boat 'Midlander'.

PUBS

🍺 **Crown** Alvechurch. Canalside, at bridge 61. Pleasant country pub serving M & B real ale. Seats outside among geraniums.

🍺 **Swan Hotel** Swan St, Alvechurch. Snacks.

King's Norton Tunnel

Leaving the reservoirs, the canal curves
through a slight cutting to Hopwood, where
there is a pub, a boatyard and a busy main road
crossing. North of here the canal enters a
cutting that leads to King's Norton Tunnel.
The ridge of hills that this tunnel penetrates
serves as an important geographical boundary;
for to the south of it is the rolling open
countryside of rural Worcestershire, while
north of the tunnel is Warwickshire, and the
southernmost indications of Black Country
industrial development. The built-up area is
revealed as soon as the canal leaves the cutting
at the north end of the tunnel: to the west is
King's Norton, while all around are new houses
and light industries. At bridge 71 (the best
access point for the village and its shops) is the
main mooring site of the local boat club; just
past it is the old canal cottage at King's Norton
Junction. Here the Stratford-on-Avon Canal
enters at right angles—the guillotine
mechanism of the celebrated King's Norton
Stop Lock can be seen a few hundred yards
along it. Boats heading for the south east should
turn off down the Stratford Canal here (*see page
173*). Meanwhile the Worcester & Birmingham
Canal continues towards Birmingham, under a
roving bridge at the junction, then under an
inelegant steel bridge that connects a canalside
factory with its car park. Another turnover
bridge (73) is encountered: there is a telephone
box near it and a further industrial stretch just
beyond.

King's Norton
*West Midlands. P.O. Tel. Stores, garage, bank,
station.* The village has done well to survive as a
recognisable entity, for the suburbs of
Birmingham have now extended all around it,
and the amount of urban traffic passing through
the village leaves one gasping. But it *is* still a
village, and the small village green, the old
grammar school buildings and the soaring spire
of the church ensure that it will remain so. The
church is set back a little from the green in an
attractive churchyard, and is mainly of the
14thC, although 2 Norman windows can still be
seen. The grammar school is even older—it was
probably founded by King Edward III in 1344.
An interesting puzzle is that the upper storey is
apparently older than the ground floor. . . .
The school declined during the last century and
was closed in 1875. Now restored it is an
ancient monument.
King's Norton Tunnel Otherwise known as
Wast Hill or West Hill Tunnel, this 2726yd
bore is one of the longest in the country. It is
usually difficult to see right through the tunnel,
and there are plenty of drips from the roof in
even the driest weather. A steam-powered
—and later a diesel—tunnel tug service used to
operate in the days of horse-drawn boats (there
is no towpath). The old iron brackets and
insulators that still line the roof were installed
to carry telegraph lines through the tunnel.
Grandiose bridges (nos 69 and 70) span the
cutting at either end.
Hopwood
West Midlands. Tel. Garage. Provisions
available at mobile home site, 200 yds NW of
bridge 67. More a name than a village,
Hopwood is merely a small settlement. There
are buildings near the canal which may be
useful to canal travellers; a pub, a boatyard, a
petrol station. A fast main road bisects the area.

BOATYARDS
Ⓑ **Marine Sales & Service** Birmingham Rd,
Hopwood, near Alvechurch, Birmingham. (021
445 2595). Ⓡ Ⓦ Ⓟ Ⓓ Small slipway, light boat
repairs. Outboard and inboard engine repairs.
Boatbuilding and fitting out. Gas, mooring,
chandlery, winter storage.

PUBS
● **Navigation Inn** King's Norton, 100yds west
of bridge 71.
● **Hopwood House** Hopwood. Canalside, at
bridge 67. Food *Mon–Sat.*

Edgbaston

Just north of King's Norton Junction, the canal
enters an industrial area. Access is closed off at
most of the bridges. Canal veterans will
recognise this as typical of an approach to the
great city of Birmingham and will doubtless
resign themselves to 10 miles of this kind of
scenery. But, thankfully, it does not last, for
the canal seems to hold the industries at bay on
one side, while a railway line (the main line
from Worcester and the south west to
Birmingham) draws alongside on its west flank.
Canal and railway together drive through the
middle of Cadbury's Bournville works, which is
interesting rather than oppressive. Beyond it is
the rather tired-looking Bournville station,
followed by a cutting. Soon the railway
vanishes briefly behind the buildings of Selly
Oak; the canal goes through this suburb, but
access is closed off at the road bridge (80).
Between this and the next, skewed, railway
bridge is the site of the junction with the
Dudley Canal, but no trace remains here now of
either the junction or the canal itself. North of
here the canal and railway together shrug off
industry and town, and head off on an
embankment towards Birmingham in splendid
isolation and attractive surroundings. Below on
either side is the green spaciousness of
residential Edgbaston, its botanical gardens and
woods. A hospital is on the west side. The
University of Birmingham is on the east side;
among its many large buildings the most
conspicuous is the Chamberlain campanile
tower, which was erected in 1900. At one of the
bridges near the University, 2 Roman forts
used to stand; but most evidence of them was
obliterated by the building of the canal and
railway. Only a reconstructed part of the larger
fort exists now. Past the University's moorings,
canal and railway enter a cutting, in which their
enjoyable seclusion from the neighbourhood is
complete; the charming old bridges are high,
with no access possible, while the cutting is
steep, and always lined by overhanging foliage.
It is a remarkable approach to Birmingham,
and quite unrivalled by any other waterway.
The railway is the canal's almost constant
companion, dipping away here and there to
reappear a short distance further on; but trains
are not too frequent, and in a way their
occasional appearance heightens the remoteness
that attaches to this length of canal. At one
stage the 2 routes pass through short tunnels
side by side: the canal's tunnel is the
northernmost of the 5 on this canal and the only
one with a towpath through it. It is a mere
150yds long.

Edgbaston
A desirable residential suburb of Birmingham,
Edgbaston is bisected but unnoticed by the
canal, and there is little contact between them.
However, for those who contrive to be on the
'landward' side of Edgbaston, there are several
things to be visited.
Cannon Hill Park Edgbaston, about 1½ miles
east of the University. Formal gardens
including a Japanese Garden of Contemplation;
tropical and sub-tropical plants adjacent.
Birmingham Zoo is now housed here.
Cannon Hill Museum Pershore Rd,
Edgbaston. Designed primarily for children.
Illustrated leisure-time pursuits including
bird-watching, bee-keeping, fishing and pets.
Safari hut around which the sounds, sights and
smells of the African bush are re-created. *Open
daily. Closed Sun morning.*
Geological Department Museum The
University, Edgbaston. Collection of
palaeontology, stratigraphy, petrology,
mineralogy and physical geology, including the
Holcroft collection of fossils and the Lapworth
collection of graptolites. *Open daily by
arrangement.* (021 472 1301).
Botanical Gardens Edgbaston. Founded over
100 years ago. Alpine Garden, lily pond and a
collection of tropical birds. *Open daily.*
Perrott's Folly Monument Rd, Edgbaston. 7
storey tower built in 1758 by John Perrott. One
theory as to its origin is that Mr Perrott could,
from its height, gaze on his late wife's grave 10
miles away. Since the late 1800s it has been
used an observatory.

The Dudley Canal This canal used to join the Worcester & Birmingham at Selly Oak, thus providing a southern 'bypass' round Birmingham. The eastern end of the canal has been closed for many years, and will certainly remain so. The tremendously long (3795yd) Lappal Tunnel (now collapsed) emerged 2 miles from Selly Oak. This bore was more like a drain pipe than a navigable tunnel—it was only 7ft 9in wide, a few inches wider than the boats that used it, and headroom was limited to a scant 6ft. Boats were assisted through by a pumping engine flushing water along the tunnel, but it must still have been a nightmarishly claustrophobic trip for the boatmen.

Bournville Garden Factory The creation of the Cadbury family, who moved their cocoa and chocolate manufacturing business south from the centre of Birmingham. The Bournville estate was begun in the late 1800s and is an interesting example of controlled suburban development. The old canal wharves can be clearly seen, but nowadays most of the ingredients travel by rail—the shunting engines are painted in the familiar Cadbury's livery.

Selly Manor and **Minworth Greaves** Bournville. 2 half-timbered Birmingham houses of the 13th and early 14thC re-erected in the 1920s and 1930s in Bournville. They contain a collection of old furniture and domestic equipment. *Open Tue, Wed, Fri afternoons.* Enquiries to the Curator, 44 Mulberry Rd, Bournville, Birmingham, B30 1TA. *The nearest point of access from the canal is at Bournville station: walk west to the Cadbury's entrance. There is a public right of way (Birdcage Walk) through the works: bear right at the fork, then turn right at the village green. The 2 houses are close by, on the left.*

The leafy Worcester & Birmingham Canal. *David Perrott*

Birmingham

The Worcester & Birmingham Canal now
completes its delightful approach to
Birmingham, and in only the last few hundred
yards to Worcester Bar Basin (Gas Street Basin)
does it assume the appearance of a typical
Birmingham waterway. The railway disappears
underneath in a tunnel to New Street station,
while the canal suddenly makes a 90-degree
turn left to the basin. The terminus of the
Worcester & Birmingham Canal is the former
stop lock; this is known as Worcester Bar, for
originally there was a physical barrier here
between the Worcester & Birmingham Canal
and the much older Birmingham Canal: the
latter refused to allow a junction, and for
several years goods had to be transhipped at
this point from one canal to the other. This
absurd situation was remedied by an Act of
Parliament in 1815, by which a stop lock was
allowed to be inserted to connect the two
canals. Nowadays the stop gates are kept open
and one can pass straight through, on to the
Birmingham Canal. This canal goes under a
short tunnel (or a long bridge) with a church on
top of it, to Farmer's Bridge Junction. From
here the Birmingham Canal aims off north west
towards the body of the Birmingham Canal
Navigations network (*see book 2*).

*The route described below is the Birmingham &
Fazeley Canal from Farmer's Bridge to Salford
Junction, where it links up with the canals
described in book 2 of this series.*

Turning north east off the main line of the
Birmingham Canal, one arrives shortly at
Cambrian Wharf—a startlingly attractive canal
basin with a modern canal pub, BWB moorings
and a generally smart and tidy appearance, all
overlooked by 4 big blocks of flats. There are
some well-painted locks too, for from this point
the Farmer's Bridge flight of 13 locks descends
steeply into the heart of Birmingham. Many of
the locks were built very close together and so
the intervening pounds were expanded as much
as possible in every direction. This results in
one side of each lock becoming like a peninsula,
flanked by water. The course of the flight is
mainly dark and mysterious, for over the years
the canal has become so frequently crossed by
bridges, and even roofed over by vast
buildings, that it becomes like a subterranean
journey—and not always an easy one, working
through locks where daylight is never
abundant. The canal is, however, totally cut off
from the town that jostles it so closely: all access
places have been sealed off, and consequently
towpath walkers are rarely seen. After passing
the base of Birmingham's Post Office Tower
and under the great arch of the now closed
Snow Hill station, the canal levels out as the
locks come to an end. But soon comes Aston
Junction, marked by the old iron turnover
bridge, on which is cast 'Horseley Iron Works
Staffordshire 1828'. To the north east is the
main line of the Birmingham & Fazeley, falling
through the 11 Aston locks to Salford Junction.
The scenery is typical Birmingham, and is not
very prepossessing: the canal banks are lined by
the back walls of industries, the old private
canal arms and basins are piled off or choked
with weeds. One of the bridges along here has
girders that restrict the headroom to 7ft 9in;
nearby is a canalside petrol station. At the
second lock from the bottom is a lock keeper's
cottage: its gate onto the road gives access to a
small grocery, a petrol station and a pub. This
is probably the only access point between
Farmer's Bridge and Salford Junction: a pity
since, as on the rest of the Birmingham canals,
the towpath is in excellent condition. Towards
Salford Junction itself, the buildings become
fewer and lower. A half-sunken narrow boat
along here provides a wonderful natural
water-garden for many flowering weeds.

Salford Junction At this unusual junction the
Birmingham & Fazeley arrives from
Birmingham, crossing the dirty River Tame on
an aqueduct and bearing half right (east)
towards Minworth and Fazeley. Meanwhile the
short Birmingham & Warwick Junction Canal
(the Saltley Cut) appears from the Grand Union
Canal to the south, also crossing the River

Tame on a low aqueduct. The straight canal entering the junction from the north-west is the Tame Valley Canal, part of the BCN system. However, this intersection of waterways is of little significance compared to what is going on overhead, for this is the site of the notorious Gravelly Hill interchange—the most elaborate urban road junction in Britain. So the whole area of Salford Junction is completely overpowered by the mass of concrete pillars and decking carrying the lines of unseen vehicles in all directions. The sky is truly filled with roads, while the little-known canals creep along underneath. The noise is a little disheartening, but it is a fascinating way to see this remarkably lavish piece of civil engineering.

The Digbeth Branch This leaves the Birmingham & Fazeley main line at Aston Junction, and descends through 6 locks to Bordesley Basin, now disused, where it meets the former Warwick & Birmingham Canal, which became part of the Grand Union Canal when the G.U.C. Company was formed in 1929. There was a stop lock—called Warwick Bar—at the junction by Bordesley Basin. One of the lesser-known tunnels on the canal system is on the Digbeth branch—this is Ashted Tunnel, a short and gloomy tube in the middle of the Ashted locks. There is a narrow towpath through the tunnel, protected by railings and with a corrugated surface for the towing horses to get a good grip on.

Cambrian Wharf The winner of a Civic Trust award in 1970, this development is a promising vision of what can be done to revive Birmingham's canals and create an exciting new townscape for the inhabitants. The construction of 4 new tower blocks of flats near Farmer's Bridge (very close to the centre of Birmingham) provided the incentive for BWB to dredge out and restore the basins at the beginning of the former Newhall branch canal; for Birmingham City Council to make a pleasing canalside walk and restore 2 18thC terraces of cottages in the nearby Kingston Row; and for a local brewery company to build an inspired new canal pub with an extra bar in a floating narrow boat. The overall effect is excellent. Apart from Gas Street Basin, Cambrian Wharf is the best place—the only place—to leave a boat moored safe from the

attentions of wandering vandals. There are permanent moorings available here. For walkers, it is unfortunately impossible to go by canal from Cambrian Wharf to Gas Street Basin (*see below*), since the towpath is sealed off at Cambrian Wharf. One must therefore go through the streets, and the route is as follows: Cambrian Wharf, Kingston Row, St Martin's Place, Cambridge Street, straight across Broad Street, down Gas Street and turn left through a small opening. This leads down onto the towpath at the Basin.

Worcester Bar Basin Unofficially known as Gas Street Basin, it is an amazing contrast with Cambrian Wharf. For, whereas the latter is smart and new, Gas Street is old, comfortable, secluded and very crowded. It is full of delightful narrow boats in working trim but mostly out of work now. The basin is shaped like a flat triangle, with a causeway across the middle. Once hemmed in by original canal warehouses of all kinds, Gas Street Basin had an authentic atmosphere that is now unfortunately diminished by their demolition.

BOATYARDS

Ⓑ **Brummagem Boats** Sherborne St Wharf, Oozell's Street Loop west of Farmers Bridge Junction (021 643 8397). Ⓡ Ⓢ Ⓦ Ⓔ Pump-out, boat hire, gas, boat building & repairs, chandlery, toilets. Safe overnight mooring. *Closed Sun in winter.*

BOAT TRIPS

Second City Canal Cruises Trips from Gas Street Basin on *Suns and B. Hols.* Details from 021-643 4384.

PUBS

🍺 **Duke of Wellington** near the second lock from Salford Junction, on the Birmingham & Fazeley Canal. The only pub easily accessible from the canal between Farmer's Bridge and Salford.

🍺 **Long Boat** Cambrian Wharf, Birmingham. Canalside, near the top lock. Large canal pub, whose 'garden furniture' includes an old canal crane and dock gates. Interior fittings include an original Bolinder engine and butty boat rudders. One of the bars is in a floating narrow boat. Food usually available at bar.

The Birmingham & Fazeley Canal. The towing path rises here over one of the many derelict basins leading off the canal in Birmingham: the rib formation of the cobble stones was designed to assist the towing horses get a firm grip on the slope.

A BRIEF HISTORY OF BRITISH CANALS

River navigations, that is rivers widened and deepened to take large boats, had existed in England since the Middle Ages: some can even be traced back to Roman times. In 1600 there were 700 miles of navigable river in England, and by 1760, the dawn of the canal age, this number had been increased to 1300. This extensive network had prompted many developments later used by the canal engineers, for example, the lock system. But there were severe limitations: generally the routes were determined by the rivers and the features of the landscape and so were rarely direct. Also there were no east-west, or north-south connections.

Thus the demand for a direct inland waterway system increased steadily through the first half of the 18thC with the expansion of internal trade. Road improvements could not cope with this expansion, and so engineers and merchants turned to canals, used extensively on the continent.

One of the earliest pure canals, cut independently of existing rivers, was opened in 1745, at Newry in Northern Ireland, although some authorities consider the Fossdyke, cut by the Romans to link the rivers Trent and Witham, to be the first. However, the Newry is more important because it established the cardinal rule of all canals, the maintenance of an adequate water supply, a feature too often ignored by later engineers. The Newry Canal established the principle of a long summit level, fed by a reservoir to keep the locks at either end well supplied. Ten years later, in England, the Duke of Bridgewater decided to built a canal to provide an adequate transport outlet for his coal mines at Worsley. He employed the self-taught James Brindley as his engineer, and John Gilbert as surveyor, and launched the canal age in England. The Bridgewater Canal was opened in 1761. Its route, all on one level, was independent of all rivers; its scale of operations reflected the new power of engineering, and the foresight of its creators. Although there were no locks, the engineering problems were huge; an aqueduct was built at Barton over the River Irwell, preceded by an embankment 900yds long; 15 miles of canal were built underground, so that boats could approach the coal face for loading—eventually there were 42 miles underground, including an inclined plane—the puddled clay method was used by Brindley to make the canal bed watertight. Perhaps most important of all, the canal was a success financially. Bridgewater invested the equivalent of £3 million of his own money in the project, and still made a profit.

Having shown that canals were both practical and financially sound, the Bridgewater aroused great interest throughout Britain. Plans were drawn up for a trunk canal, to link the 4 major rivers of England: the Thames, Severn, Mersey and Trent. This plan was eventually brought to fruition, but many years later than its sponsors imagined. Brindley was employed as engineer for the scheme, his reputation ensuring that he would always have more work than he could handle. The Trent and Mersey, and the Staffordshire and Worcestershire canals received the Royal Assent in 1766, and the canal age began in earnest.

Canals, like the railways later, were built entirely by hand. Gangs of itinerant workmen were gathered together, drawn by the comparatively high pay. Once formed these armies of 'navigators'—hence 'navvies'—moved through the countryside as the canal was built, in many cases living off the land. All engineering problems had to be solved by manpower alone, aided by the horse and the occasional steam pump. Embankments, tunnels, aqueducts, all were built by these labouring armies kept under control only by the power of the section engineers and contractors.

The Staffordshire and Worcestershire Canal opened in 1770. In its design Brindley determined the size of the standard Midlands canal, which of course had direct influence on the rest of the English system as it was built. He chose a narrow canal, with locks 72ft 7in by 7ft 6in, partly for reasons of economy, and partly because he realised that the problems of an adequate water supply were far greater than most canal sponsors realised. This standard, which was also adopted for the Trent and Mersey, prompted the development of a special vessel, the narrow boat with its 30-ton payload. Ironically this decision by Brindley in 1766 ensured the failure of the canals as a commercial venture 200 years later, for by the middle of this century a 30-ton payload could no longer be worked economically.

The Trent and Mersey was opened in 1777; 93 miles long, the canal included 5 tunnels, the original one at Harecastle taking 11 years to build. In 1790 Oxford was finally reached and the junction with the Thames brought the 4 great rivers together. From the very start English canal companies were characterised by their intense rivalries; water supplies were jealously guarded, and constant wars were waged over toll prices. Many canals receiving the Royal Assent were never built, while others staggered towards conclusion, hampered by doubtful engineering, inaccurate estimates, and loans that they could never hope to pay off. Yet for a period canal mania gripped British speculators, as railway mania was to grip them 50 years later. The peak of British canal development came between 1791 and 1794, a period that gave rise to the opening of the major routes, the rise of the great canal engineers, Telford, Rennie and Jessop, and the greatest prosperity of those companies already operating. At this time the canal system had an effective monopoly over inland transport: the old trunk roads could not compete, coastal traffic was uncertain and hazardous, and the railways were still a future dream. This period also saw some of the greatest feats of engineering.

An early photograph of the Foxton 'staircase'.

A contemporary view of canal promoters. *Eric de Maré.*

The turn of the century saw the opening of the last major cross-country routes; the Pennines were crossed by the Leeds and Liverpool Canal between 1770 and 1816, while the Kennet and Avon (opened in 1810) linked London and Bristol via the Thames. These 2 canals were built as broad navigations: already the realisation was dawning on canal operators that the limits imposed by the Brindley standard were too restrictive, a suspicion that was to be brutally confirmed by the coming of the railways. The Kennet and Avon, along with its rival the Thames and Severn, also marks the introduction of fine architecture to canals. Up till now canal architecture had been functional, often impressive, but clearly conceived by engineers. As a result the Kennet and Avon has an architectural unity lacking in earlier canals. The appearance of architectural quality was matched by another significant change: canals became straighter, their engineers choosing as direct a route as possible, arguing that greater construction costs would be outweighed by smoother, quicker operation, whereas the early canals had followed the landscape. The Oxford is the prime example of a contour canal, meandering across the Midlands as though there were all the time in the world. It looks beautiful, its close marriage with the landscape makes it ideal as a pleasure waterway, but it was commercial folly.

The shortcomings of the early canals were exploited all too easily by the new railways. At first there was sharp competition by canals. Tolls were lowered, money was poured into route improvements; 14 miles of the Oxford's windings were cut out between 1829 and 1834; schemes were prepared to widen the narrow canals; the Harecastle Tunnel was doubled in 1827, the new tunnel taking 3 years to build (as opposed to 11 years for the old). But the race was lost from the start. The 19thC marks the rise of the railways and the decline of the canals. With the exception of the Manchester Ship Canal, the last major canal was the Birmingham and Liverpool Junction, opened in 1835. The system survived until this century, but the 1914–18 war brought the first closures, and through the 1930s the canal map adopted the shape it has today. Effective commercial carrying on narrow canals ceased in the early 1960s, although a few companies managed to survive until recently. However, with the end of commercial operation, a new role was seen for the waterways, as a pleasure amenity, a 'linear national park 2000 miles long'.

Water supply has always been the cardinal element in both the running and the survival of any canal system. Locks need a constant supply of water—every boat passing through a wide lock on the Grand Union uses 96,000 gallons of water. Generally 2 methods of supply were

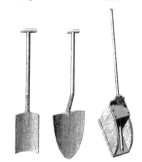

The rudimentary tools of the early 'navvies'. *Hugh McKnight*

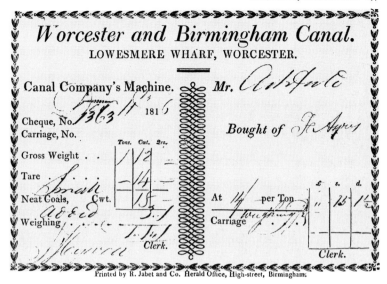

Worcester and Birmingham Canal Company toll ticket dated 1816. *Hugh McKnight*

used: direct feed by rivers and streams, and feed by reservoirs sited along the summit level. The first suffered greatly from silting, and meant that the canal was dependent on the level of water in the river; the regular floods from the River Soar that overtake the Grand Union's Leicester line show the dangers of this. The second was more reliable, but many engineers were short-sighted in their provision of an adequate summit level. The otherwise well-planned Kennet and Avon always suffered from water shortage. Where shortages occurred, steam pumping engines were used to pump water taken down locks back up to the summit level. The Kennet and Avon was dependent upon pumped supplies, while the Birmingham Canal Navigations were fed by 6 reservoirs and 17 pumping engines. Some companies adopted side ponds alongside locks to save water, but this put the onus on the boatman and so had limited success. Likewise the stop locks still to be seen at junctions are a good example of 18thC company rivalry; an established canal would ensure that any proposed canal wishing to join it would have to lock *down* into the older canal, which thus gained a lock of water each time a boat passed through.

Where long flights or staircase locks existed there was always great wastage of water, and so throughout canal history alternative mechanical means of raising boats have been tried out. The inclined plane or the vertical lift were the favoured forms. Both worked on the counterbalance principle, the weight of the descending boat helping to raise the ascending. The first inclined plane was built at Ketley in 1788, and they were a feature of the West Country Bude and Chard canals. The most famous plane was built at Foxton, and operated from 1900–10. Mechanical failure and excessive running costs ended the application of the inclined plane in England, although modern examples work very efficiently on the continent, notably in Belgium. The vertical lift was more unusual, although there were 8 on the Grand Western Canal. The most famous, built

at Anderton in 1875, is still in operation, and stands as a monument to the ingenuity shown in the attempts to overcome the problems of water shortage.

Engineering features are the greatest legacy of the canal age, and of these, tunnels are the most impressive. The longest tunnel is at Standedge, on the now derelict Huddersfield Narrow Canal. The tunnel runs for 5456yds through the Pennines, at times 600ft below the surface. It is also on the highest summit level, 656ft above sea level. The longest navigable tunnel is now Dudley Tunnel, 3154yds, which was re-opened in 1973 after being closed for many years. Others of interest include the twin Harecastle Tunnels on the Trent and Mersey, the first 2897yds, and now disused, the second 2926yds; Sapperton, which carried the Thames and Severn Canal through the Cotswolds and Netherton on the Birmingham Canal Navigations. This last, built 1855–58, was the last in England, and was lit throughout by gas lights, and at a later date by electricity.

The Netherton Tunnel was built wide enough to allow for a towing path on both sides. Most tunnels have no towing path at all, and so boats had to be 'legged', or walked through.

The slowness and relative danger of legging in tunnels led to various attempts at mechanical propulsion. An endless rope pulled by a stationary steam engine at the tunnel mouth was tried out at Blisworth and Braunston between 1869 and 1871. Steam tugs were employed, an early application of mechanical power to canal boats, but their performance was greatly limited by lack of ventilation, not to mention the danger of suffocating the crew.

An electric tug was used at Harecastle from 1914 to 1954. The diesel engine made tunnel tug services much more practical, but diesel-powered narrow boats soon put the tugs out of business: by the 1930s most tunnels had to be navigated by whatever means the boatman chose to use. Legging continued at Crick, Husbands Bosworth and Saddington until 1939.

Until the coming of the diesel boats, the

Islington Tunnel during construction. *Hugh McKnight*

horse reigned supreme as a source of canal power. The first canals had used gangs of men to bow-haul the boats, a left over from the river navigations where 50–80 men, or 12 horses, would pull a 200-ton barge. By 1800 the horse had taken over, and was used throughout the heyday of the canal system. In fact horse towage survived as long as large-scale commercial operation. Generally 1 horse or mule was used per boat, a system unmatched for cheapness and simplicity. The towing path was carried from one side of the canal to the other by turnover bridges, a common feature that reveals the total dominance of the horse. Attempts to introduce self-propelled canal boats date from 1793, although most early experiments concerned tugs towing dumb barges. Development was limited by the damage caused by wash, a problem that still applies today, and the first fleets of self-propelled steam narrow boats were not in service until the last quarter of the 19thC. Fellows, Morton and Clayton, and the Leeds and Liverpool Carrying Co ran large fleets of steam boats between 1880 and 1931, by which time most had been converted to diesel operation. With the coming of mechanical power the butty boat principle was developed: a powered narrow boat would tow a dumb 'butty' boat, thereby doubling the load without doubling the running costs. This system became standard until the virtual ending by the late 1960s of carrying on the narrow canals. Before the coming of railways, passenger services were run on the canals; packet boats, specially built narrow boats with passenger accommodation, ran express services, commanding the best horses and

the unquestioned right of way over all other traffic. Although the railways killed this traffic, the last scheduled passenger service survived on the Gloucester and Berkeley Canal until 1935.

The traditional narrow boat with its colourful decoration and meticulous interior has become a symbol of English canals. However this was in fact a late development. The shape of the narrow boat was determined by Brindley's original narrow canal specification, but until the late 19thC boats were unpainted, and carried all male crews. Wages were sufficient for the crews to maintain their families at home. The increase in railway competition brought a reduction in wages, and so bit by bit the crews were forced to take their families with them, becoming a kind of water gipsy. The confines of a narrow boat cabin presented the same problems as a gipsy caravan, and so the families found a similar answer. Their eternally wandering home achieved individuality by extravagant and colourful decoration, and the traditional narrow boat painting was born. The extensive symbolic vocabulary available to the painters produced a sign language that only these families could understand, and the canal world became far more enclosed, although outwardly it was more decorative.

As the canals have turned from commerce to pleasure, so the traditions of the families have died out, and the families themselves have faded away. But their langauge survives, although its meaning has mostly vanished with them. This survival gives the canals their characteristic decorative qualities, which make them so attractive to the pleasure boater and to the casual visitor.

FISHING

Many anglers start their fishing careers on the canals and navigable rivers, mainly because our system of waterways has always offered excellent opportunities for the thousands of angling enthusiasts throughout Great Britain.

Most of these cross-country waterways have natural reed-fringed and grassy banks, and in addition to the delightful surroundings the fishing is generally good. In most areas there has been a steady improvement in canal fishing in recent years and in many places new stocks of fish have been introduced. The popular quarry are roach, perch and bream, but the canals also hold dace, tench, chub and carp in places, in addition to pike and other species in particular areas.

Canals afford good hunting grounds for those seeking specimen fish (that is, fish above average size) and these are liable to be encountered on almost any water. The canals also make good venues for competition fishing, and in most places nowadays matches are held regularly at weekends throughout the season.

The Statutory Close Season for coarse fish is March 15 to June 15 inclusive, but in some areas, notably the Yorkshire River Authority, the Close Season is from February 28 to May 31. The Close Season for pike in some areas is March 15 to September 30.

Permits and fishing rights

Most parts of the waterways system are available to anglers. The big angling associations—e.g. the London AA, Birmingham AA, Reading & District AA, Coventry & District AA, Nottingham AA plus many smaller clubs—rent fishing rights over extensive areas on the system. In most cases, day tickets are available.

On arrival at the water-side it is always advisable to make enquiries as to who holds the fishing rights, and to obtain a permit if one is required *before* starting to fish. Remember, also, that a River Authority rod licence is usually required in addition to a fishing permit. It is essential to obtain this licence from the relevant River Authority *before* starting to fish. Some fishing permits and licences are issued by bailiffs along the bank, but local enquiry will help to determine this.

A canalside pub or a local fishing tackle shop are good places to enquire if permission or day tickets are required for the local stretch of water. Canal lock keepers are usually knowledgeable about the fishing rights in the immediate locality, and often a lock keeper may be found who issues day tickets on behalf of an angling association, or owner. It is likely that he will also know some of the better fishing areas, as well as local methods and baits which may be considered most successful.

The fishing rights on most canals are owned by the British Waterways Board and many miles of good fishing are leased to clubs and angling associations. They also issue day tickets on certain lengths, so it is worth enquiring at the local British Waterways office when planning a trip. Special arrangements are made for fishing from boats, again, enquire with the BWB locally.

'Private fishing' notices should *not* be ignored. If the owner's name and address is on the board then application can be made for permission for a future occasion. Once permission has been obtained it would be advisable to find out if there are any restrictions imposed, since some clubs and associations ban certain baits, or have restrictions on live-baiting for pike: and on some fisheries pike fishing is not allowed before a specified date.

Other restrictions may concern size-limits of fish, and this certainly applies to the London AA canal fisheries. Some River Authority bye-laws prohibit the retention of under-sized fish in keep nets. A local club holding the fishing rights may have imposed their own size-limits in order to protect certain species. Such restrictions are generally printed on permits and licences.

Tackle

In the slow moving, sluggish waters of canals the float tackle needs to be light and lines fine in order to catch fish. When fishing for roach and dace lines of 1½lb to 2lb breaking strain are the maximum strength normally needed in order to get the fish to take a bait—particularly when the water is clear, or on the popular reaches that are 'hard-fished'.

Fine tackle also means small hooks, sizes 16 and 18—or even as small as 22 at times. Such light gear is also effective when fishing for the smaller species, such as gudgeon and bleak. This tackle will require a well-balanced float to show the slightest indication of a bite.

Bait

Baits should be small, and maggots, casters (maggot chrysalis), hempseed, wheat, tiny cubes of bread crust, or a small pinch of flake (the white crumb of a new loaf) may take fish. It always pays to experiment with baits; bait that is effective on one occasion will not necessarily prove to be as effective the next. With slight variations, similar fishing methods can be used effectively on the majority of waterways.

Northern anglers who regularly compete in contests on canals use bloodworms as bait. They have become extremely skilful in using this tiny bait and often take fish on bloodworms when all other baits fail. Bloodworms are the larvae of a midge, and are a perfectly natural bait. The anglers gather the bloodworms from the mud and, apart from a wash in clean water, the baits are ready for use.

A popular groundbait that has had great success is known as 'black magic'! This is a mixture of garden peat and bread crumbs mixed

Barbel

Bleak

Common Bream

Bullhead

Common Carp

Chub

Dace

Freshwater Eel

Gudgeon

River Lamprey

Perch

Minnow

Roach

Pike

Ruffe

Rudd

Stickleback

Tench

Brown Trout

dry and carried to the water. When dampened and mixed it can be thrown in in the usual way. The basis of most groundbaits is bread, and many other materials may be added, although stodgy mixtures should be avoided when canal fishing. Canals are not waters which respond to heavy groundbaiting tactics. It is far better to use a cloud-bait, and this can be purchased ready for use. Some successful Midland anglers wet their cloudbait with milk instead of water to increase the cloud effect.

Methods

Once the swim—that is the area of water to be fished—has been decided upon, and the tackle set up, use a plummet to find the depth and adjust the float, but be cautious when doing so in clear waters. At times it may be best to find the depth by trial and error. Often most fish will be caught from around mid-water level, but always be prepared to move the float further up the line in order to present the bait closer to the bottom, where the bigger fish are usually to be found. At frequent intervals toss a few samples of the hook-bait into the top of the swim to keep the fish interested.

Fish in different waters may vary in the way they take a bait and this creates a different bite registration. It may be found that fish take the hook-bait quickly, causing the float to dip sharply or dive under the surface. The strike should be made instantly, on the downward movement. On some canals the fish are even quicker—and perhaps gentler—not taking the float under at all, and in this case the strike should be made at the slightest unusual movement of the float.

Roach and dace abound in many lengths and although working the float tackle down with a flow of water takes most fish, better quality fish—including bream—are usually to be taken by fishing a laying-on style, with the bait lying on the bottom. This method can often be best when fishing areas where there is no flow at all. This is done with float tackle, adjusted to make the distance from float to hook greater than the depth of water, so that when the float is at the surface the bait and lower length of line are lying on the bottom.

The alternative method of fishing the bottom is by legering, the main difference in the methods being in the bite indication. Without a float a bite is registered at the rod-tip where, if need be, a quiver-tip or swing-tip may be fitted. These bite detectors are used extensively on Midland and Northern waters. Legering is a method often used in the south, where in some southern canals barbel and chub are quite prolific. These species grow to good sizes in canal waters—chub up to 7lb and barbel up to 14lb have been taken—but these are exceptional and the average run of fish would be well below those weights. Nevertheless, both species are big fish and big baits and hooks may be used when fishing for them.

Many bigger than average fish—of all species—have been taken by fishing the bait on the bottom. Whatever the style of leger fishing, always choose the lightest possible lead weight, and position it some 12 to 18in up from the hook. There are no hard and fast rules governing the distance between lead and hook, so it pays to experiment to find the best to suit the conditions.

Anglers who regularly fish the Northern and Midland Canals invariably use tiny size 20 and 22 hooks, tied to a mere ¾lb breaking strain line, and when float-fishing use a tiny quill float—porcupine or crow quill. A piece of peacock quill is useful because it can be cut with scissors to make it suit prevailing conditions. Such small floats only need a couple of dust-shot to balance them correctly, and usually the Midland anglers position this shot on the line just under the float so that the bait is presented naturally. Once the tackle has been cast out, the bait falls slowly through the water along with hook-bait samples, which are thrown in at the same time. This is called 'fishing on the drop'. A fine cloud-bait is also used with this style.

Canals which have luxuriant weed growth harbour many small fish, which are preyed upon by perch. These move in shoals and invariably the perch in a shoal are much the same size. Usually the really big perch are solitary, so it pays to rove the canal and search for them. They are to be caught from almost any canal and although they may be caught by most angling methods, the most effective is simple float-fishing. The fishing depth can vary according to conditions, time of year, and actual depth of the canal, so it pays to try the bait at varying depths. The usual baits for perch are worms, small live-baits (minnows etc) and maggots. Close by wooden lock gates is often the haunt of large perch.

In certain places canals and rivers come together and take on the characteristics of the river (i.e. with an increased flow) and different methods are needed. These places are often noted for splendid chub (and somtimes barbel) in addition to roach and other species. Trotting the stream is a popular and effective fishing style.

Weather

Weather conditions have to be taken into consideration. Canals usually run through open country and catch the slightest breeze. Even a moderate wind will pull and bob the float, which in turn will agitate the baited hook. If bites are not forthcoming under such conditions then it may be best to remove the float and try a straightforward leger arrangement.

When legering, the effects of the wind can be avoided by keeping the rod top down to within an inch or two of the water level—or even by sinking the rod-tip below the surface. Anglers in the North and Midlands have devised a wind-shield for legering that protects the rod-tip from the wind and improves bite detection. Nevertheless, in some circumstances a slight wind can be helpful because if a moderate breeze is blowing it will put a ripple on the water, and this can be of assistance in fishing in clear waters.

Where to fish

Most canals are narrow and this makes it possible to cast the tackle towards the far bank, where fish may have moved because they had been disturbed from the near bank. Disturbance will send the fish up or downstream and often well away from the fishing area. So always approach the water quietly, and remember to move cautiously at all times. When making up the tackle to start fishing it is advisable to do so as far back from the water as possible to avoid scaring the fish. It pays to move slowly, to keep as far from the bank as possible, and to avoid clumping around in heavy rubber boots. If there is cover along the bank—shrubs, bushes, tall reeds and clumps of yellow flag iris—the wise angler will make full use of it.

There are some canals that are no longer navigable, and these are generally weedy. At certain times in the season the surface of the water disappears under a green mantle of floating duckweed, which affords cover and security for the fish. It is possible to have the best sport by fishing in the pockets of clear water that are to be found.

Some canals have prolific growths of water lilies in places, and are particularly attractive for angling. They always look ideal haunts for tench, but they can also be rather difficult places from which to land good fish. Tench are more or less evenly distributed throughout the canals and the best are found where weed growth is profuse. It may be best to fish small areas of clear water between the weeds. Groundbait can encourage tench to move out from the weed beds, and to feed once they are out. Sometimes it is an advantage to clear a swim by dragging out weeds or raking the bottom. This form of natural groundbaiting stirs the silt, which clouds the water and disturbs aquatic creatures on which the fish feed.

Bream seem to do well in canals and some fairly good fish up to 5lb may be taken. Any deep pools or winding holes (shown as ⌐ on map) are good places to try, particularly when fishing a canal for the first time.

Other places worth fishing are 'cattle drinks' regularly used by farm animals. These make useful places to fish for bream, roach and dace. The frequent use of these drinking holes colours the water, as the animals stir up the mud, and disturb various water creatures. The coloured water draws fish into the area—on the downstream side of the cattle drink when there is the slightest flow.

Pike are to be found in every canal in the country—they are predators, feeding on small fish (which gives a sure indication of the most effective baits). Any small live fish presented on float tackle will take pike. The best places to fish are near weed beds and boats that have been moored in one place a long time.

Many of our canals are cut through pleasant and peaceful countryside, and this enables anglers to spend many delightful hours along the banks—and always with the chance of making a good catch. As a general rule, never fish in locks on navigable canals, or anywhere that could obstruct the free passage of boats. Remember that you will inconvenience yourself as well as the boatman if you have to move in a hurry, or risk a broken line. Never leave discarded line or lead weights on the bank, and never throw these items into the water. Waterfowl become entangled in the line, and are poisoned by the lead shot, which they swallow when grubbing for food. All responsible anglers take their spoilt tackle and litter home with them, where it can be disposed of properly.

The BWB Fisheries Officer at Watford welcomes specific enquiries about fishing on BWB canals from individuals, associations and clubs. He will also supply the names and address of the current Secretary of each Angling Association.

FURTHER READING

Reference works:

Canals and Rivers of Britain	Andrew Darwin	Dent
Shell Book of Inland Waterways	Hugh McKnight	David & Charles
Canal Architecture in Britain	Frances Pratt	BWB
Inland Waterways of Great Britain and Northern Ireland	L. A. Edwards	Imray
A General History of Inland Navigation (reprint from 1805)	J. Phillips	David & Charles
Historical Account of Navigable Rivers & Canals of Great Britain (reprint from 1831)	J. Priestley	David & Charles
Bradshaw's Canals & Navigable Rivers of England and Wales (reprint from 1904)	Henry de Salis	David & Charles

General books:

British Canals	Charles Hadfield	David & Charles
The Canals of the East Midlands	Charles Hadfield	David & Charles
The Canals of the West Midlands	Charles Hadfield	David & Charles
The Canals of South & South East England	Charles Hadfield	David & Charles
The Canals of Yorkshire & North East England (2 volumes)	Charles Hadfield	David & Charles
The Canals of North West England (2 volumes)	Charles Hadfield	David & Charles
The Canals of Eastern England	Charles Hadfield	David & Charles
The Canals of South Wales and the Border	Charles Hadfield	David & Charles
James Brindley Engineer, 1716–1772	C. T. G. Boucher	Goose & Son
The Decorative Arts of the Mariner	G. F. Cook (ed.)	Cassell'
Slow Boat Through England	Frederic Doerflinger	Allan Wingate
English Canals (3 volumes)	D. D. Gladwin & J. M. White	Oakwood Press
The Canal Age	Charles Hadfield	David & Charles and Pan Books
Canals and Their Architecture	Robert Harris	Hugh Evelyn
A Tour of the Grand Junction Canal in 1819 (reprinted 1968)	J. Hassell	Cranfield & Bonfiel
Journeys of the Swan	John Liley	Allen & Unwin
The Canals of England	Eric de Maré	The Architectural Press
Discovering Canals	L. Metcalf & J. Vince	Shire Publications
Narrow Boat	L. T. C. Rolt	Eyre & Spottiswoode
Navigable Waterways	L. T. C. Rolt	Longmans
The Inland Waterways of England	L. T. C. Rolt	Allen & Unwin
Thomas Telford	L. T. C. Rolt	Longmans
James Watt	L. T. C. Rolt	Batsford
Lost Canals of England and Wales	R. Russell	David & Charles
Voyage into England	John Seymour	David & Charles
Lives of the Engineers (3 volumes—reprint from 1862)	Samuel Smiles	David & Charles
Maidens Trip	Emma Smith	Penguin
The Flower of Gloster (reprint from 1911)	Temple Thurston	David & Charles
River Navigation in England 1600–1750	T. S. Willan	F. Cass
The Kennet & Avon Canal	Kenneth R. Clew	David & Charles
Waterways to Stratford	C. Hadfield & J. Norris	David & Charles
London's Lost Route to Basingstoke	P. A. L. Vine	David & Charles
London's Lost Route to the Sea	P. A. L. Vine	David & Charles

Not all of these books are in print—your local library will help you obtain those not readily available.

There are also 3 more volumes in this series, providing complete coverage of all the popular cruising waterways.

2: Central
3: North
River Thames (including the River Wey).

BRITISH WATERWAYS BOARD OFFICES

HEADQUARTERS
Melbury House, Melbury Terrace, London NW1 6JX ((01)262 6711). General and official enquiries.

Willow Grange, Church Road, Watford, Herts WD1 3QA (Watford 26422). Pleasure craft licences and registration, mooring permits and angling enquiries.

AREA OFFICES
Will deal with enquiries regarding stoppages, long term moorings and specific problems on a particular canal.

Birmingham Area Amenity Assistant Reservoir House, Icknield Port Road, Birmingham B16 0AA. (021-454 7091)
Grand Union Canal (north)
Oxford Canal (north)

Stratford-on-Avon Canal (north)
Worcester & Birmingham Canal

Gloucester Area Amenity Assistant Dock Office, The Dock, Gloucester GL1 2EJ. (Gloucester 25524)
Kennet & Avon Canal
Monmouthshire & Brecon Canal
Gloucester & Sharpness Canal
River Severn

London Area Amenity Assistant 53 Clarendon Road, Watford, Herts WF1 1JE. (Watford 31363)
Grand Union Canal (south)
Lee & Stort Rivers
Oxford Canal (south)

Other navigation authorities are listed in the appropriate place in the text.

BWB Tardebigge Yard. *David Perrott*

INDEX